PRIMAL REBELLION

Escaping the System: A Journey Back to Your Becoming

By **Cashea Earls**

ISBN: 979-8-9989094-2-9
Cover Design: Cashea Earls
Interior Design & Layout: Cashea Earls
Printed in the United States of America.
First Edition

Dedication

For the ones who always sensed—deep in their spirit—that they were made for more.
For the ones who couldn't ignore the quiet stirring within— the holy unrest that called them out of the life they were taught to settle for.

For the ones who left the box,
even when it cost them comfort, connection, or control— because God was whispering, *"Follow Me."*

For the ones who chose truth over approval,
freedom over fear,
faith over familiarity.

This is for you.
For us.
For the ones who are still becoming—
not by the world's standards,
but by God's hand.

You are the called.
The set apart.
The ones He chose to rise.

"You will know the truth, and the truth will set you free."
— John 8:32

An Invitation to the Ones Who Are Ready

This is not a book for the faint of heart.
It will not hand you quick fixes, polished affirmations, or a formula for perfection.
It will not teach you how to earn your worth or shrink yourself into someone the world finds easier to love.

Because you were never created to fit inside a box that keeps you small.
You were created by a God who makes no mistakes—
a God who formed you in love,
on purpose,
for a purpose.

This book is not about performance.
It is about permission.
A holy invitation to come home to the one God made you to be.

It's for the ones who are ready.

Ready to look beneath the surface.
Ready to ask the hard questions, even when the answers unravel everything.
Ready to sit in the discomfort of truth, rather than cling to the illusion of safety.
Ready to unlearn what the world taught—
and remember who God says they are.

You are not broken.
You are not too late.
You are not too far gone.

You are being called higher.
Not to hustle harder—
but to surrender deeper.

This book is a rebellion against the lies you were sold,
a remembering of what your soul always knew,
and a return to the One who never left your side.

You don't need to have it all figured out to begin.
You just need a willing heart—
and the courage to follow the still, small voice that has been whispering,
"Come back."

You were made for more—
More truth.
More grace.
More freedom that doesn't cost your soul.
More love that doesn't require your self-abandonment.

And if something stirs in you as you read these words,
if something rises up in your spirit and says *"This is it..."*—
know this isn't coincidence.

It's a calling.
A divine appointment.
An answer to the prayer you didn't even know you were praying.

This is the moment you stop performing and start listening.
The moment you stop striving and start surrendering.

The moment you remember who you belong to—
and what you were made for.

If you've been waiting for a sign—
this is it.

Welcome to the edge.
Welcome to the awakening.
Welcome to the sacred ground of your own becoming.

Welcome home.

Introduction

I didn't set out to write this book.
I set out to survive.

For most of my life, I followed the script I was given — the one that promised safety, success, love, and health if I just did things "right."
I followed the rules.
I trusted the experts.
I played the roles.
I silenced my body.
And I ignored the quiet knowing that something deeper — something truer — was calling me.

Until I couldn't anymore.
Until my health collapsed.
Until the systems I relied on crumbled.
Until my body whispered... then screamed: *Enough.*

What followed wasn't a graceful rise.
It was a raw unraveling.
A sacred dismantling of everything I thought I had to be.

It wasn't healing in the way we're taught to imagine it.
It wasn't linear. It wasn't tidy.
It was a messy, painful, beautiful process of unlearning.

Unlearning what I believed about health, work, success, relationships, identity, and worth.
Unlearning the idea that my body was the problem.

Unlearning the scripts that kept me small, obedient, disconnected, and sick.

And somewhere in that unraveling, I began to remember.
Remember my body's wisdom.
Remember my instincts.
Remember the parts of me that had been buried beneath layers of conditioning and performance.

This book was born in that remembering.
It is not a manual.
It's not a 10-step formula or a blueprint for a perfect life.
It's a rebellion.
A return.
A conversation about what becomes possible when you begin to question everything — and decide to trust yourself again.

This book is for anyone who's ever felt like they were living someone else's life.
For the ones who've stared at their relationships, their career, their reflection — and whispered, *There has to be another way.*

There is.
But it won't be a straight line.
It will be a spiral.
A journey of unlearning, relearning, grieving, becoming, and finally living — not as you were taught to, but as you were always meant to.

If you're holding this book, I believe some part of you already knows that.
Some part of you is ready.
Some part of you is tired of waiting for permission.

So let this be your invitation to begin.
It won't be easy.
It won't be neat.
But it will be real.
It will be yours.
And it will set you free.

Table of Contents

Part One:

The Box We Were Put In

It took me nearly four decades to realize I had been living inside a box — not one made of walls, but of beliefs. It was shaped by the roles I played, the rules I followed, the approval I chased, and the silence I kept. For most of my life, I did what I was taught to do: I trusted the experts, obeyed the systems, swallowed the pills, and showed up in environments that drained me. I wore the smile, performed the part, and pushed through the exhaustion, all while ignoring the quiet voice inside that whispered, *something isn't right.*

I didn't know there was another way. Like many of us, I had internalized the idea that my safety and success depended on compliance. I had been conditioned to trust logic over instinct, evidence over intuition, and structure over sensation. The more I silenced my body and my inner knowing, the more disconnected I became. I lived almost entirely in my mind, believing it was the only trustworthy authority. But the truth is, the mind can be shaped by fear, conditioning, and repetition. The body, however, holds a different kind of truth — one that cannot be faked or forgotten.

Over time, I began to understand that the body doesn't lie. It remembers everything — every trauma, every suppression, every time we overrode our needs to meet someone else's expectations. The primal intelligence that once guided our ancestors to survive, to heal, to rest, to protect, and to connect still exists within us. But in our modern world, that intelligence has been buried beneath layer after layer of programming that tells us our worth is measured by how well we obey, how much we produce, and how little we question.

This, I came to see, is the box. A box built by cultural narratives, family dynamics, institutional systems, and internalized fear. It trains us to dismiss our instincts, ignore our bodies, and outsource our truth. And while it may appear safe, it is often the very thing making us sick, anxious, disconnected, and lost.

But here's what's most important: once you become aware of the box, you can never truly go back. Once you recognize the invisible framework shaping your choices, your identity, and your health, you begin to unravel it. And from that unraveling, something new — something real — can finally begin.

This section is about seeing clearly. About calling out the scripts we were handed and the stories we never chose. Because the moment we name them, we reclaim our power to choose something different. And that moment — that awareness — is the beginning of liberation.

Chapter 1:

The Inherited Belief Systems —
Stories We Never Chose

"The most dangerous cages are the ones we cannot see."

— Brené Brown

We are born into stories long before we ever speak. From our earliest days, the world begins whispering into us — not with words we can remember, but with patterns we learn to obey. These whispers become the background noise of our lives, subtly informing who we should be, how we should act, what we should want, and which parts of ourselves are safe to express. We absorb them without question, because we're wired to belong. Because survival once depended on our ability to adapt to the environment around us.

These stories don't come from nowhere. They are passed down — through generations, institutions, and everyday interactions. Parents model them. Teachers reinforce them. Doctors name them. Religion blesses them. Media magnifies them. Culture normalizes them. And slowly, without realizing it, we begin to live by them.

They shape how we see the world. They shape how we see ourselves. They tell us what is acceptable, what is admirable, and what is shameful. They influence how we measure our worth, how we make decisions, how we define health, happiness, and success. They determine the boxes we place ourselves in — and the ones we place others in too.

Most of these stories are presented as unquestionable truths. But they are not truths. They are scripts — written and reinforced by people, systems, and societies that often benefit from our compliance. Scripts that thrive when we stay quiet, stay small, and stay in line. And so, we do. We memorize our lines. We play the part. We become who we're expected to be.

At first, these scripts may feel like safety. They offer predictability. They provide a framework to navigate life. For a time, they might even bring comfort — a sense of control, identity, or acceptance. But eventually, for many of us, they stop working. The life we were told would make us happy begins to feel hollow. The achievements we were taught to chase leave us exhausted. The roles we were expected to play no longer fit.

And then something starts to crack. A faint discomfort. A quiet resistance. A sense that we are living someone else's life. That maybe — just maybe — we never chose these stories to begin with.

That's the moment the cage becomes visible.

And once it is, everything begins to change.

The Master Belief Systems We Were Sold

Unlearning Begins with Awareness

The first step toward freedom isn't action — it's awareness.
Before we can reclaim our lives, we have to see the systems
that shaped them.
Before we can rebel, we must remember what we're
rebelling against.

Most of us weren't handed rulebooks or overt
commandments about how to live. Instead, we were shown.
We learned through the unspoken — through the patterns
of approval and disappointment, through subtle rewards for
compliance and quiet consequences for defiance. We
absorbed messages not from what was said, but from what
was withheld. Expectations. Praise. Silence. Conditional
love. These messages were everywhere — in our
classrooms, in our places of worship, in our living rooms, in
exam rooms, on screens, in social circles, and within the
walls of our workplaces.

They weren't always named, but they were felt — deep in
our bones. Over time, they became internalized truths.
Inherited codes of conduct. The silent agreements we didn't
remember making but somehow believed we had to uphold
in order to be safe, accepted, successful, or loved.

We were taught who we were supposed to be — and which
parts of ourselves needed to be hidden, shamed, or
sacrificed in order to belong. We learned to suppress our

needs, override our intuition, and mold ourselves to fit into systems that were never designed for our wholeness.

But the truth is: these beliefs were never ours.
They were handed to us by a world that benefits from our self-abandonment — from our silence, our striving, and our shame. And the more disconnected we became from ourselves, the easier we were to control, manipulate, and keep small.

These beliefs are not personal failings.
They are societal scripts.
Cultural programs.
Inherited systems of conditioning.

And until we name them, we will keep living them — unconsciously, on autopilot, wondering why we feel stuck, exhausted, or broken.

This section is not about blame — it's about illumination.
It's about stepping out of the fog of conditioning and into the clarity of truth.
It's about meeting the lies we inherited with compassion — not only for ourselves, but for the generations who handed them down without questioning them, simply because they too were trying to survive.

This is where we begin the work.
With honesty. With tenderness. With the willingness to get uncomfortable.
Because naming what was never true is the first step toward remembering what has always been.

Below are the ten core belief systems that many of us were sold. Each one holds ideas we were taught to accept without question. Each one is woven into the fabric of how we think, feel, and move through the world. And each one is ready to be re-examined.

1. **Health & Wellness Beliefs** — That health is weight, symptoms are problems, and your body must be controlled to be loved.
2. **Work & Productivity Beliefs** — That your worth is tied to your output, and rest is laziness.
3. **Social & Relationship Beliefs** — That loneliness is failure and love must be earned through self-sacrifice.
4. **Education & Knowledge Beliefs** — That authority knows best, and learning ends when school does.
5. **Financial Beliefs** — That wealth equals success, debt is normal, and financial literacy is only for the elite.
6. **Time & Aging Beliefs** — That life is measured by milestones, and aging is decline.
7. **Spirituality & Purpose Beliefs** — That obedience is holiness and doubt is sin.
8. **Body & Appearance Beliefs** — That your body is an object to fix, perfect, or shame into submission.
9. **Consumer & Materialism Beliefs** — That more equals better, and buying equals belonging.
10. **Self-Worth & Identity Beliefs** — That you must earn love, prove your value, and deny your truth to be accepted.

These beliefs have shaped how we see ourselves. How we see each other. How we see the world.
But just because they were handed to us doesn't mean we have to keep carrying them.

You are allowed to put them down.
You are allowed to ask better questions.
You are allowed to write something new.

Let this be the moment you begin to see clearly — not just
the world around you, but the world within you.
Let this be the beginning of your great remembering.

Health & Wellness Beliefs

#1: Health is the Absence of Disease

For most of us, this belief was never directly taught — it was
absorbed. Through silent cues and systemic structures, we
learned that as long as we weren't *sick*, we were "fine." If
the labs looked good, if there was no fever, no diagnosis, no
obvious malfunction, then we were told we were healthy.
Never mind the chronic exhaustion, the anxiety that lived in
our chest, the sleep that never felt restorative, or the gut
that flared up under stress — if we could still go to work,
keep up appearances, or take care of everyone else, then
surely, we must be healthy.

This belief has roots in a system designed around managing
illness, not cultivating wellness. Western medicine, in its
primary role of emergency care, often views the body like a
machine — diagnose, treat, suppress the symptom. It rarely
asks *why* the body is speaking, only how to make it quiet.

And so we internalize that health is the absence of breakdown, rather than the presence of vitality.

But the impact of this belief runs deeper than we realize. It conditions us to ignore the subtle whispers of the body until they become screams. It normalizes burnout, pain, and numbness as part of everyday life. Psychologically, it makes us question ourselves — are we just being dramatic? Lazy? Overly sensitive? We gaslight our own experience because our symptoms don't "look" like illness. And in that disconnection, our bodies carry the weight of what's unseen: tight shoulders that never release, a gut in knots, a heart that beats fast for no reason, a nervous system always stuck in "on."

The truth is, health isn't defined by a diagnosis — it's defined by your experience of being alive. True health includes joy, rest, digestion, emotional expression, mental clarity, connection, safety in your own skin. It's not just the absence of disease — it's the presence of harmony. Of flow. Of resilience.

In this new paradigm, the body is no longer a machine to be fixed — it's a living intelligence to be partnered with. Symptoms aren't failures; they're messengers. Fatigue may be a sacred invitation to rest. Anxiety may be your body's way of telling you something doesn't feel safe. Even illness, in this light, becomes an opportunity to listen more deeply and return to balance.

Health becomes a relationship, not a checklist. It's dynamic, evolving — shaped by how you eat, breathe, move, connect, feel, and rest. It's your emotional health, your nervous system state, your spiritual alignment, your community, your pleasure, your peace. It's remembering that you are not separate parts — you are a whole, interconnected system with the power to heal, adapt, and thrive.

You don't need to wait until something breaks to care for your body. You don't need permission from a lab report to begin healing. You are allowed to feel good. You are allowed to seek more than just *not being sick*.

You are allowed to want to feel fully alive.

Reflection:
Where have I confused functioning with thriving?
What parts of my body or being have I dismissed because "nothing is wrong"?
If I redefined health as the full aliveness of my system, what would I begin to do differently?
What does "health" feel like in my body — not just look like on paper?

#2: Doctors and Pharmaceuticals Are the Ultimate Authority on Health

From a young age, many of us were taught to place our trust in white coats and prescription pads. The doctor knows best. The expert has the answers. The cure comes in a bottle. Whether it was antibiotics for every childhood infection, pills for every symptom, or a growing list of diagnoses and dosages as we aged, we were conditioned to believe that healing was something external — something given to us, prescribed to us, decided for us.

This belief didn't arise in a vacuum. It's the result of a culture that reveres institutional knowledge while devaluing embodied wisdom. It comes from a medical system that was built on authority, hierarchy, and often — profit. And while many doctors are deeply committed to helping people heal, the system they operate within often leaves little room for root-cause thinking, whole-person care, or honoring the patient's lived experience.

So we learn to outsource our inner knowing. We silence our gut instincts. We ignore the side effects that don't fit the textbook. We question ourselves before we question the person in the lab coat. We become passive participants in our own health journey — nodding, complying, and hoping someone else has the map.

Psychologically, this creates a deep disempowerment. We stop asking questions. We fear speaking up. We feel ashamed when medications don't work or when we still feel unwell, as though *we* failed. Somatically, the body holds this powerlessness — the tension in the chest when dismissed by a provider, the stomachache before an appointment, the frozen stillness of not knowing how to advocate for yourself.

But the truth is: your body is the ultimate authority on your health. The sensations you feel, the patterns you notice, the intuition you carry — these are not irrelevant. They are data. They are wisdom. They are a language that only *you* can fully interpret.

The new paradigm invites a radical shift in power: from passive patient to active participant. It doesn't mean rejecting all doctors or medicine — it means remembering that you are not a problem to be solved, but a person to be understood. It means partnering with practitioners who honor your voice, who co-create care with you, not over you. It means understanding that pharmaceuticals may offer temporary relief, but true healing often asks deeper questions: *Why is the body speaking? What has it been carrying? What has it been denied?*

This paradigm reclaims health as a collaboration — between your body, your story, and the support you choose. It asks you to remember that while expertise is valuable, it's not infallible. That while credentials matter, so does lived experience. That the most important relationship you'll ever have in your health journey... is with yourself.

You are not broken. You are not crazy. You are not imagining it.
You are allowed to know what's best for your body. You are allowed to lead.

Reflection:
When have I silenced my intuition in favor of someone else's authority?
What has that cost me — emotionally, physically, spiritually?
What might shift if I saw myself as the expert of my own experience?
What kind of support would truly *honor* the wisdom of my body?

#3: Aging Automatically Equals Decline and Illness

Somewhere along the way, we stopped honoring aging and started dreading it. We learned to equate growing older with falling apart — more pain, more pills, more problems. Wrinkles were seen as flaws. A slower pace became something to fight. Aging was no longer seen as a sacred evolution, but as a slow, inevitable slide into irrelevance, fragility, and decline.

This belief runs deep. It lives in advertising, in medicine, in culture. Entire industries profit from our fear of aging. We're told to fight it, hide it, reverse it. To mask the symptoms and silence the signs. To stay youthful at all costs — as if youth is the only currency that holds value.

But when we internalize this belief, the consequences are profound. Psychologically, we begin to fear our own future. We associate each birthday with a step closer to brokenness. We stop imagining what's *possible* in later years and instead start bracing for what might go wrong. Somatically, this belief becomes a self-fulfilling prophecy — the body responds to chronic stress, fear, and disengagement with real physical symptoms. We shrink. We stiffen. We disconnect from the vibrant life force still moving within us.

But here's the deeper truth: aging is not a diagnosis. It's a process — natural, sacred, and layered with potential. Yes, the body changes. Yes, we slow down. But that slowing is not always loss — sometimes, it's wisdom. Sometimes, it's presence. Sometimes, it's the shedding of everything that no longer needs to be carried.

In this new paradigm, aging becomes a deepening, not a deterioration. It's a time of increased self-knowledge, of emotional refinement, of reorientation toward what actually matters. It's the body asking to be treated with more reverence, not fear. It's the invitation to build strength in new ways — strength of spirit, clarity of mind, softness of heart.

You are not a machine wearing out. You are a soul inhabiting a living, breathing body that has carried you through every chapter — and still has so much to offer. The aches may come. The recovery may take longer. But there is also beauty here. There is resilience. There is the possibility of aging with *vitality*, with meaning, with power.

Your future is not a sentence. It's a canvas. And the brush is still in your hand.

Reflection:
What fears or assumptions have I carried about growing older?
How have those beliefs shaped how I care for — or abandon — my body?
Can I imagine a version of aging that feels nourishing, empowered, and alive?
What would it look like to honor my body as it is, right now, in this season?

#4: Weight Alone Defines Health

We live in a world where the number on the scale has become a moral compass. Where thinness is praised and larger bodies are pathologized — often without question. From childhood doctor visits to media messages to diet culture disguised as wellness, we've been taught to equate weight with worth, and health with appearance.

This belief isn't just cultural — it's institutional. Medical charts categorize bodies by BMI, a metric never meant to measure health. Doctors prescribe weight loss like it's a cure-all, often without exploring deeper causes or listening to the patient's lived experience. We're told to chase an "ideal" body type, regardless of genetics, context, or mental health. And so we internalize it: if I gain weight, I must be failing. If I lose weight, I must be succeeding. The scale becomes our scorecard.

But this narrow lens harms more than it helps. Psychologically, it breeds shame, obsession, and disconnection. It makes people afraid of food, afraid of rest, afraid of being seen. It convinces us that our bodies are projects to be fixed rather than homes to be lived in. And somatically, the body absorbs this message — through constant stress, cortisol dysregulation, restrictive eating, and the nervous system swinging between fight and collapse. The result isn't health. It's a body that feels unsafe and unseen.

The deeper truth is: health is not a shape. It's not a size. It's not a specific weight. It's a *state of being*. Real health includes metabolic function, hormonal balance, emotional resilience, nervous system regulation, joy, digestion, connection, and rest. It includes how we feel *in* our bodies — not just how we appear from the outside.

In this new paradigm, we begin to see the body as a communicator, not a scoreboard. We honor its shifts, cycles, and context. We stop assuming someone's health based on their size, and we start asking better questions: How's your energy? Your sleep? Your mood? Your digestion? How connected do you feel to yourself and your life?

We also begin to heal our relationship with nourishment. Food becomes fuel, not punishment or reward. Movement becomes a celebration of ability, not a form of control. And our bodies, in all their changing forms, become worthy of care — not because they are "ideal," but because they are *ours*.

You were never meant to shrink yourself to be seen as healthy. You were meant to *feel* healthy — in ways no number can measure.

Reflection:
When have I equated weight with value, or thinness with success?
How has that belief shaped how I nourish, move, or relate to my body?
What would it feel like to focus on how I *feel* in my body, rather than how it looks?
Can I honor my body's needs today, regardless of what the scale says?

#5: Fast Fixes Are More Effective Than Lifestyle Changes

We live in a culture addicted to urgency. Want to lose weight? Take this pill. Trouble sleeping? Try this quick remedy. Digestive issues, burnout, chronic pain? There's a protocol for that — and if it doesn't work in seven days, try the next one. We're sold solutions that promise fast relief, immediate change, instant results. The quicker, the better. The deeper, the scarier. And the slower? Unthinkable.

This belief is rooted in a system designed for speed, not depth. A system that rewards productivity over presence, symptom suppression over root cause healing. In that system, fast fixes are seductive — they promise us control, certainty, and relief without the discomfort of true transformation. But what they often deliver is temporary silence, not sustainable change.

And so we learn to chase outcomes instead of listening inward. To bypass the messy middle. To treat the body like a problem to solve instead of a teacher to learn from. We try protocol after protocol, supplement after supplement, hoping this next one will finally "fix" us. When it doesn't, we blame ourselves. We feel broken. Discouraged. Desperate.

But what if the issue isn't *you* — what if it's the belief that healing should be fast?

The truth is, real healing is not linear — and it's rarely quick. It's cyclical, layered, and deeply personal. It asks us to slow down, to look inward, to engage in the daily, unsexy, sacred work of nourishment and regulation. It asks us to rebuild our foundations — sleep, breath, safety, food, connection — and to tend to them like a garden, not a checklist.

This new paradigm doesn't chase fast fixes. It honors *slow medicine*. It honors the body's timeline, not society's. It trusts that sustainable change grows from consistency, compassion, and curiosity — not pressure or punishment.

It's not about perfection, but about alignment. It's about learning the language of your body and building a life that supports your wellness long-term.

And here's the radical truth: the lifestyle shifts you once saw as optional or insignificant — the morning sunlight, the food that truly nourishes, the walk that grounds you, the boundaries that protect your peace — these are the real medicine. They're not quick. But they're lasting.

You don't need to fix yourself fast.
You need to love yourself steadily — and build a life that loves you back.

Reflection:
Where have I prioritized speed over sustainability in my healing?
What parts of me still believe that "quicker" means "better"?
What would change if I trusted the process — even when it's slow, nonlinear, or hard?
What small, loving choice could I make today that supports lasting change?

#6: Mental Health Is Separate from Physical Health

For too long, we've been taught to treat the mind and the body as separate entities — as if what we feel emotionally has no bearing on our physical health, and what we experience physically doesn't touch our inner world. Mental health? That's in your head. Physical health? That's in your body. Different departments. Different doctors. Different treatments. Different conversations.

This separation runs deep. It's built into our healthcare systems, our language, our insurance codes. It's why someone can be treated for panic attacks with no inquiry into blood sugar or trauma. It's why chronic illness patients are told "it's all in your head" when tests come back "normal." It's why many of us don't even realize that our back pain might be grief, or our fatigue might be anxiety wearing a physical mask.

When we internalize this belief, it fragments us. We start compartmentalizing our symptoms — a headache here, a sadness there, a digestive issue we can't explain. We treat them like isolated issues rather than interconnected signals. Psychologically, we become confused, ashamed, or dismissed. Somatically, the nervous system lives in a constant tug-of-war — caught between suppression and survival, never feeling truly seen or safe.

But the truth is: there is no such thing as "just mental" or "just physical." Everything is connected. Every thought, every emotion, every trauma, every belief — it all lands in the body. And everything in the body — every ache, imbalance, and dis-ease — echoes back into the mind and heart.

In the new paradigm, we stop asking, *Is this mental or physical?* and begin asking, *What is my whole system trying to tell me?* We understand that anxiety can live in the gut. That unresolved trauma can show up as inflammation. That chronic pain can be the body's language of unprocessed emotion. We recognize that nervous system regulation, emotional processing, spiritual connection, and physical care are not separate practices — they are one integrated path to wholeness.

When you tend to your inner world, your body softens. When you nourish your body, your mind feels safer. Healing happens when we stop fragmenting ourselves — and start listening to the full conversation within.

You are not pieces.
You are not separate parts stitched together.
You are one, whole, intelligent being — and your healing begins where your connection to yourself is restored.

Reflection:
Where have I been separating my mental and physical experiences?
What symptoms or patterns might be trying to bridge that gap?
What would it feel like to care for my emotions and my body as one?
Where can I begin to listen to the whole of me — not just the parts that hurt the loudest?

Work & Career Beliefs

#1: Productivity Equals Self-Worth

It starts early. Gold stars for finishing your work. Praise for being "such a hard worker." Approval when you're busy. Disappointment when you rest. Somewhere along the way, we absorb the message: the more you *do*, the more you *are*.

Hustle becomes identity. Achievement becomes love. Productivity becomes proof that we're valuable, capable, and worthy of being seen.

In this belief system, there's no space for stillness. Rest feels suspicious. Slowness feels lazy. We measure our days in output, not in presence. And when we're not accomplishing something — not creating, building, performing, or helping — we feel guilty. Or worse: empty.

This conditioning is reinforced by culture, capitalism, and even family systems that value doing over being. In a society obsessed with performance, we become machines in human bodies — always striving, always pushing, always producing. The burnout is celebrated until it breaks us.

But the cost is steep. Psychologically, we lose touch with our inherent worth — the kind that exists even when we're not achieving. We feel anxious when we pause. We equate rest with laziness. We fear being perceived as "not enough." And our bodies? They carry it all. The racing heart. The shallow breath. The clenched jaw. The wired-but-exhausted nervous system that doesn't know how to *be* without doing.

But here's the truth: your worth was never meant to be measured in hours, hustle, or output. You are not here to be productive — you are here to be *alive*.

In this new paradigm, productivity becomes a tool — not a measuring stick. It's something you *do*, not something you *are*. Your value doesn't rise or fall based on your to-do list. You don't have to earn your right to rest, joy, or belonging. Those things are already yours.

This is where everything begins to shift. You begin to notice how much of your identity was built on doing — and you start the sacred work of unbecoming. You learn to rest without guilt. To say no without explaining. To exist without producing — and still feel whole.

You begin to remember:
You are not the job.
You are not the task list.
You are not your level of output.

You are worthy because you *exist*. Period.

Reflection:
When did I begin to believe that doing more made me more valuable?
How has this belief shaped my self-esteem, my rest patterns, or my boundaries?
What would it feel like to separate my worth from my productivity?
Where can I begin to honor my being — not just my doing?

#2: Success Is Defined by Money, Status, and Titles

From the time we're young, success is painted with a narrow brush: the corner office, the big paycheck, the fancy title, the admiration of others. We're taught to chase symbols — letters after our name, promotions on our resume, milestones that prove we've made it. Even if no one says it directly, the message is clear: *Your value increases as your status does.*

And so we run. We climb ladders we didn't choose. We wear labels that don't fit. We pursue degrees, positions, and salaries — not always because they fulfill us, but because they *validate* us. Because we've been taught that success must look impressive on paper, even if it feels hollow in our chest.

This belief is rooted in a culture that worships image over integrity. In systems that reward visibility, productivity, and accumulation, while ignoring presence, purpose, and peace. It teaches us that *who* we are matters less than *how* we're perceived. And if we're not careful, we begin to perform our lives instead of living them.

Psychologically, this belief can leave us constantly chasing — and never arriving. Because no title is ever enough. No paycheck is ever "the one." No applause ever truly fills the ache of living out of alignment. And physically, the body knows. It carries the strain of overachievement, the tension of proving, the burnout of living by someone else's definition of success.

But here's the truth: real success has *nothing* to do with optics — and everything to do with *alignment*. It's not about what you have — it's about how you feel. Are you at peace in your body? Do you wake up with purpose? Are your values reflected in your work? Can you breathe in your own life?

In this new paradigm, success is redefined as *soul satisfaction*. It's the ability to live a life that feels good on the inside — not just one that looks good on the outside. It's knowing yourself, honoring your limits, doing meaningful work, and living in a way that supports your nervous system, your joy, your relationships, and your integrity.

It's not about climbing — it's about *coming home* to what matters most.

You don't need to be a somebody to be *somebody.*
You are already enough — regardless of how the world labels you.

Reflection:
Whose definition of success have I been living by?
What have I sacrificed in pursuit of recognition, status, or financial gain?
What does success *feel like* in my body — not just look like in the world?
What would it mean to create a version of success that actually supports the life I want to live?

#3: Hustle Culture — The Only Path to Value and Success

Wake up early. Work harder. Sleep less. Grind now, rest later. If you're not busy, you're falling behind. If you're not hustling, you're not hungry enough. These messages aren't just slogans — they're the sacred rules of hustle culture. Rules that have been silently shaping how we measure worth and chase success.

We're told that ambition looks like burnout, that discipline means denying your body, and that value is proven by how much you can produce under pressure. We glorify the "always on" lifestyle — the late nights, skipped meals, jam-packed schedules — as if depletion is a badge of honor and exhaustion is a sign of dedication.

But hustle culture doesn't just shape behavior. It infiltrates identity. It whispers, *If you slow down, you'll be forgotten. If you stop pushing, you'll lose everything.* And so we stay in motion, often disconnected from why we started in the first place. We confuse urgency with purpose. We wear busyness like armor, hoping it will protect us from the fear of being invisible, replaceable, or left behind.

Psychologically, hustle culture breeds deep insecurity. It keeps us stuck in survival mode, always reaching but never arriving. And the body? It suffers — chronically activated, sleep-deprived, nutrient-depleted, stuck in a loop of "go" with no "off." The nervous system doesn't get to rest, because we've learned to equate stillness with failure.

But the truth is: hustle is not the only path. It's just the loudest.
And it's not the most effective — it's just the most praised.

In the new paradigm, value is no longer measured by how much you do, but how aligned you are with what truly matters. Success is no longer defined by how much you grind, but by how much you *feel* — peace, purpose, vitality, joy. We begin to honor *sustainable success* — the kind that doesn't cost us our health, relationships, or souls.

We learn that rest is not the reward — it's the foundation. That slowness is not weakness — it's wisdom.

That our deepest impact comes not from doing *more*, but from doing what's *aligned*.

You don't have to hustle to prove your worth.
You don't have to burn out to succeed.
You don't have to sacrifice your humanity for your goals.

You get to build a life that supports your well-being *while* supporting your dreams.

Reflection:
How has hustle culture shaped how I view success, rest, or self-worth?
What have I ignored or sacrificed in the name of "keeping up"?
What would success look like if it included my body, my relationships, and my peace?
What part of me is ready to rest — not because the work is done, but because *I* matter?

#4: The Myth of Retirement—Life's End Goal

Work hard now. Sacrifice your time, your health, your freedom — because one day, you'll retire. And *then* you'll rest. *Then* you'll travel. *Then* you'll enjoy life. It's the carrot on a stick that keeps generations moving — the golden promise at the end of decades of grind.

But here's the hard truth: many people never make it to that someday. Or if they do, they arrive too depleted to enjoy it.

Their bodies are worn. Their passions buried. Their joy postponed for so long, it forgot how to return. They were sold a vision of fulfillment that always lived in the future — never in the now.

This belief is rooted in a system designed to extract labor, not cultivate wholeness. We're conditioned to believe that worth is earned through decades of output — and only then do we "deserve" rest. Retirement becomes a reward for surviving the burnout, rather than a life
lived *through* presence, pleasure, and purpose all along the way.

Psychologically, this belief trains us to delay joy. To tolerate misery. To dismiss the voice that says *this isn't it*. We learn to endure instead of enjoy. To hold our breath instead of inhabit our lives. And somatically, our bodies hold the weight of the waiting — the tension of always pushing through, the stress of postponing needs, the nervous system living in chronic anticipation of relief that never quite arrives.

But what if retirement isn't the goal?
What if the real goal is a *life you don't feel the need to escape from?*

In the new paradigm, we stop deferring joy. We stop trading our vitality for some distant promise. We start asking: *What kind of life can I build now — one that feels meaningful, nourishing, and alive?* A life where work supports well-being, not erodes it. Where purpose isn't something you earn later, but something you live now.

Success becomes less about someday — and more about today. It becomes about creating a rhythm of life where rest, joy, connection, and contribution are woven into the *now*, not locked away for the end. You begin to see that every small choice — every boundary, every breath, every realignment — shapes your life into something worth living fully, not just surviving until it's "over."

You don't need to wait until you're 65 to feel free.
You don't need to wait until your body gives out to start listening to it.
You don't need to delay joy, purpose, or peace — they are not retirement perks.
They are your birthright.

Reflection:
How has the idea of retirement shaped the way I tolerate stress or delay joy?
Where have I postponed living in hopes of "someday"?
What would shift if I designed a life I didn't need to recover from?
What could it mean to start living *now*, not just planning for later?

#5: Stability Comes Only from Traditional 9–5 Employment (Passion is a Risk, Not a Path)

Get a "real" job. Something stable. Something with benefits. Something that looks good on paper and doesn't raise eyebrows at family dinners. Follow your passion if you must — *on the side*. But don't rely on it. That's not responsible. That's risky.

We've been taught to see the 9–5 path as the only legitimate form of stability. Structure, salary, benefits, retirement plan — all wrapped in predictability. Anything outside that box? Freelance. Creative work. Entrepreneurship. Purpose-driven callings. These are framed as unstable, unrealistic, even selfish — especially if you have a family to care for or a mortgage to pay.

And so, many of us trade our gifts for job security. We bury our dreams in practicality. We settle for "safe," even if it slowly disconnects us from ourselves. We start to believe that choosing passion means sacrificing security — that we can't have both. That fulfillment is optional, but stability is everything.

But the irony is — how many people do you know who feel truly *secure* in their traditional job? Layoffs still happen. Burnout is everywhere. Toxic work environments, chronic stress, disconnection from purpose — and still, people stay, not because it's aligned, but because it's familiar. Because we were never taught how to define *security* on our own terms.

Psychologically, this belief creates a deep inner split. The soul longs for meaning, expression, freedom — but the mind says, *that's too dangerous.* So we stay in jobs that drain us, convinced that's just "how life works." And the body? It starts to shut down. We feel numb, heavy, anxious, fatigued. Not because we're lazy — but because we're out of alignment.

Here's the deeper truth: real stability doesn't come from a paycheck — it comes from *personal power*. From knowing who you are, what you value, and how to build a life rooted in *integrity*, not just income. Passion isn't reckless — it's revealing. It shows you where your aliveness lives. And that aliveness is a compass worth following.

In this new paradigm, we stop asking, *Which path is safer?* and start asking, *Which path is mine?* We stop measuring stability only in financial terms — and begin to include nervous system regulation, creative fulfillment, freedom of time, alignment with values, and emotional sustainability.

We also allow a more nuanced truth: sometimes the 9–5 is the right fit. Sometimes it isn't. Sometimes passion becomes the career, and sometimes it stays sacred and separate. The point is not one path over the other — the point is *choice. Agency. Truth.* You don't have to trade your soul for a sense of safety. You get to define both.

You are not selfish for wanting more.
You are not irresponsible for choosing alignment.
You are not foolish for believing your passions hold wisdom.
You are allowed to create a life that feels both meaningful and stable — *on your terms.*

Reflection:
What definitions of stability have I inherited — and do they still serve me?
Where have I silenced my passion in the name of safety?
What would stability look like if I included my mental, emotional, and spiritual health?
Am I willing to trust that my passions were planted in me for a reason?

#6: Workplace Boundaries Are Unprofessional

We're praised for being the "go-to" person. The one who always says yes. The one who stays late, picks up the slack, answers emails after hours, and never complains. Somewhere along the way, we learned that our value at work increases when our boundaries disappear. That being a "team player" means self-sacrifice. That setting limits is ungrateful, uncommitted — even unprofessional.

This belief is often unspoken but deeply felt. We're rewarded for overextending and subtly shamed when we advocate for ourselves. We see rest as a privilege, not a right. We apologize for taking time off. We feel guilty for saying no. And slowly, we stop listening to our own capacity — because our workplace culture taught us that being respected means being available, agreeable, and endlessly accommodating.

But the impact is undeniable. Psychologically, we feel drained, resentful, anxious. We fear we're "too much" if we speak up, or "not enough" if we don't keep proving ourselves. The nervous system responds by living in chronic stress — tight chest, shallow breath, wired exhaustion, emotional numbness. We don't just burn out — we disconnect from ourselves entirely.

The truth is: boundaries are not a lack of professionalism — they are a *foundation for it*. Boundaries are how we stay honest, effective, and grounded. They protect our energy so we can show up with presence. They separate what we are responsible *for* from what we are responsible *to*. They create space for sustainability — not just survival.

In this new paradigm, professionalism is redefined. It's not about people-pleasing. It's about mutual respect. It's about modeling self-trust, not self-abandonment. It's about understanding that saying no to one thing is saying yes to what matters most — our well-being, our families, our integrity, our nervous systems.

Work is not supposed to deplete your humanity.
You are not a machine.
You are allowed to have needs, limits, rhythms, and values — and to build a life and career that honors them.

Boundaries are not walls. They are doors — doors that guide you back to balance, self-respect, and long-term impact.

Reflection:
Where have I been afraid to set boundaries at work — and why?
What have I been taught about saying no, resting, or protecting my time?
How has people-pleasing impacted my nervous system or emotional well-being?
What would it feel like to set boundaries not out of defense, but out of *devotion* to myself?

Social & Relationship Beliefs

#1: Loneliness Is a Consequence of Not Being Enough

There's a quiet ache that comes with loneliness — and for many of us, that ache has been internalized as shame. Not just *I feel alone*, but *I must be the reason I'm alone.* Somewhere deep inside, a belief takes root: *If I were better — more interesting, more lovable, more successful, more normal — I wouldn't feel this way.* Loneliness becomes a reflection of personal failure, not just a human experience.

This belief often begins early — in schoolyards, at family tables, or in places where our uniqueness made us feel different instead of seen. We learned that connection had to be *earned* — through performance, people-pleasing, or self-abandonment. And when those strategies didn't work, we assumed the problem was us.

As we grow older, this belief can quietly dictate our relationships. We over-give. We settle. We stay in connections that drain us, just to avoid the sting of being alone. Or we withdraw completely, convinced no one could truly understand or accept us. Psychologically, it breeds self-doubt. Somatically, it shows up as a tight chest, a clenched jaw, a hollow feeling in the belly — the body bracing for rejection even before it happens.

But here's the truth: loneliness is not a character flaw. It's not evidence that you are unworthy or broken. It is a *signal* — a sacred one — that you are wired for connection. Not surface-level attention. Not toxic attachments. *True, nourishing connection.* The kind that sees the *real* you. The kind that doesn't require you to shrink, pretend, or prove.

In this new paradigm, we begin to see loneliness not as a reflection of our inadequacy, but as a reflection of our unmet need for *authentic belonging.* We realize that being alone can be a form of protection — a pause between who we were and the relationships we are finally worthy of calling in. We start to understand that sometimes the loneliest place is inside a relationship where we can't be ourselves — and sometimes solitude is where we begin to come home.

You are not too much.
You are not hard to love.
You are not alone because you are unworthy — you are alone because you are awakening to what you *truly deserve.*

And that kind of awakening will always create a gap between the old and the new.

Reflection:
When have I believed that my loneliness was a reflection of my flaws?
What relationships or dynamics have I held onto just to avoid being alone?
What would it look like to view my solitude as sacred — as a bridge to something deeper, not a punishment?
Can I begin to believe that I am worthy of love, even when I feel unseen?

#2: Men Should Be Strong and Unemotional; Women Must Be Self-Sacrificing

We've all been shaped by stories about what it means to be a "real" man or a "good" woman. Stories that tell men to be stoic, invulnerable, providers who never break. Stories that tell women to be nurturing, accommodating, selfless — even when it costs them everything. These roles are presented as natural, honorable, even noble. But underneath the surface, they are cages.

Men learn early that emotion is weakness. That tears are embarrassing. That tenderness must be hidden or transformed into control, anger, or silence. Women, on the other hand, are praised for their ability to hold everything and everyone — often at the expense of themselves. To anticipate needs, smooth conflict, soften their truth, and make space for others, even when no one makes space for them.

This belief system doesn't just shape identity — it distorts intimacy. It keeps men emotionally walled off, unable to fully connect or express. It teaches women to ignore their own needs, to base their worth on how much they can give, and to fear being "too much" when they finally speak up. It creates relationships that are out of balance — full of performance, obligation, and unmet needs.

And the impact is deep. Psychologically, it fragments us. Men feel shame for being human — for grieving, for needing help, for feeling afraid. Women feel invisible in their own lives — burned out, underappreciated, and unsure who they are outside of others' needs. Somatically, this shows up as anxiety, fatigue, repression, shutdown, and chronic stress. The body holds what the culture refuses to honor.

But the truth is: these roles are not rooted in wholeness — they are rooted in survival. And we are allowed to outgrow them.

In this new paradigm, we honor emotional presence as strength — for *everyone*. We recognize that men are allowed to feel, to soften, to cry, to receive. That strength includes vulnerability, and leadership includes emotional literacy. And we honor that women are allowed to have needs, to say no, to rest, to take up space — and to lead with both heart and boundaries.

We begin to see relationship not as a performance of roles, but as a meeting of souls. Where masculine and feminine energy can move fluidly — within *all* of us — and where partnership is built not on sacrifice, but mutual sovereignty.

You are allowed to be fully human.
You are allowed to break the mold.
You are allowed to rewrite what masculinity and femininity mean to you.

And in doing so, you make space for relationships that are more honest, more nourishing, and more whole.

Reflection:
What messages did I receive about what it means to be a man or a woman?
Where have I abandoned myself to fit into those roles?
What parts of me have I suppressed to meet expectations of strength or sacrifice?

What would it feel like to reclaim the fullness of who I am —
beyond roles and rules?

#3: Friendships Are About Quantity, Not Quality

We live in a world that confuses connection with proximity, popularity with intimacy. We're taught that a full social calendar, a long contact list, and a high follower count are signs of being loved and accepted. That the more friends we have, the more whole we must be.

And so we strive. We collect connections. We spread ourselves thin trying to be everywhere, for everyone. We stay in surface-level friendships that leave us feeling unseen but "included." We fear being left out, so we keep showing up — even when we're shrinking inside. We trade depth for belonging, but still end up feeling alone in a room full of people.

This belief often stems from early experiences of social hierarchy — school cliques, popularity contests, or moments when being chosen meant being safe. We learn that inclusion is something we earn, not something we *receive* for simply being who we are. And when we feel lonely, we assume the solution is *more people*, rather than *more honesty*.

Psychologically, this belief leaves us craving connection, but scared to be vulnerable. We may have many "friends," but few we can truly fall apart with. Few we can be messy with.

Few who really *see* us beneath the roles we play. Somatically, the body feels the gap — the disconnect between our outward circle and our inward truth. We leave hangouts feeling drained instead of filled. Our nervous system remains on alert, performing rather than relaxing.

But the truth is: real friendship isn't measured by numbers. It's measured by *presence*. By trust. By how safe your nervous system feels in someone's presence. One soul-deep connection can be more healing than a hundred shallow ones. One person who listens without fixing, who loves without conditions, who remembers your essence when you forget — that is more than enough.

In this new paradigm, we stop trying to "keep up" and start looking for what's *real*. We give ourselves permission to release friendships that feel one-sided, obligatory, or performative. We learn to invest in the few who make us feel whole, not spread thin. We stop trying to be liked by everyone — and start being known by a few.

You are not hard to love.
You are not too much or too little.
You don't need a crowd to prove your worth — you need truth, reciprocity, and resonance.

Reflection:
Where have I prioritized being included over being truly known?
Which relationships drain me — and which ones nourish me?
What does my body feel in the presence of real connection?
Can I give myself permission to choose quality over quantity — even if it means fewer, deeper friendships?

#4: Your Partner Should Complete You

"You complete me."
It sounds romantic, even sacred — the idea that somewhere out there is a person who will fill every gap, meet every need, soothe every ache, and make you whole. We've been taught that love is the solution to our brokenness, and that a partner is the missing piece to our puzzle. That without someone else, we are somehow unfinished.

But this belief — no matter how sweet it sounds — creates a dangerous foundation. When we believe our partner is responsible for our completeness, we begin to outsource our emotional stability, self-worth, and fulfillment. We lean on them not out of love, but out of need. And over time, we lose sight of who we are without them.

It begins innocently. We look to them to calm our anxiety. To affirm our beauty. To give us purpose, identity, direction. But when they fall short — as all humans will — we feel abandoned, unworthy, betrayed. We take their limitations personally. We begin to believe the relationship is broken when really, it's the *expectation* that was flawed.

Psychologically, this belief creates dependency and emotional fragility. Somatically, our bodies feel it as tension in the chest, grasping in the gut, or a deep fear of loss that keeps us in fight-or-flight when the connection feels unstable. We mistake enmeshment for intimacy. And we call it love.

But here's the truth: you are already whole. No one can complete what was never missing.

In this new paradigm, we release the fairytale and begin the sacred work of *inner reunion*. We meet our own needs first — not to be hyper-independent, but to be rooted. We learn that partnership is not about two halves making a whole — it's about two *wholes* walking side by side, choosing each other in freedom, not fear.

We stop looking for someone to save us — and start becoming someone we trust. We stop seeing love as possession — and start seeing it as a co-creation. A mirror. A space where healing is reflected and supported, but never assigned as someone else's job.

Your partner can support you. Cherish you. Walk beside you.
But they are not your missing half. You were never broken. Love is not about completing one another — it's about witnessing, honoring, and growing together.

Reflection:
Where have I expected someone else to meet needs I've never learned to meet within myself?
What parts of me have I abandoned or ignored in the name of "love"?
What would it feel like to enter partnership from wholeness, not hunger?
Can I begin to see myself as complete — with or without someone else?

#5: You Have to Find "The One"

We're raised on the story that there's one person out there — *your other half, your soulmate, your forever* — and that your job is to find them. The One. The magical missing piece. The person who will make it all make sense, heal every wound, and finally give your life meaning. It sounds beautiful. It sounds hopeful. But it's also incredibly heavy.

Because when love is framed as a *quest for completion*, we begin to believe that wholeness is something we earn only when someone else chooses us. That if we haven't found The One, we're falling behind. That our worth, maturity, or even spiritual growth is somehow tied to being chosen by the "right" person.

This belief creates an underlying anxiety in how we date, love, and commit. We look for perfection. We second-guess every relationship: *Is this it? Is this them?* We stay in dynamics that don't serve us because we're afraid we've already "found The One" and don't want to mess it up. Or we keep searching, endlessly unsatisfied, chasing a fantasy that doesn't account for growth, seasons, or the real work of relationship.

Psychologically, this belief keeps us externally focused — always reaching, never arriving. It makes us think love is something we *find*, not something we *build*. Somatically, it can feel like restlessness in the body, disconnection from the present, and grief over imagined futures. We carry a low-grade ache that whispers, *Maybe I missed it. Maybe I'm the problem.*

But here's the truth: there is no "one" person who will rescue you from your own becoming.
There is no perfect match, no flawless partner, no eternal guarantee.
There are only humans — complex, evolving, wounded and wonderful — who are willing to meet you where you are and grow beside you.

In this new paradigm, we release the fantasy of "The One" and open to *true partnership*. We realize that love isn't about fate — it's about conscious choice. It's about compatibility, shared values, emotional safety, and the willingness to *do the work* — together.

You may have many soulmates. Or none in the way you imagined.
You may find love in unexpected places, or build it slowly over time.
But you don't need to be found. You are not lost.
You don't need to be chosen to be enough. You already are.

Reflection:
What expectations have I placed on love based on the idea of "The One"?
How has this belief impacted how I show up in relationships — or with myself?
Can I release the fantasy in favor of something more real, honest, and grounded?
What might love look like if it were chosen, nurtured, and honored — rather than chased or proven?

#6: Family Loyalty Should Override Personal Well-being

Family first. Blood is thicker than water. You only get one family. We hear these phrases growing up — woven into holidays, obligations, and unspoken rules. They sound noble, even sacred. But what's rarely acknowledged is the cost. The invisible expectation that no matter how you're treated, no matter what the dynamic is doing to your nervous system or your spirit, you *owe* your family your loyalty.

This belief is passed down through generations — especially in cultures and households where survival once depended on unity. Speaking up, setting boundaries, or walking away from toxic patterns is seen as betrayal. You become the "selfish" one. The dramatic one. The ungrateful one. So, you stay. You comply. You minimize your pain. You smile when it hurts.

And little by little, you disappear inside the performance of being the "good" daughter, son, sibling, partner. You lose access to your own truth — because it doesn't match the family story. You feel guilt for needing space. Shame for feeling resentment. Grief for wanting more. Psychologically, this belief teaches us to self-abandon in the name of love. Somatically, the body bears the burden — tension, suppression, illness, anxiety. Your system becomes the container for generations of pain no one else was willing to name.

But here's the truth: loyalty that costs you your health, peace, or truth is not love.
It is emotional debt.

And you are allowed to stop paying for someone else's comfort with your suffering.

In this new paradigm, love and boundaries are not opposites — they coexist.
You can love your family *and* hold them accountable.
You can have compassion for their pain *and* refuse to carry it.
You can honor your roots without entangling yourself in cycles that keep you small or sick.

Choosing yourself doesn't mean abandoning your family — it means refusing to abandon *you*.

You are allowed to walk away from dysfunction, even if it's wrapped in tradition.
You are allowed to rest, heal, and create a new legacy — one rooted in truth, not performance.

Reflection:
What was I taught about family, loyalty, and love — and how has that shaped me?
Where have I ignored my own well-being in the name of keeping the peace?
What boundaries feel loving *to me*, even if they are misunderstood by others?
Am I willing to believe that honoring myself is not betrayal — it's liberation?

Education & Knowledge Beliefs

#1: Success is Defined by Formal Education and Degrees

From the time we're children, we're asked, *"What do you want to be when you grow up?"* — as if the answer must fit neatly into a career path that comes with a degree, a title, and a resume full of credentials. We learn that success is linear: get good grades, go to college, get a degree, get a job. Stay on the path. Stay in the system. That's how you "make it."

And if you don't? If school never made sense to your brain? If life circumstances pulled you another way? If you chose a different path — creative, holistic, trade-based, or self-led — you're made to feel behind. Unqualified. Less than. Even if you're thriving in every other way.

This belief is rooted in systems that reward conformity over curiosity. Systems that tell us what knowledge matters — and what doesn't. That elevate institutional learning while disregarding the wisdom found in experience, intuition, creativity, embodiment, and lived survival. And when we internalize that story, we begin to question our own intelligence, even when we *know* things deeply in our bones.

Psychologically, it can make us feel like imposters — especially in spaces where we don't have the "right" letters after our name. It can keep us playing small, undercharging, or holding back from speaking up. Somatically, this belief can show up as tightness in the throat, shrinking in posture, or an inner freeze when asked to explain ourselves.

But the truth is: real intelligence has never belonged to institutions.
It lives in the body. In the heart. In the lived experience of those who have *felt* their way through life, healed themselves through presence, built skills through grit, and learned truths that no classroom could ever teach.

In this new paradigm, success is not defined by credentials — it's defined by *congruence*. Are you doing work that reflects your values? Are you using your gifts in service of something meaningful? Are you living a life that feels real, nourishing, and aligned?

Education doesn't have to be formal to be valid.
Wisdom doesn't need a certificate to be embodied.
And you don't need a degree to be worthy of respect, opportunity, or impact.

You are not unqualified — you are *uncontained* by a system that was never built for your kind of brilliance.

Reflection:
What messages did I receive about education, intelligence, and success?
Where have I felt "not enough" without formal credentials — even when I've lived through more than most?
How might I begin to honor *my* path as legitimate, meaningful, and wise — exactly as it is?
What does success mean to *me* — outside of external validation?

#2: Intelligence Is Measured Academic Performance

Smart. Gifted. Advanced. Behind. Slow. Struggling. From our earliest years, we're labeled — sometimes gently, sometimes harshly — based on how well we fit the structure of a standardized system. How quickly we learn. How neatly we follow instructions. How well we memorize, test, and perform.

And in that system, intelligence becomes a score. A grade. A number on a report card. Something that can be ranked, compared, praised — or punished. Children who color outside the lines, question the rules, or learn through movement, emotion, or intuition are often left feeling *less than* — not because they aren't intelligent, but because their intelligence doesn't fit the mold.

We grow up believing that if we struggled in school, we must not be smart. That if we didn't test well, we aren't capable. That if we don't learn the way others do, we're somehow broken. And even those who excel academically can internalize a fear of failure — as if their value depends entirely on continued achievement.

This belief limits everyone. It shames the creative mind. Silences the embodied learner. Punishes neurodivergence. And worst of all — it teaches us to mistrust our own knowing. To believe that intelligence lives *outside* of us, in a textbook or an authority figure, rather than within our own lived experience.

Psychologically, this belief creates a constant striving — to be smart *enough*, to *prove* we belong. Somatically, it can manifest as anxiety before speaking up, a clenched gut in learning environments, or a deep inner freeze around anything that feels like "school." We stop asking questions not because we don't care, but because we've learned to fear being wrong.

But here's the truth: intelligence is not a score — it's a spectrum.
It's not about how fast you absorb — it's about how deeply you understand.
It's not confined to classrooms — it exists in kitchens, forests, conversations, heartbreak, healing, and hands-on living.

In this new paradigm, intelligence becomes *multi-dimensional*.
It includes emotional intelligence. Somatic intelligence. Relational intelligence. Creative intelligence. Practical wisdom. Sacred wisdom. Intuition. Curiosity. Lived resilience.

We stop asking "How smart are you?"
And begin asking, "*How* are you smart?"

You are not less intelligent because you don't learn the way someone else does.
You are not broken because school didn't make sense to your brain.
You are a whole, intelligent being — and your way of understanding the world is sacred.

Reflection:
What messages did I receive about intelligence, learning, and worth growing up?
Where have I carried shame for not fitting into academic

systems?

How do I learn best — and what kinds of intelligence live within me?

Can I begin to redefine what it means to be "smart" — on my own terms?

#3: If You Don't Have the Answers, You Have Nothing to Offer

We've been taught to speak only when we're certain. To wait until we've mastered something before we contribute. To be an "expert" before we're allowed a voice. Uncertainty is seen as weakness. Not knowing becomes something to hide. And so, we stay quiet — not because we don't care, but because we're afraid of getting it wrong.

This belief shows up early. In classrooms where the fastest answer gets the gold star. In family dynamics where curiosity was dismissed, or where mistakes were punished. In workplaces where questions are met with condescension. Over time, we learn that if we don't have the *right* answer, we shouldn't speak at all. That offering a perspective, asking a question, or sharing from lived experience is only valid if it's backed by data, degrees, or authority.

And so we start second-guessing ourselves. We hold back. We shrink in conversations. We nod when we want to challenge. We keep our wisdom quiet — even when it could have made a difference. Psychologically, this belief creates imposter syndrome. Somatically, it feels like a constriction in the throat, a hesitation in the chest, a pull to disappear when asked to speak.

But the truth is: you don't need to have all the answers to offer something meaningful.
You don't have to be fully healed to hold space.
You don't need a solution to share your story, your question, your insight, your presence.

In this new paradigm, we reclaim the value of being *in process*. We understand that curiosity is as valuable as certainty. That asking good questions is just as powerful as offering polished answers. That vulnerability is a form of wisdom — one that invites others to be honest too.

You are not here to be perfect — you are here to be *present*.
To bring what you have, where you are, with humility and courage.
To speak from your experience, even if it's still unfolding.
To honor that what you *don't* know leaves room for connection, collaboration, and growth.

Your worth is not tied to being right. Your voice matters — even when it's unsure.
Especially when it's unsure.

Reflection:
When have I silenced myself out of fear of not knowing enough?
Where did I learn that being unsure made me unworthy or unqualified?
What would it feel like to share from my *experience* instead of from expertise?
Can I honor the value of being in process — and trust that I still have something to offer?

#4: If It's Not Scientifically Proven, It Isn't Real or Valid

We live in a world that worships evidence. If it can't be measured, published, peer-reviewed, or explained through data — it's dismissed. Unseen experiences, inner knowing, intuition, energetic shifts — these are too often labeled as pseudoscience, irrational, or untrustworthy. And slowly, we learn to distrust anything that can't be proven — even when it's happening inside our own body.

This belief is deeply rooted in a culture that elevates logic over intuition, intellect over embodiment, science over spirit. It stems from systems built to validate only what can be controlled, categorized, and repeated — even though human experience has never fit neatly inside a lab. It has silenced indigenous wisdom, feminine knowing, and body-based truth for centuries — calling them unscientific, unimportant, or "not real."

And so, when we *feel* something — a gut instinct, a deep emotional truth, a somatic knowing — we second-guess it. We want to see a study before we trust ourselves. We dismiss what we *know* in our bones because someone else hasn't written it in a textbook yet. We hand over authority, again and again, to a system that doesn't speak the language of our inner world.

Psychologically, this belief creates self-doubt and disembodiment. We intellectualize our healing. We look for answers "out there" and struggle to trust what's happening "in here." Somatically, this disconnect feels like floating above our lives, unsure how to land. We ignore the goosebumps, the tightening in the chest, the soft inner voice that always knows — because no one taught us how to listen.

But here's the truth: just because something hasn't been studied doesn't mean it isn't real.
Just because something can't be measured doesn't mean it doesn't matter.
Science is a tool — not the only one.
And you don't need permission from a study to trust your lived experience.

In this new paradigm, we reclaim *other forms of knowing*. We remember that truth can be felt. That healing can be intuitive. That our bodies are data. That ancestral wisdom and somatic experience are valid sources of insight. That the unseen doesn't have to be proven to be *powerful*.

You are allowed to believe in what you feel.
You are allowed to trust what you know — even if no one else has named it yet.
Your body, your spirit, your intuition — these are not irrational. They are ancient. They are real.
And they are *yours*.

Reflection:
When have I dismissed my experience because it wasn't backed by science?
Where did I learn that my inner knowing wasn't trustworthy?
What would it feel like to believe my body and intuition, even when no one else does?
What other ways of knowing have I inherited, ignored, or silenced — and am I ready to reclaim them?

#5: Learning Ends After School

Get your education, they say — as if learning is a phase you move through and then leave behind. As if growth has a graduation date. We're taught that school is where you "get smart," and once you're done, you're supposed to have it all figured out. Degree in hand, answers intact, future secured.

But what they don't say is that some of the most important lessons — the ones that shape your soul — don't come from a classroom. They come from heartbreak. From illness. From starting over. From building something from nothing. From losing everything and discovering who you really are.

When we internalize the belief that learning ends after school, we unconsciously start to fear growth. We see mistakes as failures rather than invitations. We stop asking questions. We feel shame for not knowing something, as if we're "too old" or "too far along" to be figuring things out. We feel behind — not because we are, but because we were told the learning part was supposed to be over by now.

Psychologically, this belief creates stagnancy or shame. We resist change because we associate it with incompetence. Somatically, we may feel heavy, stuck, or numb — as if we're carrying the pressure to already be "complete," when the soul is still in motion. But the truth is: you were *never meant to stop learning*. You were meant to evolve.

In the new paradigm, we remember that life *is* the classroom — and every season is a teacher.
Your body is teaching you.
Your relationships are teaching you.

Your failures, your shifts, your resistance, your curiosity —
all of it is part of your unfolding.

You are allowed to reinvent yourself.
To ask questions at 40 that you didn't ask at 20.
To learn new skills, new truths, new parts of yourself —
again and again.
You are not behind. You are becoming.

Learning isn't a chapter you close. It's the heartbeat of your
life.
Stay curious. Stay teachable. Stay open.
Because *you* are your own curriculum — and your growth is
sacred.

Reflection:
Where have I felt ashamed or "behind" for still learning,
questioning, or evolving?
How has the belief that I'm supposed to "have it all
together" limited my curiosity?
What would it feel like to honor my growth as ongoing,
natural, and meaningful — no matter my age or stage?
What am I learning right now — and can I celebrate that,
even if it's messy?

#6: Youth Means You Lack Wisdom

They say "you'll understand when you're older," or "you're
too young to get it," as if wisdom only comes with age — as
if young people can't see clearly, feel deeply, or know truth
in their bones. We've been taught that children and youth
are blank slates — empty vessels to be filled, corrected,

shaped — not already whole beings with insight, intuition, and inner knowing of their own.

This belief shows up subtly but consistently: in families where kids are told to "stay in a child's place," in schools where obedience is prioritized over curiosity, and in a culture where youth are often seen as a problem to manage rather than a generation to learn from. And so, we grow up learning that our voices don't matter until we've accumulated enough years, degrees, or hard knocks to be taken seriously.

But the truth is: wisdom doesn't only live in age. It lives in presence. In clarity. In soul.
It lives in the child who cries when something feels off.
In the teenager who questions the system.
In the young adult who senses that there's more to life than what they were handed.

When we dismiss youth, we also dismiss the part of *ourselves* that still remembers. The intuitive part. The emotionally honest part. The wild, imaginative, unconditioned part that hasn't yet learned to perform, suppress, or comply. That part — the one we all started with — is where so much of our truth lives.

Psychologically, this belief teaches us to mistrust our own early knowing. To look back at our younger selves with shame or judgment, rather than reverence. Somatically, we may carry regret, internalized dismissal, or fear of speaking up unless we're seen as "qualified." But in truth, some of our deepest insights arrived long before the world told us who to be.

In this new paradigm, we honor wisdom as something that isn't bound by age — but by awareness.
We listen to children when they speak with clarity.
We trust the knowing of teenagers and the fire of young leaders.
We also return to our own inner child — the part of us that knew, before the world interrupted.
We stop asking *"What do you want to be when you grow up?"* and start asking *"What do you already know?"*

You were never naive — you were *sensitive*.
You were never ignorant — you were *intuitive*.
You were never wrong for knowing too much, too soon.
You were wise before the world taught you how to forget.

Reflection:
Where have I dismissed or doubted the wisdom of my younger self?
How have I silenced the inner voice that knew things before it was "appropriate"?
What messages did I receive about my worth being tied to age or experience?
Can I honor the insight, sensitivity, and truth I carried even when I was young?

Financial Beliefs

#1: More Money Equals More Happiness and Security

From a young age, we're taught that more money means more freedom. More respect. More safety. More happiness. That success can be measured by the size of your house, the make of your car, the number in your bank account. That if we just had *more*, life would finally feel okay.

And so we chase it. Not always out of greed — but out of fear. Out of conditioning. Out of the hope that maybe, just maybe, we'll finally feel calm, confident, or worthy when we hit that next financial milestone. But what no one tells us is that for many, the finish line keeps moving. And sometimes, the more we accumulate, the more we fear losing it.

This belief is rooted in systems that have equated wealth with value — not just economic value, but *personal* value. Capitalism has taught us that money fixes everything. That success is happiness. That struggle is shameful. That poverty is personal failure. So we keep striving, climbing, and comparing — believing that *more* is the answer.

Psychologically, this belief creates anxiety, scarcity, and chronic dissatisfaction — no matter how much we have. We fear slowing down. We feel behind. We tether our self-worth to our net worth. Somatically, the body reflects it too — constant tension, a never-ending to-do list, sleepless nights, a sense that we're never quite "there."

But here's the deeper truth: money can create options —
but it doesn't create peace.
It can buy convenience, comfort, even temporary relief —
but it cannot buy rootedness.
It cannot replace connection, purpose, nervous system
safety, or a life that feels aligned.
Real security comes from within — not from a number.

In this new paradigm, we begin to untangle money from
meaning.
We learn to see money as a tool, not a reflection of our
worth.
We begin to ask: *What am I really craving? Is it money* — or
is it freedom? Rest? Joy? Safety? Belonging? And how can I
begin to cultivate those feelings now, even before I "arrive"?

We still honor money. We respect its power. But we no
longer worship it.
We reclaim our happiness, not as a destination money leads
us to — but as a state of being that begins inside.

You are not more worthy when you earn more.
You are not more lovable with a bigger bank account.
You are not safer just because you have savings — if you've
never felt safe in your own body.

Reflection:
Where have I equated more money with more happiness,
love, or peace?
What emotions do I hope money will finally make me feel —
and can I start cultivating those now?
Where do I feel unsafe or unworthy around money, and is
that really about the money itself?
What would it feel like to pursue a relationship with money
that is rooted, balanced, and conscious?

#2: Debt Is a Normal Part of Life

Everyone has debt. Student loans, credit cards, mortgages, car payments. We hear it all the time — it's just the way the world works. It's positioned as a rite of passage, a necessary evil, the cost of adulthood. And over time, we begin to accept it not just as common — but as inevitable.

This belief is embedded in a system that thrives on people living just beyond their means. Where delayed gratification is rare, and long-term planning is buried under short-term urgency. A system that makes higher education, home ownership, and even basic survival feel out of reach without borrowing. So we sign on the dotted line, again and again — and call it normal.

But what's "normal" doesn't always mean healthy.
What's expected doesn't always mean aligned.

Debt becomes more than a financial tool — it becomes a chronic weight. It can shape how we feel about ourselves, our decisions, and our future. Psychologically, debt can feel like shame. Like failure. Like we're always trying to catch up. We see our balances rise and internalize them as proof that we're irresponsible or "bad with money."

Somatically, this stress isn't abstract — it's *felt*. In the gut. In the jaw. In the nervous system's fight-or-flight response every time another bill is due. We live in survival mode, constantly chasing relief, constantly hustling to pay back a system that was designed to keep us dependent.

But here's the truth: while debt is *common*, it doesn't have to be *your normal*.

You are allowed to question the systems that told you debt is just a part of life.
You are allowed to create a new relationship with money — one that doesn't include carrying guilt, fear, or the weight of owing.

In the new paradigm, we begin to see debt not as a personal failing — but as a reflection of systemic imbalance.
We shift from avoidance to awareness.
From shame to strategy.
We take small, intentional steps toward liberation — not through punishment or deprivation, but through clarity, healing, and self-respect.

You are not a bad person for having debt.
You are not behind.
You are not stuck.
You are allowed to walk a new path — one that leads to sovereignty, not just survival.

Reflection:
What beliefs have I internalized about debt — and how have they shaped how I feel about myself?
Have I accepted financial bondage as normal, simply because it's familiar?
What would it feel like to move toward financial peace without shame — even if it's one small step at a time?
Am I willing to rewrite my story around debt — from burden to breakthrough?

#3: Poverty Is Due to Laziness or Lack of Effort

We've been told a story — that people are poor because they didn't try hard enough. Because they're irresponsible, unmotivated, or made bad choices. That success is simply the reward for hard work, and if you're not succeeding financially, you must not be working hard enough.

This story is dangerous. It's been weaponized to protect systems of power, dismiss suffering, and justify inequality. It ignores generational trauma, systemic barriers, medical debt, educational gatekeeping, mental health struggles, and the thousands of invisible factors that shape someone's access to opportunity. It reduces human lives to economic output — and calls it accountability.

But when we internalize this belief — whether we've lived in poverty or not — it begins to shape how we see ourselves and others. It creates a deep fear of *becoming poor*, and with it, a deep shame for ever needing help. We distance ourselves from those struggling financially, not out of superiority, but out of terror: *If it could happen to them, it could happen to me.*

Psychologically, this belief breeds judgment and disconnect. Somatically, it creates a constant low-grade panic — that if we don't perform, achieve, or grind enough, we'll fall through the cracks. We tie our worth to our productivity. Our safety to our bank account. And our compassion becomes conditional — reserved only for those who've "earned" it.

But here's the truth: poverty is not a moral failure. It's not proof of laziness.
It's often the result of structural inequity, intergenerational trauma, and a society that prioritizes profit over people.
And those experiencing poverty often work *harder* than most — juggling multiple jobs, raising families, navigating survival, all while carrying the weight of stigma and shame.

In the new paradigm, we begin to see worth as inherent — not tied to income.
We recognize that effort does not always equal opportunity.
That wealth is not the only measure of success, and poverty is not proof of weakness.
We begin to extend compassion — not pity, not saviorism, but real human empathy.

You are not more valuable because you earn more.
You are not more evolved because you escaped struggle.
And if you've known poverty — you are not broken. You are not less than. You are not to blame.

You are worthy. Full stop.

Reflection:
What stories was I told — explicitly or implicitly — about people living in poverty?
Where have I internalized shame or superiority around financial struggle?
How might I begin to see worth, intelligence, and dignity as separate from wealth?
What would it look like to create a world — and a life — where success includes *all* of us?

#4: The Invisible Pyramids — How Society Forces Us to Obey

There are rules we all agree to without ever really questioning them.
You go to school. You get the job. You get the house. You pay the insurance. You buy the retirement plan. You do the dance. You stay in line.
And in return, you're promised safety. Stability. A future.

But beneath the surface of this "normal life" is a quiet system of control — a pyramid, carefully designed. You give your time, your health, your energy, your creativity — and in return, you get just enough to keep going. Not enough to thrive, not enough to opt out — just enough to keep playing.

This belief isn't one we consciously choose. It's baked into everything:
Student loans that start before your career does.
Healthcare tied to employment.
Retirement accounts you can't touch until you're old — even if you need them to survive now.
Rising costs of living with stagnant wages.
Tax systems that benefit the wealthy and punish the working.
A housing market that keeps you locked into 30-year chains while rent keeps you afraid to leave.
All while being told it's your fault if you can't "make it work."

This system teaches obedience disguised as opportunity.
It's not a conspiracy — it's design.
And when we internalize this structure, we begin to blame ourselves for our struggle.

We feel guilt for not thriving. Shame for not saving enough. Anxiety that we'll never catch up.

Psychologically, it creates burnout, hopelessness, and chronic comparison.
Somatically, we carry the weight of powerlessness — in our gut, our chest, our breath.
We live on edge, trying to play a game that was never built for our liberation.

But here's the radical truth: it's not *you* that's broken — it's the system.
You are not failing for feeling trapped.
You are not weak for wanting out.
You are not crazy for questioning the game.

In this new paradigm, we begin to see these invisible pyramids for what they are:
Structures designed to keep us compliant — not free.
We begin to challenge the myth that obedience equals safety.
We start redefining success not as compliance, but as *sovereignty*.
We ask better questions:
What am I building — and who benefits from it?
What would it look like to live in alignment, not just survival?

You don't owe your life to systems that demand your burnout and call it success.
You get to design a new way.
One rooted in truth, transparency, community, and inner authority.

Reflection:
What systems have I participated in without ever

questioning?
Where have I felt trapped or powerless — and blamed myself instead of the structure?
What would it look like to reclaim my agency in a system designed to keep me small?
Am I willing to see the invisible — and choose differently?

#5: Financial Literacy Is Too Complicated or Not for People Like Me

Numbers. Budgets. Investments. Taxes. Terms that trigger overwhelm, shame, or shutdown. For so many of us, financial literacy feels like a foreign language — one we were never taught but somehow expected to speak fluently. And if we can't? We assume it must be because we're not "that kind of person." Not smart enough. Not responsible enough. Not wired for money.

This belief is not an accident — it's a byproduct of a system designed to make financial power feel exclusive. Complex jargon. Gatekeeping. Elitist messaging. Generational silence. If you didn't grow up in a household that talked about money — or worse, if money was a source of stress or secrecy — chances are, you learned to fear it. Or avoid it. Or believe it wasn't for *people like you*.

And so we defer. We stay quiet in conversations about money. We let others manage it. We avoid checking accounts or opening bills. We feel too far behind to start — or too ashamed to ask for help. Psychologically, this belief creates a freeze response. Somatically, it shows up as avoidance, constriction, or shutdown around money decisions, even simple ones.

But here's the truth: you are not bad with money — you were simply never given the tools.
You are not incapable — you were uninvited.
You are not irresponsible — you were overwhelmed by a system that made financial literacy feel out of reach on purpose.

In the new paradigm, financial literacy becomes a reclamation.
Not about perfection, but empowerment.
Not about mastering every detail, but understanding enough to stand in your own power.
You don't have to become a finance expert to be financially well.
You just have to be willing to *engage* — gently, consistently, and with self-compassion.

You are allowed to learn.
You are allowed to ask questions.
You are allowed to start from exactly where you are.
And no matter what you've been told — financial wisdom belongs to *everyone*.

Reflection:
What stories have I told myself about my ability to understand or manage money?
Where did I learn that financial literacy was "too hard" or "not for me"?
What small, empowering step could I take today to begin engaging with my finances from a place of curiosity, not shame?

Am I willing to believe that I am capable — and that money is not beyond me?

#6: Abundance Is a Mindset, Not Just a Bank Balance

We're taught that abundance is measured in dollar signs. That it shows up in luxury. In excess. In accumulation. And if we don't *see* it in our accounts, our homes, our lifestyles — we assume it must not be real. We equate wealth with safety. Overflow with success. And scarcity with failure.

But here's the part that often gets missed: many people have money and still live in fear. Still hoard. Still never feel like it's enough. And others have very little and still feel nourished, supported, and rich in what truly matters. So maybe the question isn't just *how much do I have?* — but *how deeply do I trust that what I need is available to me, now and in the future?*

This belief shifts the foundation. It reminds us that abundance is not something we achieve — it's something we cultivate. It's not just about your income — it's about your inner world. Your nervous system. Your ability to receive. Your ability to feel supported, connected, and safe without needing proof in the form of a number.

That doesn't mean money doesn't matter — it does. It feeds, shelters, liberates. But in this new paradigm, we begin to see that true abundance *starts before* the paycheck. It begins with presence. With sufficiency. With the belief that life is generous, that we are provided for, that we can create from trust instead of fear.

Psychologically, this mindset expands us. It opens creativity, possibility, and grounded confidence. Somatically, the body softens. The breath deepens. The shoulders drop. We stop gripping, rushing, hoarding — and begin flowing, receiving, giving. We begin to see abundance in non-monetary forms: time, rest, joy, connection, opportunity, breath.

In this new way, we stop outsourcing abundance to external milestones.
We root it in how we *live.*
We build our relationship with money — yes — but also with trust, with enough-ness, with the feeling of being supported by something deeper than numbers.

Abundance becomes not just what we have — but who we are willing to *be.*

You don't have to wait until you "make it" to feel abundant.
You don't have to hustle your way into wholeness.
You are allowed to feel rich in love, time, wisdom, rest, and purpose — right here, right now.

Reflection:
What have I believed abundance should look like — and has that brought me peace?
Where have I tied abundance to proof, rather than presence?
What would it feel like to embody abundance today — before anything changes externally?
Can I redefine wealth to include how supported, grounded, and fulfilled I feel in my life?

Time & Aging Beliefs

#1: Youth Is the Peak — Everything After Is Decline

We live in a culture that worships youth. Smooth skin. Fast metabolisms. Boundless energy. Infinite potential. We're told that our twenties are our prime — that we should look our best, perform our best, *be* our best early — and if we don't, we've somehow missed our moment. The rest? It's downhill. Manage the symptoms. Slow the decline. Fade gracefully.

This belief shows up everywhere. In anti-aging marketing. In career timelines. In the way we talk about milestones. It's the invisible pressure that tells women their worth is tied to youth and beauty. It's the message that men must prove their success while they're still virile, powerful, productive. And it's the underlying fear that once we pass a certain age, we become irrelevant — or worse, invisible.

Psychologically, this belief fuels urgency, regret, and comparison. We rush to hit life's checkboxes — afraid that if we fall behind, we'll never catch up. We grieve aging not because of what's lost — but because of what we never got to experience when we were "supposed to." Somatically, we hold this in the body as anxiety, tension, and resistance. The body begins to feel like a betrayal, rather than a trusted home.

But here's the truth: youth is not the peak — it's a chapter.
And decline is not the inevitable next one — *depth* is.

In the new paradigm, we begin to see aging not as
diminishment, but as a *becoming*.
We begin to value the slow wisdom of lived experience.
The beauty of knowing ourselves — not just performing for
others.
The freedom that comes when we stop living for approval,
and start living in alignment.

Yes, youth is vibrant. But so is midlife clarity. So is the
courage of reinvention. So is the soul-rich wisdom of your
40s, 50s, 60s, and beyond. Every season brings gifts — not
just the ones that get photographed, praised, or celebrated
by culture.

You don't age out of magic.
You don't expire when the world stops watching.
You get deeper. Wiser. Freer. More *you*.
And that... is not a decline. It's an arrival.

Reflection:
What messages have I absorbed about aging and worth?
Where have I feared getting older — and what do I believe
I'll lose?
What might I *gain* as I grow into new seasons of life?
Can I release the idea that my "best years" are behind me —
and claim the beauty of where I am now?

#2: Time Is Running Out — It's Too Late to Change

There's a clock we've all been handed.
It's invisible but loud.
It tells us when we're supposed to fall in love. Build a career.
Have kids. Find our purpose. Heal our wounds.
And if we miss those windows? If we wake up at 30, 40, 55
and realize we want something *different* — the voice
whispers: *It's too late.*

This belief is one of the most haunting. It quietly convinces
us to settle. To shrink. To stay in the life we've outgrown
because the shame of starting over feels heavier than the
pain of staying stuck. We feel like we're behind — not
because we are, but because we're measuring our journey
against someone else's map.

Psychologically, this belief can crush possibility. We feel like
change is only for the young. That reinvention is reserved
for people who "got it right" earlier in life. Somatically, the
body absorbs the pressure — tension in the chest,
exhaustion in the bones, a heaviness that feels like defeat.
We confuse aging with fading. Time with threat.

But here's the truth: time is not your enemy — it's your
companion.
And there is no expiration date on becoming.

In the new paradigm, we throw away the old timelines.
We stop asking, *"Am I too late?"* and start asking, *"What am I
being called to now?"*
Because your life doesn't move in straight lines — it unfolds

in seasons.
And each season has its own kind of awakening.

Some people don't find their voice until their 50s.
Some people don't heal until after their kids are grown.
Some people don't fall in love with life until they lose everything first.
And some people restart — again and again — and become more alive with each turn.

You are not behind.
You are not too late.
You are right on time — for *you*.
And that is all that matters.

Reflection:
Where have I believed I missed my chance — and who gave me that timeline?
What have I felt was "too late" to begin — and is that really true?
What would it look like to honor my own timing, even if it doesn't match the world's?
Am I willing to believe that change is available to me — at any age, in any season?

#3: Rest Is Wasted Time

We live in a world that praises hustle and shames stillness.
Where full calendars are a badge of honor, and burnout is worn like a gold star.
Where slowing down is seen as falling behind — and rest is something you have to *earn* through exhaustion.

From school to the workplace to home life, we've been conditioned to equate busyness with value. To feel guilty when we're not producing, performing, or pushing through. Rest becomes a luxury — not a right. A weakness — not a wisdom. And over time, we begin to believe that if we're not doing something "productive," we're wasting our lives.

Psychologically, this belief creates a deep sense of restlessness and unworthiness. Even when we *want* to slow down, we feel guilt creep in. We feel anxious when we're still. We fear being seen as lazy, selfish, or falling behind. And somatically, our bodies bear the cost — adrenal fatigue, chronic tension, inflammation, sleep disorders, and nervous systems stuck in "go" with no safe place to land.

But here's the truth: rest is not wasted time — it is *repair*.
It is restoration.
It is remembering that you are not a machine.

In the new paradigm, rest becomes sacred.
It's no longer something you do only when you crash — it becomes part of your rhythm, your resilience, your relationship with self.
You begin to see that rest is where insight emerges, healing happens, and creativity is reborn.
That the most powerful shifts in your life might come *not* when you're striving — but when you're still enough to *receive*.

Rest is not the opposite of productivity — it's the foundation of it.
It softens the body. Calms the mind. Reconnects you with your breath.
And it reminds you that your worth has *never* been

measured by how much you can carry — but by how deeply you're willing to *care for yourself*.

You don't have to hustle for permission to rest.
You don't need to prove your exhaustion.
You are allowed to pause. To breathe. To restore. To *be*.

Reflection:
What messages have I received about rest, laziness, and productivity?
Where do I feel guilt or resistance when I slow down?
What would it look like to build rest into my life as a necessity — not an afterthought?
Am I willing to believe that rest is not wasted time, but a return to my true self?

#4: Slowing Down Means Falling Behind

There's a quiet panic that follows us through life — a whisper that says, *Keep going. Keep pushing. Don't stop. Don't fall behind.* We measure our worth in speed. Our success in how much we can juggle. Our relevance in how quickly we can respond, react, achieve.

Slowing down? That's risky. That's lazy. That's for people who can afford to pause. And most of us have been conditioned to believe that if we dare to step back, to breathe, to listen inward — the world will move on without us.

This belief is rooted in a culture obsessed with acceleration. Faster results. Faster growth. Faster healing. Faster

everything.
We glorify urgency and confuse pace with progress. We're taught to chase timelines that weren't even ours to begin with.

Psychologically, this belief creates a deep inner pressure. A fear of stillness. An inability to rest without guilt. It disconnects us from our own pace — from the cycles, seasons, and signals of our body. Somatically, the body responds with burnout, tension, insomnia, adrenal overload, and a constant state of "not enough."

But here's the truth: slowing down doesn't mean falling behind — it means *coming back home*.
To yourself. To your rhythm. To what actually matters.

In the new paradigm, we begin to honor *right timing* over fast timing.
We realize that slowing down often brings clarity.
That pause is not weakness — it's wisdom.
That rushing can take us further from our truth, while stillness often brings us right to it.

You are not falling behind when you move at your own pace.
You are not missing out — you are tuning in.
To your nervous system. To your soul. To the next right step that cannot be heard in the noise of constant motion.

Slow is sacred.
And your worth is not measured by how quickly you move — but by how deeply you live.

Reflection:
Where have I internalized urgency as a measure of value?

What am I afraid might happen if I slow down?
When have I made my most aligned decisions — during chaos, or in stillness?
Am I willing to trust that slowing down may actually *move me forward* in ways speed never could?

#5: Prioritizing Your Time Over Others' Needs Is Selfish

Be available. Be helpful. Be generous. Be selfless.
From a young age, we're praised for putting others first — for making ourselves small to make others comfortable. We're taught that being a "good" person means being endlessly accessible. That saying yes is noble, and saying no is cold. That if someone else needs you, your time is no longer yours.

And slowly, we learn to equate self-sacrifice with virtue. We feel guilty for wanting space. We apologize for having boundaries. We feel selfish when we protect our energy. Even when we're drowning, we convince ourselves it's our job to stay afloat *for everyone else.*

This belief is deeply tied to identity. It's especially embedded in how we're conditioned by gender, religion, family roles, and cultural expectations. And over time, it wires us to ignore our own time-based needs — rest, focus, solitude, spaciousness — in service of others' comfort or approval.

Psychologically, this belief erodes our sense of sovereignty. It creates resentment, burnout, emotional fatigue, and an underlying belief that *my time doesn't belong to me*. Somatically, it shows up as overwhelm, tension, chronic busyness, or the inability to rest even when we desperately need it.

But here's the truth: your time is not selfish — it's sacred. It is not greedy to protect it. It is *wise*.
Because when your time is always being given away, your life becomes someone else's.

In the new paradigm, we reclaim our right to choose how we spend our hours, our days, our energy.
We stop equating worth with availability.
We understand that boundaries don't separate us from people — they *deepen* connection by honoring truth.

You are allowed to prioritize your own time.
You are allowed to say no, even if it disappoints someone.
You are allowed to choose rest over obligation. Wholeness over performance. Alignment over approval.

Protecting your time isn't selfish — it's how you teach the world that your life matters, too.

Reflection:
Where have I felt guilty for needing time to myself?
What have I been taught about saying no or setting time-based boundaries?
What parts of me have I silenced to meet others' expectations?
Am I willing to believe that honoring my time is not rejection — but self-respect?

#6: Life Is Measured by Milestones and Timelines

By 18, you should know what you want to do.
By 25, you should have a career.
By 30, be married.
By 35, have kids.
By 40, be established.
By 50, be secure.
By 60, be winding down.

There's a silent scorecard we're handed — filled with deadlines, milestones, and invisible benchmarks. And if we miss one? If we're "late" to the party? We feel like we've failed. Even if we've lived, learned, and grown deeply in ways no timeline could ever account for.

This belief is everywhere. It's written into education systems, career ladders, family expectations, and social media highlight reels. It convinces us there's a right time for everything — and if we don't hit the mark, we must be broken, lost, or running out of time.

Psychologically, this belief creates quiet panic. The constant sense of being behind. The shame of not keeping up. The pressure to force things before they're ready. Somatically, we carry it as tension in the chest, a racing mind, and the exhaustion of trying to meet deadlines we never agreed to in the first place.

But here's the truth: your life is not a checklist.
You are not a project to be completed on schedule.
You are a soul unfolding in divine time — and that timeline is *yours alone*.

In the new paradigm, we release the myth of milestones as measures of worth.
We stop rushing, comparing, and forcing.
We honor the seasons of becoming — the detours, the pauses, the reinventions, the sacred delays that shaped us far more than any timeline ever could.

Maybe your life isn't late.
Maybe it's just *true*.
And maybe the "milestone" isn't a moment the world can measure — but the moment *you* come home to yourself.

You are not behind.
You are on time for your own becoming.
And that is more than enough.

Reflection:
Where have I felt like I was "behind" in life — and whose timeline was I following?
What milestones have I judged myself for missing — and do they even reflect what I *truly* value?
What has grown in me *off the beaten path* — and how can I honor that?
Can I release the pressure to arrive — and instead trust the rhythm of where I am now?

Spirituality & Purpose Beliefs

#1: Purpose Must Come from Achievements

We've been taught that purpose is something you *prove*.
That it's tied to a career title, a resume, a legacy.
That in order for your life to matter, you must *do* something impressive, measurable, or meaningful enough to be recognized by the world.

This belief is baked into our culture — where productivity is praised, impact is public, and worth is tied to visibility. We begin to believe that unless we're doing something "big," we must not be living in our purpose. That unless our work is changing lives, leaving a mark, or breaking ceilings, we're somehow falling short of why we're here.

And so we chase it — this elusive "purpose" — believing it lives at the end of achievement. We burn out trying to be significant. We question our path every time we pause or pivot. We feel lost when life slows down, as if stillness means our life has lost its meaning.

Psychologically, this belief leaves us empty, disconnected, and always reaching. Somatically, we feel the pressure in our chest, the tight grip in our gut, the constant buzz of urgency — as if our value is always *one step away*.

But here's the truth: purpose is not something you chase — it's something you *live*.
It's not reserved for the extraordinary.
It's found in the everyday.

In how you love. In how you show up. In the quiet, sacred way you move through the world with intention.

In the new paradigm, we begin to see purpose not as performance — but as *presence*.
Your purpose may not have a job title. It may not win awards.
It might be found in the way you raise your children, hold space for someone's pain, grow food from the earth, create beauty, or heal a lineage that no one else could.

Purpose doesn't always look like impact.
Sometimes it looks like alignment.
Sometimes it looks like *being exactly who you are*, without apology or performance.

You don't have to earn your purpose through achievement.
You *are* your purpose — embodied, breathing, becoming.

Reflection:
Where have I equated purpose with success, visibility, or productivity?
Have I overlooked the quiet ways my life already carries meaning?
What lights me up — not because it's impressive, but because it feels true?
Am I willing to believe that I don't need to do more to be purposeful — I simply need to *be more of myself*?

#2: Spirituality Is the Same as Religion

For many of us, the only doorway we were ever shown to connect with something greater was through religion. A building. A book. A set of rules. We were taught that God had a specific name, voice, and gender. That faith meant obedience. That belonging required belief in someone else's version of the truth.

And if we didn't fit into that box? If we asked too many questions, if we loved differently, if we doubted, struggled, or simply felt disconnected from the structure — we were told we had walked away from God. From truth. From our soul.

So we carried guilt. Or shame. Or silence. Some of us stayed, trying to shrink ourselves to fit. Others left, and felt like we had to choose between our freedom and our faith. We learned to associate "spirituality" with control, hierarchy, or trauma — not with love, intimacy, or peace.

The truth is, Jesus hated religion—he often challenged it due to religious leaders tendencies to twist God's word for power, or personal gain. From a young age many of us heard the teachings of the Bible, but what we witnessed in the lives of those teaching it often didn't align.

The hypocrisy was confusing, even disheartening, making it hard to know what—or who—to trust.

Over time, this disconnect can cause us to pull away, sensing something deeply inauthentic and unsafe in the versions of faith we are often shown.

Psychologically, this belief creates spiritual exile. We feel like there's no place for us in the divine. Somatically, it creates fear in the body — fear of being judged, rejected, or punished by something that was meant to love us unconditionally. Our spirit longs for connection — but our nervous system remembers the pain.

But here's the truth: religion and spirituality are *not* the same — and they never were.

Religion is a container. Spirituality is the *current*.
Religion is the language. Spirituality is the *truth behind the words*.
Religion can be beautiful, sacred, healing — *if* it points you back to love. But if it disconnects you from yourself, from others, or from grace — it's not the way.

In the new paradigm, spirituality is reclaimed as something personal. Intimate. Direct.
It's a personal relationship with The Father, The Son, and the Holy Spirit — in a way that feels honest and alive.
It's not about being perfect. It's about being present.
It's not about knowing all the answers. It's about asking better questions.

You don't have to follow a religion to be deeply spiritual.
You don't have to follow "religious" rules to be close to God.
You don't have to choose between freedom and faith.
You get to come home to your own sacred connection — one that's rooted in love, truth, and *belonging without conditions*.

Reflection:
What messages did I receive about religion and spirituality growing up?

Where did I feel safe — and where did I feel silenced?
What does spirituality mean to *me*, now — if I define it on
my own terms?
Am I willing to believe that I don't need a middleman to be
close to God — I can go directly, and be received exactly as I
am?

#3: Science and Spirituality Cannot Coexist

Choose a side, they say.
Are you logical or intuitive? A believer or a skeptic?
Grounded in data, or guided by faith?
For centuries, we've been taught that science and
spirituality live in different worlds — even different people.
That you can either trust what can be measured *or* what can
be felt — but never both.

This divide was never about truth. It was about control.
Spirituality was dismissed as superstition. Science was
weaponized to strip mystery from the sacred. Institutions
told us that to be intelligent, we must detach from the
unseen — and to be spiritual, we must reject reason. And in
that split, something vital was lost: *wholeness.*

Psychologically, this belief fractures the self. It creates
internal conflict — between head and heart, between
knowing and believing. We second-guess our insights. We
distrust the data if it challenges our faith, and distrust our
faith if it isn't backed by data. Somatically, we feel this split
as disconnection — the discomfort of having to choose
between our analytical mind and our mystical soul.

But here's the truth: science and spirituality are not enemies — they are mirrors.
They are different languages describing the same mystery.
Science explains the *how*. Spirituality honors the *why*.
Science explores the mechanics. Spirituality holds the meaning.

In the new paradigm, we allow both to inform us.
We see that the nervous system's responses are physiological *and* sacred.
That breathwork, prayer, fasting, meditation, somatic release — they are both ancient wisdom *and* evidence-based healing.
We trust our bodies *and* our beliefs.
We listen to research *and* revelation.

You don't have to choose between being grounded and being guided.
You don't have to silence your intuition to honor your intelligence.
You don't have to abandon spirituality to be informed — or abandon science to be free.

You are allowed to be fully human — and deeply connected to something greater.
You are allowed to *know* with your mind and *feel* with your spirit.
You are allowed to let truth live in more than one place.

Reflection:
Where have I felt like I had to choose between intellect and intuition?
What stories have I been told about spirituality being irrational, or science being soulless?
What would it feel like to integrate both — to honor the

evidence *and* the unseen?
Am I willing to let truth be layered, expansive, and more whole than I've been taught?

#4: Living Your Purpose Means You Always Know Where Your Going

We've been taught that purpose comes with a plan. That when you're "on the right path," you'll be clear, confident, and moving forward in a straight line. That certainty is proof of alignment — and if you're confused, lost, or in transition, you must have taken a wrong turn.

This belief is so seductive — especially in a world that values direction over depth. We idolize clarity. We equate vision with virtue. And we internalize the idea that if we don't *know* exactly what we're doing with our life, then we must not have one.

So we chase certainty.
We pressure ourselves to figure it all out.
We bypass rest, detours, and rediscovery — all in the name of "finding our purpose."

Psychologically, this belief creates anxiety and shame. We fear the unknown. We judge ourselves for not having answers. We silence our curiosity in favor of control. Somatically, it manifests as tightness in the chest, shallow breathing, or a low-level panic that hums beneath our daily decisions. A constant whisper of, *"I should know by now."*

But here's the truth: living your purpose doesn't always feel like knowing — it often feels like *trusting*.

It's not a neatly paved road. It's a wilderness.
It's not a destination. It's a devotion.
It's not clarity that defines your purpose — it's your willingness to *show up anyway*.

In the new paradigm, we allow purpose to unfold in seasons, not schedules.
We honor the messy middle. The becoming. The pauses. The pivots.
We stop waiting for certainty to take the next step — and begin listening for what feels *true*, even when the whole path isn't visible.

Purpose isn't something you "figure out" once and for all.
It's something you *live into* — again and again.
Through your presence.
Through your honesty.
Through your courage to take the next right step, without needing the whole map.

You don't have to know where you're going to be walking in purpose.
Sometimes, the not-knowing *is* the sacred part.
The part where you meet yourself — and God — in a whole new way.

Reflection:
Where have I felt pressure to "have it all figured out"?
How has uncertainty made me question my worth or purpose?
Can I name a time when I found meaning in the middle of confusion?

Am I willing to trust that my purpose is alive — even when the path isn't clear?

#5: Being Spiritual Always Means Feeling Peaceful

We're often sold a sanitized version of spirituality — all light, no shadow.
A version where being "high vibe" means never being angry.
Where calmness equals enlightenment.
Where discomfort means you're not aligned — or not evolved enough.

This belief turns spirituality into performance.
It teaches us to bypass what's real in favor of what looks serene.
To suppress rage, grief, fear, or frustration in the name of being "spiritually mature."
It rewards politeness over honesty, stillness over movement, and smiles over rawness.

Psychologically, this belief teaches us to mistrust our emotions. To feel guilt or shame anytime we're struggling. To disconnect from our truth in order to uphold an image of peace. Somatically, it creates internal tension — we tighten, repress, and silence parts of ourselves that don't "fit" the mold.

But here's the truth: being spiritual doesn't mean being peaceful all the time.
It means being *present* — even in the chaos.

It means feeling it *all* — the joy and the grief, the love and the anger, the awe and the ache — and staying open, honest, and connected through it.

Spirituality is not about staying above the mess — it's about being anchored through it.
It's sitting with your sadness instead of running from it.
It's allowing your anger to move without burning down your life.
It's feeling deeply, truthfully, and without shame — knowing that every emotion has something sacred to show you.

In the new paradigm, we release the pressure to be peaceful at all costs.
We recognize that real spiritual growth doesn't always feel good — sometimes it feels like breaking. Like shedding. Like coming undone so something deeper can emerge.

You are not less spiritual because you're feeling overwhelmed.
You are not broken because you're having a hard time.
You are human — and that *is* the path.

The most powerful peace doesn't come from avoiding life's storms —
It comes from learning how to stay grounded in yourself and trust God in the midst of it all.

Reflection:
Where have I judged myself for not feeling peaceful enough?
What emotions have I silenced in the name of "being spiritual"?
What would it look like to honor my full emotional experience as sacred?

Am I willing to let go of spiritual perfection — and embrace spiritual *presence* instead?

#6: Spiritual Bypass Is the Same as Spiritual Growth

"Everything happens for a reason."
"Just focus on the positive."
"Let it go. Forgive. Move on."

On the surface, these phrases sound helpful — even enlightened. But beneath them often lives a dangerous distortion: the idea that true spirituality means transcending pain, skipping the hard stuff, and staying above the mess of being human.

This is spiritual bypass — using spiritual ideas to avoid emotional reality.
It's when positivity replaces processing.
When "love and light" silence grief, rage, trauma, or truth.
When we rush to "forgive and forget" without ever fully *feeling*.

Many of us learned this in spiritual spaces that feared emotion or discomfort. We were told that anger was low-vibration. That sadness meant we weren't trusting God. That questioning was a sign of spiritual immaturity. So we stuffed it down. We smiled through it. We tried to ascend our way out of what needed to be faced and healed.

Psychologically, spiritual bypass creates deep repression.
It disconnects us from our inner world — and from others.

We start to feel ashamed for struggling, unsafe to be honest, and unsure if our pain has a place.
Somatically, it creates dissonance: the body knows what's real, even when the mind tries to override it with spiritual scripts.

But here's the truth: spiritual growth isn't about bypassing — it's about *being with*.

Real growth is raw. Unpolished. Honest.
It's sitting in the ashes of what you lost before trying to rise again.
It's letting grief have its voice. Letting anger be witnessed.
It's choosing to stay present through discomfort — not in spite of your faith, but *because of it*.

In the new paradigm, we reclaim a spirituality that welcomes all of you.
One that knows you can cry and still be connected to God.
That your doubts can lead you deeper into truth.
That your pain isn't a barrier to the sacred — it's often the doorway.

You are not less spiritual when you feel broken.
You are not failing if you're still healing.
You don't have to fake peace to be whole.

Growth isn't in escaping the wound — it's in holding it with tenderness, staying with it long enough to understand its message, and walking with it toward integration.

Reflection:
Where have I used spiritual ideas to avoid facing something real within me?
What emotions or truths have I skipped over in the name of

being "high vibe"?
What would it look like to bring more honesty into my spiritual life?
Am I willing to believe that the messy, human parts of me are not obstacles to growth — they *are* the growth?

Body & Appearance Beliefs

#1: Beauty Standards Are Universal

Somewhere along the way, we were told there is one kind of beauty — and everything else is just... trying.
One skin tone. One hair texture. One body shape. One face. One age.
The message wasn't always loud, but it was consistent:
This is what desirable looks like. This is what valuable looks like. This is what "beautiful" looks like.

And if you don't look like that?
Then you better shrink, smooth, lighten, sculpt, cover, or contort until you do.

This belief isn't rooted in truth. It's rooted in profit.
Industries are built on convincing you that you are not enough — but you *could be* if you just bought the right product, lost the right weight, or fixed the right "flaw."
It's manufactured insecurity, sold to us as motivation.

Psychologically, this belief fractures our sense of self.
It makes us compare, compete, and criticize.
It teaches us to see ourselves through the lens of lack —
always measuring, always falling short.
Somatically, we feel it as tension in the mirror. A flinch
when the camera's on. A subtle self-hatred that feels normal
because it's so common.

But here's the truth: beauty is *not* a narrow mold to fit into
— it is a diverse, living, breathing expression of *being fully
you.*

There is no single standard of beauty. There never was.
Beauty is cultural. Seasonal. Personal. Spiritual.
It's in the stories carved into your skin.
It's in the joy behind your smile.
It's in the radiance of someone who's at home in their body
— not because they were told they should be, but because
they chose it.

In the new paradigm, we stop outsourcing our worth to an
imaginary standard.
We stop chasing someone else's definition of desirable.
We begin asking deeper questions:
*What feels beautiful to me? What makes me feel most like
myself? What if beauty isn't something I have to earn — but
something I get to claim?*

You are not behind. You are not broken. You are not a
before-picture.
You are not here to be palatable.
You are here to be *true* — and truth is magnetic.

Reflection:
What messages have I received about beauty — from media,

family, culture?
Where have I compared myself to an invisible standard and come up short?
What does beauty feel like when I'm not performing or conforming?
Am I willing to believe that beauty is not universal — it's personal, and I get to define it?

#2: Cosmetic Procedures Are Necessary for Aging Bodies

There's a quiet panic that seeps in around a certain age.
A wrinkle here. A shift in skin tone there.
And suddenly the world offers you a dozen ways to erase what's been lived.
Tighten it. Freeze it. Fill it.
Because God forbid you look like you've *been here.*

This belief doesn't come from vanity — it comes from survival.
Aging in our culture isn't just seen as natural. It's seen as a threat to value, desirability, even credibility. Especially for women.
We're told that to remain visible, relevant, or lovable, we must stay frozen in time — or at least try our best to.

The industries that profit from this narrative call it "confidence," "prevention," "modern wellness."
But often, beneath the glossy ads and filtered faces, what they're really selling is the fear of being forgotten.

Psychologically, this belief tells us that our worth has an expiration date.
That youth equals value — and aging must be managed, hidden, or "fixed."
Somatically, it creates a deep disconnection. We start to view our natural features as problems to solve. We flinch at our reflection. We grieve changes that were never meant to be shameful.

But here's the truth: aging is not a flaw — it is a privilege. Your lines are not a failure of maintenance — they are a record of your laughter, your grief, your years of *living*.

In the new paradigm, we don't shame those who choose cosmetic procedures — but we question the system that made them feel like they *had* to.

We return to reverence.
We honor the softness that comes with time, the gravity-earned wisdom in our eyes, the changing rhythms of our bodies.
We realize we were never meant to stay frozen.
We were meant to evolve — and to be loved through every season of that becoming.

You do not owe anyone your youth.
You do not have to earn beauty by resisting nature.
You are not fading — you are *deepening*.

Reflection:
What have I been taught to fear about aging?
Where have I internalized the message that growing older makes me less valuable?
How might I begin to view my aging body with reverence instead of resistance?

Am I willing to rewrite the story — not to reject others'
choices, but to reclaim my own power in how I relate to my
changing self?

#3: Self-Worth Is Tied to Appearance Only

From the earliest age, we were praised for how we looked.
"Look how cute you are."
"You're so pretty."
"That outfit is adorable."
The compliments came easy when we looked "right." And
often went quiet when we didn't.

Slowly, the message sunk in: *how you look determines how
you'll be treated.*
Beauty brings approval. Attraction brings belonging.
Thinness brings admiration.
And anything outside of that?
Silence. Criticism. Rejection. Or worse — invisibility.

So we began to attach our worth to our reflection.
We measured our value in photos, pants sizes, and passing
comments.
We started to believe that being seen *was* being loved —
and that changing our bodies was the gateway to feeling
worthy.

Psychologically, this belief creates a fragile self-image, one
built on external validation.
It makes us scan for flaws, seek approval, and equate our
appearance with our goodness.
Somatically, it lives as a low hum of self-surveillance —

sucking in, smoothing out, hiding what we've deemed "unacceptable," even from ourselves.

But here's the truth: your body is *not* the currency of your worth.

You are not more lovable when you weigh less.
You are not more deserving when you're attractive.
You are not more valuable when you're being seen.

Your worth is *inherent*. It is the marrow of your being — not a reward for fitting a mold.

In the new paradigm, we start to ask: *What if I am enough, even when I don't feel beautiful? Even when I'm overlooked? Even when I'm simply existing, not performing?*

We start building our worth on deeper ground — on our integrity, our softness, our truth.
On the way we show up, the way we care, the way we choose to come back to ourselves, again and again.

Self-worth isn't something you win by perfecting your appearance.
It's something you remember — and reclaim.

Reflection:
When did I first learn that appearance determined my value?
Where have I performed beauty to feel accepted or loved?
What would it feel like to unhook my worth from how I look?
Am I willing to explore who I am beyond the mirror — and believe that *who I am* is already enough?

#4: Movement and Exercises Are Only for Weight Loss

"Burn the calories."
"No pain, no gain."
"Summer bodies are made in winter."

Somehow, movement — the purest form of self-expression — got hijacked by shame.
We were taught that exercise is something you *have* to do to be good, to be thin, to be acceptable.
Not something you *get* to do to feel alive.

This belief turns movement into punishment.
It disconnects us from joy, intuition, and embodiment.
It teaches us to ignore our body's cues and push through pain in the name of progress.
It glorifies exhaustion. It moralizes thinness. It strips movement of pleasure and replaces it with pressure.

Psychologically, this belief warps our relationship with our bodies.
We start to believe that we don't deserve rest.
That movement only "counts" if it's hard, extreme, or yields a visible result.
Somatically, it conditions us to override the body — to push instead of partner, to punish instead of listen.

But here's the truth: your body was born to move — not to be managed.

Movement isn't a debt you owe for what you ate.
It's a celebration of your aliveness.
It's dancing in the kitchen. Stretching with the sunrise.

Taking a walk to clear your mind.
It's shaking off the day. Releasing the tension. Returning to yourself.

In the new paradigm, movement becomes a form of *care*, not control.
It becomes a conversation — not a command.
It becomes intuitive, responsive, *joyful*.

We remember that movement isn't about fixing a body — it's about *feeling* it.
It's about being in it, with it, for it.

You do not have to earn your worth in sweat.
You do not have to prove your discipline through pain.
You can move because it feels *good*, because it helps you *connect*, because it brings you *home*.

Reflection:
What messages have I received about movement and body image?
When have I used exercise to punish rather than nourish myself?
What forms of movement feel joyful, grounding, or healing to me?
Am I willing to move my body not to change it — but to *honor* it?

#5: The Perfect Body Is Meant to Be Permanent

We chase it like a finish line — the "perfect" body.
Maybe we hit a number on the scale, see the abs show through, zip the jeans we never thought we'd wear again.
And for a moment, we feel invincible.
But then comes the fear: *Can I keep this up?*
What happens if I slip?

We were never told that the body is seasonal. That it responds to life — to grief, to motherhood, to stress, to healing.
Instead, we were told that once we "make it," we must *maintain* it. That backsliding is failure. That change is weakness.

So we start to cling.
To routines that burn us out.
To eating habits that leave us depleted.
To identities that no longer match the rhythm of our lives.

Psychologically, this belief locks us into rigidity.
It makes our sense of worth conditional — one injury, one hormonal shift, one life change away from collapse.
Somatically, it creates distrust. We stop listening to our body's changing needs. We try to freeze it in time, even as it whispers for rest, softness, or space.

But here's the truth: the "perfect" body is a myth.
And permanence was never the point.

Your body is not a sculpture to be preserved.
It is a living system — dynamic, adaptive, sacred.

It will stretch, soften, scar, heal, change shape. It's supposed to.

In the new paradigm, we stop worshiping consistency as a virtue.
We honor the body as cyclical, responsive, and wise.
We stop making health a snapshot in time, and start making it a lifelong relationship.

You are not failing if your body changes.
You are not broken if you can't maintain a version of yourself from five years ago.
You are human — evolving, expanding, learning to love yourself through each iteration.

The goal was never to stay the same.
The goal is to stay *connected.*

Reflection:
Where have I believed that once I reached a goal with my body, I had to maintain it forever?
How has that belief shaped the way I treat myself?
What would it look like to embrace my body as seasonal — to allow change without shame?
Am I willing to build a relationship with my body that can evolve, instead of clinging to a version of it that no longer fits?

#6: Only Certain Bodies Are Allowed to Be Seen

There's an unspoken rule in our culture:
If your body doesn't fit the standard — stay quiet, stay covered, stay invisible.

We learn this early.
We notice who gets celebrated, and who gets shamed.
Who is centered in the media, and who's left out.
Who is told they're "brave" for wearing a swimsuit — and who's simply called beautiful.

And so, many of us shrink.
We pull at our clothes. We sit a certain way. We hide from photos.
We wait until we "fix" ourselves before we allow ourselves to be seen.

This belief isn't just about beauty — it's about *permission*.
Who gets to take up space. Who is allowed to be visible.
Who is granted the dignity of presence.

Psychologically, this belief creates a fractured sense of self.
We internalize shame that doesn't belong to us.
We start to believe that our existence is too much — or not enough — for the world to witness.
Somatically, it's felt in the hunch of the shoulders, the tension in the jaw, the shrinking of the breath.
The body physically responds to a lifetime of messages saying, *"You don't belong here."*

But here's the truth: **every body belongs.**

Your body is not a problem to be fixed before it deserves to be seen.
You don't need permission to take up space.
You don't need validation to exist fully, freely, and unapologetically in the skin you're in.

In the new paradigm, we reject the lie that visibility is earned.
We challenge the systems and stories that try to gatekeep worth.
We allow softness, scars, stretch marks, curves, mobility aids, wrinkles, bellies, and bodies of all kinds to be *seen and celebrated.*

We begin to show up as we are — not because we've "made it," but because we've stopped abandoning ourselves to fit someone else's mold.

Your existence is not a disruption.
Your presence is not a mistake.
You were never meant to shrink for comfort. You were meant to *shine for truth.*

Reflection:
Where have I held back from being seen because of how my body looks?
What messages have I received about which bodies are allowed to be visible, celebrated, or free?
Am I willing to begin showing up as I am — not when I'm "ready," but because I already *belong?*
What might it feel like to take up space without apology?

Consumer & Materialism Beliefs

#1: Owning More Leads to Happiness

We grow up swimming in messages that whisper — or scream — that our worth is measured by what we own. The sleek car, the bigger house, the trendiest outfit, the latest tech. We're told that joy comes wrapped in a box, delivered in two days or less. That if we could just buy the next thing, *then* we'd feel whole. *Then* we'd be seen. *Then* we'd finally arrive.

It's a lie dressed in luxury, sold through curated commercials and filtered feeds. And it works—because it hooks us where we're most vulnerable: the desire to feel like we matter.

This belief didn't come out of nowhere. It was built intentionally. In the rise of industrial capitalism, mass production outpaced demand. So marketing evolved—not just to sell products, but to sell emotions. Commercials didn't just show you a car; they showed you a man with confidence, friends, admiration. Advertisements didn't just sell soap—they sold love, belonging, a sense of being "enough."

The "American Dream" became the perfect backdrop: work hard, buy more, be happy. But no one mentioned the fine print—that you'd always be chasing. That satisfaction would always sit just out of reach.

And so we hustle. We compare. We spend. We scroll. We convince ourselves that the next purchase will be the one that finally fills the emptiness. And when it doesn't, we try again. Bigger, better, faster.

Psychologically, this creates a loop of dissatisfaction. We measure our lives against highlight reels. We believe success is visible, tangible, ownable. And when we don't measure up, we internalize it as failure. On a deeper level, we start to numb. We avoid stillness, avoid the real questions, avoid our unmet needs—because that kind of truth can't be purchased.

Our bodies feel it too. The stress of chasing. The fatigue of never arriving. We sacrifice rest, connection, even health for another paycheck, another upgrade. The nervous system stays wired, tense, exhausted. And for what? A fleeting dopamine hit from a delivery notification?

Eventually, some of us wake up. Sometimes it takes a breakdown, a health scare, a moment of raw clarity—where the panic sets in and we realize: *None of this made me feel alive.*

Because the truth is, joy doesn't live in things.
It lives in presence.
In simplicity.
In a quiet morning with your kids.
In deep belly laughter around a dinner table.
In creating, in connecting, in remembering who you are when no one's watching.

The new paradigm isn't anti-comfort. It's pro-consciousness. It's asking not "How much do I have?" but "Does what I have reflect who I really am?" It's choosing to measure abundance in time, energy, and truth—not just transactions.

You don't need to own more to be more.
You don't need to impress to be enough.
You don't need a full closet or a five-figure income to access joy.

You need to come home to what actually matters.

Reflection:
What messages did I absorb about success, happiness, and what it looks like?
Where in my life have I believed that more stuff equals more worth?
What would it feel like to release the chase and root myself in sufficiency?
What might I discover if I let go of what I thought I needed—and made space for what I truly value?

#2: Buying Convenience and Comfort Will Solve Discomfort

We live in a world that tells us discomfort is a problem to be fixed—immediately. Feeling tired? Order takeout. Feeling anxious? Add to cart. Feeling overwhelmed? Distract yourself with a show, a drink, a scroll, a "treat."

We're sold the promise that comfort can be purchased. That ease lives in two-day shipping and digital checkouts. That if life feels heavy, there must be something we can buy to lift the weight.

And so we do. We buy the candle, the skincare, the takeout, the new outfit, the upgraded app. We chase relief in tiny dopamine hits and temporary escapes. But the discomfort always returns—louder, deeper, more persistent. Because it was never asking for a product. It was asking for *presence*.

This belief—that buying convenience will make us feel better—was carefully planted. As life sped up, capitalism evolved to meet us in our exhaustion and exploit it. Marketing became more than persuasion; it became emotional manipulation. Slogans like *"You deserve it," "Treat yourself,"* and *"Why wait?"* turned coping into consumption. And instead of listening to our bodies, we learned to silence them with purchases.

But in silencing them, we stopped listening to ourselves.

Psychologically, this belief fragments us from our inner world. It teaches us that struggle means failure, that pain means pause, and that healing should be outsourced. We forget how to *be* with ourselves. We lose the muscle of resilience. And over time, we begin to equate peace with distraction, and nourishment with indulgence.

Our bodies keep the score. When we override fatigue with caffeine, or stuff emotions down with sugar, or numb loneliness with online shopping, the nervous system becomes disoriented. Instead of moving through discomfort, we get stuck in a loop: soothe, suppress, repeat. Eventually, that loop creates symptoms—chronic stress, tension, bloating, fatigue, compulsive habits. Not because we are broken, but because we are bypassing the truth of what we actually need.

But discomfort isn't the enemy. It's the compass.

Discomfort says, *"Slow down."*
"You're not aligned."
"You're not tending to something that matters."

When we stop outsourcing our pain and start listening to it, we find wisdom. We find unmet needs. We find ourselves.

The new paradigm invites us back into relationship with our discomfort—not to fix it, but to *honor* it.
To ask, *"What are you trying to show me?"*
To realize that real comfort doesn't come from consumption—it comes from connection.
Connection to body.
Connection to rhythm.
Connection to presence.

It's not about rejecting all convenience. It's about remembering that no product can replace the healing power of being with yourself.

True comfort doesn't numb.
It nourishes.
It softens.
It returns you to yourself.

Reflection:
When I feel discomfort—emotional, physical, or spiritual—
what is my first instinct?
What am I reaching for that might actually be a substitute
for what I really need?
What would it feel like to *stay* with the discomfort long
enough to hear its message?

#3: You Are What You Own

From an early age, we're conditioned to associate our
identity with what we possess. The car we drive, the
neighborhood we live in, the brands we wear—each
becomes a quiet but powerful symbol of value. It's not just
about what we like or need anymore; it's about who we
believe we have to be in order to be respected, admired, or
loved.

This belief isn't accidental. It was carefully manufactured by
decades of consumer marketing that gradually shifted the
narrative from function to identity. Products stopped being
tools for living and started becoming statements of worth. A
handbag wasn't just a handbag—it was confidence. A home
wasn't just shelter—it was status. The more we bought, the
more we believed we were becoming someone "better."

And then came social media, intensifying this belief tenfold. We no longer compared ourselves to neighbors or coworkers—we began measuring our lives against curated feeds, where perfection was filtered, and value was painted in aesthetics. If your life didn't match the standard, it was easy to feel behind, less than, or invisible.

Psychologically, this creates a fragile foundation for identity. We begin to perform rather than live. The chase for the next upgrade or image of success becomes relentless, and the deeper truth of who we are starts to fade beneath the surface of what we think we're supposed to be. We lose connection to our inner compass in favor of outer approval.

Over time, this disconnect shows up in the body. The nervous system, constantly striving, rarely settles. There's a low-grade hum of stress that comes from never feeling "there" yet—always needing to do more, have more, become more. This can manifest in anxiety, restlessness, digestive issues, fatigue, and even compulsive behaviors like overworking or overspending. The body aches for rest, for authenticity, for the permission to stop proving.

But the truth is, your worth has never lived in what you own. It was never housed in your wardrobe or bank account or square footage. It lives in your essence—your presence, your resilience, your heart, your capacity to love and connect.

You don't need to perform your value. You just need to remember it.

The new paradigm isn't about rejecting all material comfort—it's about detaching your identity from it. It's about knowing you are whole, even when your life doesn't look polished. It's about reconnecting with the parts of you that were never for sale: your joy, your integrity, your peace. When we stop letting things define us, we return to who we've always been beneath it all—free.

Reflection:
Have you ever shaped your identity around your belongings or image?
What would it feel like to live for yourself instead of for appearance?
Who are you when no one's watching?

#4: Spending Equals Self-Care

Somewhere along the way, we started confusing self-care with spending. It wasn't always this way. Once, care meant tending to ourselves gently, intentionally—through nourishment, rest, boundaries, or stillness. But in today's world, it often looks like shopping carts full of skincare, takeout meals ordered after a long day, or the latest wellness subscription. The message we're sold is simple: if you love yourself, you'll buy something that proves it.

This belief didn't appear by accident. It was designed— rooted in a system that benefits when we're tired, disconnected, and searching for relief. As marketing evolved, it learned to prey on our pain points, turning healing into a product and wholeness into a price tag. Advertisements shifted from showing us what we might *need* to convincing us that what we *lack* can be filled through consumption. Especially for women, "treat yourself" became a slogan of liberation, even as it tethered us to a cycle of temporary comfort and long-term depletion.

But when we look closer, this belief reveals itself as a thief. It steals our presence and replaces it with performance. It teaches us to soothe without listening, to cope without asking questions. We start chasing the next purchase instead of the next breath, numbing discomfort instead of getting curious about it. And while the dopamine hit of spending feels like a momentary high, the crash comes soon after—sometimes as financial stress, sometimes as emotional emptiness, and often as the quiet ache of still not feeling seen, known, or tended to.

Our bodies are not fooled by this pattern. They register the absence of true care. They feel the fatigue of chasing ease in all the wrong places. When we ignore the signals— hunger, loneliness, exhaustion, overwhelm—and try to quiet them with convenience, the nervous system begins to fray. Sleep suffers. Digestion slows. Emotions flatten. The very vessel we're trying to care for becomes dysregulated, not because we're broken, but because we're bypassing the very things it's asking us to notice.

Real self-care doesn't demand a receipt. It asks for your attention. It asks you to stop and ask: What do I actually need right now? Not what will make me feel better in the moment, but what will anchor me in wholeness over time. Sometimes the answer is movement. Sometimes it's stillness. Sometimes it's letting yourself cry without rushing to fix it. Self-care, at its core, is about coming home to yourself—not performing wellness, but practicing it in a way that restores your humanity.

The truth is, you don't have to earn rest through spending. You don't have to buy your way into being worthy of care. You are worthy right now—messy, tired, overwhelmed, imperfect. When you begin to meet your needs with presence instead of performance, everything begins to shift. You realize that the most radical form of self-love is listening. And that the most nourishing form of self-care often costs nothing at all.

Reflection:
When I feel the urge to spend in the name of self-care, what am I truly needing beneath that impulse?
What might it feel like to care for myself without reaching for anything external—just presence, breath, and compassion?

#5: Advertising Equals Truth

We don't just consume products—we consume messages. From the moment we're old enough to recognize a jingle or a logo, we're being taught what to believe: about our bodies, our worth, our needs, and our place in the world. Advertisements don't just sell us things—they sell us identities, fears, fantasies, and illusions of control. And somewhere along the way, we start mistaking these curated, manipulative messages for truth.

This belief—that what we see in ads must be trustworthy—comes from decades of repetition. Corporations have spent billions crafting images that feel familiar, safe, aspirational. They borrow the language of health, empowerment, and authenticity, even as they manipulate our deepest insecurities. They show us what "normal" looks like. What beauty looks like. What success, love, and happiness are supposed to look like. And because we're surrounded by these images so constantly, we begin to internalize them as reality. We believe the models are that flawless. We believe the lifestyle is that attainable. We believe the problem they've named in us is real—and that their product is the only solution.

Psychologically, this breeds a quiet erosion of self-trust. We stop looking inward and start deferring to the curated lens of advertising to define what we should want, how we should look, and who we should be. It creates a constant comparison loop, where our real lives never quite measure up to the glossy versions we're shown. This gap between reality and illusion breeds shame, anxiety, and a hunger that never feels satisfied—because it was never meant to be. That's how the system works. If we believed we were whole, it wouldn't profit.

Our bodies feel this too. They register the constant barrage of "not enough." They carry the tension of trying to meet impossible standards. They hold the stress of trying to fix problems that were invented to sell us something. And over time, the nervous system learns to stay in a state of subtle urgency—always reaching, always comparing, always doubting. This stress can manifest in chronic fatigue, digestive imbalance, hormonal shifts, and disconnection from our body's true signals. When the mind is filled with noise, the body's voice is drowned out.

But here's the truth: advertising is not truth. It is strategy. It is a mirror designed to reflect back a distorted version of yourself, just convincing enough to keep you buying. Real truth doesn't sell to your insecurities—it speaks to your wholeness. It invites you to turn away from the noise and return to your own knowing. The most powerful rebellion in a world built on manipulation is to see clearly. To ask questions. To come back to the quiet voice within that says, *I don't need to be fixed—I need to be remembered.* You were never meant to be a consumer first. You were meant to be a human being, fully alive, fully aware, and deeply rooted in your own truth.

Reflection:
What beliefs have I internalized that may have come from advertising or media rather than lived experience?
Where have I outsourced my sense of truth to companies, brands, or influencers—and what might it feel like to take that truth back?

#6: Success Must Be Visible

Somewhere along the way, success stopped being a feeling and became a performance. It became something we had to prove, show, and share. Not just to ourselves, but to the world. The house, the title, the social media post, the carefully curated image—we were taught that unless others can see it, validate it, and applaud it, it doesn't count. Quiet success—like peace of mind, deep healing, or choosing rest—became invisible, and therefore, insignificant in the eyes of a world addicted to optics.

This belief is deeply woven into a culture that equates visibility with value. From early schooling, we're rewarded for measurable outcomes: grades, achievements, gold stars. As we grow, the markers shift—followers, salaries, external recognition. We're taught to seek worth through external benchmarks. The world rarely pauses to ask: *But how do you feel? Are you fulfilled? Are you free?* Because in a society driven by production and appearances, the process doesn't matter—only the perception does.

But this constant need to be seen and validated takes a toll. Psychologically, it detaches us from the quieter, truer parts of ourselves. We start making choices for optics, not alignment. We prioritize what looks good over what feels right. And in doing so, we can lose touch with our own inner compass. We chase goals that don't nourish us and perform roles that drain us, all in the hope that if others see us as successful, we might start to feel that way, too.

The body feels the pressure of this performance. It carries the weight of comparison, the anxiety of judgment, the exhaustion of proving. Chronic stress, burnout, adrenal fatigue, and emotional disconnection can all emerge when we live out of alignment with our authentic selves. The nervous system remains in a state of vigilance, constantly scanning for approval and fearing the loss of it. And over time, even accomplishments feel hollow, because we were never doing it for us in the first place.

But real success doesn't live on a resume or a screen. It lives in the body. It lives in how you sleep at night, how deeply you breathe, how freely you laugh, how fully you show up in your life. The new paradigm asks us to redefine success—not as something to be proven, but something to be lived. It invites us to honor the invisible victories: setting a boundary, choosing rest, walking away from what no longer serves us, healing generational wounds. These are the successes that truly change our lives—but they rarely come with applause.

Reflection:
What version of success have I been chasing—and who taught me to value it?
What would success look and feel like if it didn't need to be seen by anyone but me?

Self-Worth & Identity Beliefs

#1: Loving Yourself Is Selfish or Indulgent

Many of us grew up with the quiet, insidious message that loving ourselves was wrong—that it meant we were arrogant, self-absorbed, or self-centered. We were praised for selflessness, for putting others first, for being agreeable, accommodating, humble to a fault. Love, we were told, should pour out of us endlessly—but turning that love inward? That was indulgent. That was pride. That was something to be ashamed of.

This belief has roots in cultural, religious, and generational conditioning. For centuries, especially for women and marginalized communities, worth was tied to sacrifice. To be lovable was to be useful, helpful, invisible when necessary. Even spiritual teachings were often misinterpreted to imply that self-denial was virtue and that humility meant self-erasure. Somewhere along the way, we began to confuse martyrdom with love and self-abandonment with goodness.

But psychologically, this creates a dangerous split. When self-love is viewed as wrong, we disconnect from our own needs, desires, and voice. We silence the inner knowing that says "I matter too." We bend, overextend, and exhaust ourselves trying to prove we are enough by being everything to everyone. And yet, no amount of external approval can fill the void left when we've abandoned ourselves.

The body remembers this betrayal. It feels the sting of being overlooked—especially by the one person who's supposed to care for us most: ourselves. Over time, this shows up as anxiety, depression, autoimmune symptoms, chronic pain, or fatigue. When love is always directed outward and never inward, the nervous system remains in survival mode, striving for connection but never feeling safe or whole.

The truth is, loving yourself isn't selfish. It's sacred. It's the root from which all other love can grow. When you love yourself, you show up more fully, more honestly, more sustainably for the people and places you care about. Real self-love isn't about indulgence—it's about nourishment. It's not about exclusion—it's about inclusion, making room for your own heart in a world that taught you to leave yourself out.

This is the new paradigm: You are allowed to take up space. You are allowed to rest. You are allowed to speak, to feel, to want. You are allowed to come home to yourself—and call that holy. When we love ourselves, we don't love others less. We love more truthfully, without resentment or depletion. Because we're no longer loving from a wound— we're loving from wholeness.

Reflection:
When did I first learn that loving myself was "too much"?
What would change in my life if I treated self-love as
essential, not optional?

#2: Your Identity Is Fixed and Defined by Your Past or Your Trauma

For many of us, the story of who we are has been written in
ink made from our past wounds. We're taught—sometimes
subtly, sometimes blatantly—that our identity is shaped by
what happened to us, by the labels we've worn, the
mistakes we've made, or the roles we've been forced into.
We begin to believe that our trauma, our failures, our pain,
or even our diagnoses are the sum total of who we are. As if
growth is a betrayal of our story. As if healing means erasing
something instead of evolving from it.

This belief is often reinforced in a world that prefers linear
narratives. You're either broken or healed. This or that.
People crave categories and clarity, so we learn to shrink
ourselves into digestible versions of who we were—victim,
survivor, addict, angry, anxious, too much, too sensitive.
And over time, we internalize this confinement. The idea of
change feels disloyal, even dangerous. We forget that we
are more than the hardest things we've lived through.

Psychologically, this belief keeps us tethered to the past like
a ghost we can't release. It clouds our sense of agency,
making us feel powerless to become something new. We
begin to expect pain, sabotage joy, and anticipate failure—
because that's who we think we are. The nervous system

adapts to this identity too. It wires itself around survival, expecting threat, bracing for impact, rarely experiencing the safety required for expansion. And even when life offers something new, we struggle to trust it.

But here's what's true: you are not your trauma. You are not your diagnosis. You are not the worst thing that ever happened to you. You are not the choices you made from pain, fear, or survival. You are a living, breathing, ever-evolving being who is allowed to change, to soften, to grow, and to rewrite the narrative. You're allowed to hold your past with compassion and still decide that it does not get to define your future.

The new paradigm reminds us that healing is not forgetting. It's remembering who you were before the world told you who to be. It's allowing all parts of your story to inform you—but not to imprison you. Identity isn't static—it's fluid, layered, and sacred. You are not here to be the same version of yourself forever. You're here to transform, again and again, until your truth feels like home.

Reflection:
What parts of your identity are still being defined by old pain or past experiences?
What would it feel like to believe that you are allowed to become someone new?

#3: Changing Who You Are Means You're Being Fake or Disloyal

Change is often met with suspicion—not just from others, but from within ourselves. We've been conditioned to believe that who we've always been is who we're supposed to stay. That consistency equals integrity, and any shift—whether in values, beliefs, boundaries, or expression—means we're being fake, rebellious, or ungrateful. Especially if that shift disrupts family dynamics, social expectations, or long-held roles.

For those of us who were taught to equate loyalty with self-sacrifice, change can feel like betrayal. If we soften our edges, we worry we're abandoning our strength. If we set boundaries, we fear we're hurting the people who once depended on our silence. If we leave the roles that kept us safe—people pleaser, peacemaker, overachiever—we feel as though we're turning our backs on everything that once helped us survive.

But what if staying the same is what's actually inauthentic? What if the real betrayal is abandoning ourselves in order to keep everyone else comfortable?

This belief keeps us small, cautious, and stuck. Psychologically, it reinforces the idea that worth is tied to how well we maintain the image others have of us. And when we grow, when we evolve, when we start choosing differently—it threatens the systems we were once part of. The nervous system, too, reacts to this perceived threat. Shifts in identity or behavior—especially when met with criticism or rejection—can trigger guilt, fear, and deep anxiety. Our bodies brace for disapproval and social disconnection, even when the change is aligned with our truth.

But growth is not betrayal. It is the most loyal thing you can do for your soul. Changing doesn't mean you're becoming someone fake—it means you're finally becoming someone real. You're allowed to evolve beyond the stories you outgrew. You're allowed to want more, need less, or change direction completely. You're allowed to let your healing change you. That's not disloyalty. That's honesty.

The new paradigm invites you to honor the truth that change is a sign of life. Nothing in nature stays the same— and neither should you. Integrity isn't about never changing. It's about staying true to what's real for you now. And sometimes, the most courageous thing you can do is become someone your past self wouldn't recognize— because that means you're no longer living from survival. You're living from sovereignty.

Reflection:
Where have you feared that changing would make you disloyal or "fake"?
What if evolving is the most honest thing you could ever do?

#4: Confidence Is Arrogant

Many of us were taught to dim our light—not because we didn't have something beautiful to offer, but because somewhere along the way, we learned that shining too brightly made others uncomfortable. We were told to be humble, but what they really meant was "Be small." Speak softly. Don't brag. Don't take up space. Confidence, especially in women or marginalized voices, was framed as arrogance—something unbecoming, something to be ashamed of.

This belief seeps in quietly. It whispers that if we walk with certainty, we're full of ourselves. That if we name our gifts, we're seeking attention. That if we dare to feel proud, we're crossing some invisible line of acceptability. We learn to preface our achievements with disclaimers. We downplay our talents. We self-deprecate before others can bring us down first. And when others praise us, we deflect it like it's too heavy to hold.

But this isn't humility. It's fear disguised as modesty. It's a survival strategy that teaches us to betray ourselves before anyone else can. Culturally, this belief is reinforced through systems that reward compliance and penalize self-assuredness—especially in those who were never meant to lead according to the old paradigm. Confidence becomes a threat to control. A challenge to the status quo.

Internally, this belief disconnects us from our power. It conditions the nervous system to associate visibility with danger and success with rejection. We brace ourselves before speaking. We edit ourselves mid-sentence. We shrink our bodies and our voices, not because we lack brilliance—but because we've been taught that brilliance is dangerous.

But the truth is: confidence isn't arrogance. It's self-trust made visible. It's a deep knowing—not that you are better than anyone—but that you are no less. Confidence doesn't compete, it radiates. It doesn't seek approval, it walks in truth. And when it's rooted in love, not ego, it invites others to rise with you—not shrink beneath you.

The new paradigm reminds us that humility and confidence are not opposites—they are allies. You can own your voice and still listen deeply. You can celebrate your gifts and still remain grounded. You can take up space and still hold space for others. You are not here to apologize for your presence. You are here to embody it—fully, freely, and without shame.

Reflection:
Where did you learn that confidence was something to be ashamed of?
What would it look like to trust your voice and your gifts without shrinking or softening them?

#5: Your Value Depends on How Others Perceive You

From an early age, many of us learn to measure our worth through the eyes of others. Approval becomes the mirror in which we search for ourselves. We shape-shift to fit the roles that earn us love, praise, or belonging—student, caretaker, achiever, peacemaker. The message is clear: if others think highly of you, you're worthy. If they don't, something must be wrong.

This belief trains us to live from the outside in, rather than the inside out. We become experts in scanning the room, reading the mood, adjusting our tone. We seek validation like a lifeline, handing over our self-worth to likes, compliments, or subtle nods of acceptance. And when we don't receive it? We spiral. We question. We contort ourselves into more pleasing shapes, more acceptable versions—less bold, less sensitive, less *us*.

Over time, this need for perception-based validation fractures our identity. We lose sight of what we actually want, believe, or feel. We fear rejection not just as a social discomfort, but as an existential threat. The nervous system learns to equate disapproval with danger, and so we over-perform, over-explain, and over-apologize just to feel safe. Our energy goes into managing how we're seen rather than nurturing who we truly are.

But perception is fickle. It's filtered through projections, pain, and preferences that have nothing to do with us. Basing your worth on someone else's lens is like trying to see yourself clearly in a broken mirror—it distorts you every time. The truth is, your value is not contingent on being understood, liked, or validated. It lives in your being, not your branding. It's intrinsic, not performative.

The new paradigm invites you to come home to yourself. To reclaim your worth as a birthright, not a reward. To stop outsourcing your enough-ness and start anchoring it in your truth. You are not here to be easily digested or universally approved of. You are here to live honestly, deeply, and fully—in a way that feels like integrity, not performance.

Reflection:
When have you shaped yourself to match what others expected of you?
What would it feel like to trust your worth even when it isn't mirrored back to you?

#6: You Must Earn Love Through Perfection, Sacrifice, or Self-Abandonment

Somewhere along the way, many of us learned that love isn't something you simply receive—it's something you earn. Through being the "good one," the strong one, the quiet one, the selfless one. We absorbed the belief that love comes with conditions: Be less. Be more. Be what they need. But don't be too much of yourself. Because if you are, you might lose the approval, the affection, or the safety you've come to depend on.

This belief often begins in childhood, when survival depends on connection. If love felt inconsistent or tied to achievement, compliance, or emotional caretaking, we internalized the message that our inherent self wasn't enough. And so we learned to over-function. We became the fixer, the peacekeeper, the high achiever—the one who made things easier for others, often at the cost of our own needs.

Over time, this survival strategy becomes a pattern of self-abandonment. We say yes when we mean no. We tolerate what hurts. We silence our intuition and override our body's signals, because deep down we fear that if we stop performing, we'll be rejected—or worse, forgotten. The nervous system stays on high alert, constantly monitoring for signs that we've disappointed someone. We measure our lovability by how much we give, how well we please, and how little we need.

But love that must be earned through sacrifice is not love—it's a transaction built on fear. True love, the kind that heals and sustains, does not require the erasure of your essence. It does not demand perfection or endless giving. It meets you where you are and invites you to bring your whole, messy, human self to the table.

The new paradigm offers a radical truth: You are worthy of love simply because you exist. Not because of what you do for others. Not because of how flawless you appear. But because you are a living, breathing, feeling being deserving of compassion and care. Real love doesn't ask you to abandon yourself—it calls you back home to who you really are.

Reflection:
In what ways have you tried to earn love through perfection or self-sacrifice?
What might shift if you began to believe you are lovable exactly as you are—no performance required?

The Cost of Staying in the Box

The beliefs we just walked through — they may seem like
ideas or values passed down innocently, but they are far
from harmless. They've shaped us in quiet, persistent ways.
They've dictated how we define ourselves, how we relate to
others, how we set boundaries (or don't), how we handle
rest, how we process pain, and even how we see God.
These beliefs weren't simply taught — they were absorbed.
Internalized through repetition, modeled in our families,
reinforced in institutions, and rewarded by culture. Over
time, they became the silent frameworks that dictated how
we moved through life.

We stopped questioning them because they became
familiar. Predictable. Normal. We didn't call them beliefs —
we called them reality. But underneath the surface, these
beliefs have been shaping not just our thoughts, but our
health, our energy, our relationships, our choices, and our
capacity for joy.

And they come with a cost.

Not a vague, philosophical cost — a real one. These beliefs
slowly erode our vitality. They disconnect us from
ourselves. They dull our intuition, suppress our expression,
and distort our sense of worth. They cost us joy. They cost
us peace. They cost us connection — with our bodies, with
others, and with God. They flatten our experiences, drain
our spirit, and tell us to smile while we wither.

They whisper that love must be earned. That stillness is
laziness. That discomfort means you're failing. That your
body is a problem. That your worth is conditional. And

slowly, without even realizing it, we begin to shrink. We stop trusting ourselves. We stop listening to our needs. We override what we feel. We numb what we can't bear to face.

We learn to wear the mask. To play the role. To be palatable and pleasing, even if it means abandoning what's real inside of us. And on the surface, it may look like success — but underneath, we're exhausted. Disconnected. Afraid to slow down because we don't know what might rise to the surface if we do.

I know this because I've lived it. I stayed in the box far longer than I'd like to admit. I followed every rule, earned the praise, and met the expectations. I did everything "right" — and still found myself empty, sick, burned out, and wondering if life was supposed to feel this heavy. At one point, it nearly cost me everything — my health, my voice, my will to keep going, and almost my life.

When you live by these beliefs, you don't always realize the damage being done. It feels like exhaustion is just part of adulthood. Like anxiety is just your personality. Like pushing through is strength. Like emotional detachment is maturity. Like striving is noble. Like constant self-sacrifice is love. And because everyone around you is doing the same, it starts to feel normal.

But it's not normal.
It's just common.
It's the result of a culture of disconnection.
It's the cost of a system that asks us to trade wholeness for performance.

Eventually, you begin to wake up. You start to feel the ache of misalignment. The restlessness. The grief. The sense that maybe... just maybe... the life you built isn't truly yours. And in that moment, a choice emerges.

You can stay in the box.
Keep contorting yourself to fit someone else's narrative.
Keep striving for worthiness you were born with.
Keep overriding the truth that lives inside your body.

Or you can break the box.
You can let the old structures collapse.
You can let yourself grieve the years spent performing.
You can start questioning everything you were told was necessary to be loved, to be safe, to be good.

And in doing so, you begin the slow, sacred return to yourself.

Breaking the box isn't rebellion for rebellion's sake.
It's healing.
It's liberation.
It's the reclamation of your voice, your body, your truth.
It's choosing presence over performance.
It's choosing alignment over approval.
It's choosing the voice of God within you over the noise of culture around you.

And it's worth it.
Because the cost of staying in the box — the real cost — is your life.

Exercises for Chapter 1: The Cost of Staying in the Box

This chapter may have stirred something in you—memories, questions, emotions, resistance.

That's okay.
That's actually the point.

Now is your chance to slow down and listen.
These exercises are here to help you process, not just read.

They're not about getting it "right"—they're about being real.

1. My Inherited Belief Audit

Take a few moments to revisit the nine belief system categories in this chapter. These systems—*Health, Work, Relationships, Education, Finances, Time, Spirituality, Body Image, and Self-Worth*—hold the blueprints you were handed.

Instructions:
- Under each category, write down the beliefs you inherited from family, school, religion, culture, or media.
- Circle the ones that feel heavy or restrictive.
- Star the ones you feel ready to question or let go of.

Reflection Prompt:
What patterns do you notice across the categories?

Which beliefs feel like they no longer serve the version of you you're becoming?

2. The Body Check-In

Most of the time, your body knows before your mind does. These beliefs didn't just shape your thoughts—they shaped your nervous system, your posture, your digestion, your stress patterns. Let's give your body a say.

Instructions:
- Find a quiet space. Close your eyes or soften your gaze.
- Slowly read each belief (or the ones that stood out to you) out loud.
- As you do, gently scan your body. Ask yourself:
    - Where do I feel tension, tightness, or constriction?
    - Is there a sensation of sadness, grief, anger, or numbness?
    - What happens in my breath, chest, jaw, or gut as I read this belief?
- Let your body respond. No need to fix it—just notice.

Reflection Prompt:
What did your body reveal that your mind hadn't noticed?

3. Letter to Your Younger Self

There's a younger version of you who believed these things without question. Not because you were naive, but because it's what you were taught. That version of you deserves compassion—not shame.

Instructions:
- Write a letter to a younger version of yourself (choose any age that feels relevant).
- Speak from the place you're in now.
- Tell them what belief you wish they hadn't carried. Tell them the truth you now know.
- Offer love, validation, and maybe even an apology— for the years you didn't know what you didn't know.

Reflection Prompt:
If your younger self could hear you now, what would they feel? Relief? Sadness? Freedom?

Optional Add-On Exercises

Here are two additional options you might include if you want to deepen the chapter further:

4. "Whose Voice Is That?" Journaling Prompt

Pick one belief that feels especially loud in your life. Write freely for 5–10 minutes answering the question: *"Whose voice is this?"*
Is it your mother's? A teacher's? A pastor's? A cultural script?

Trace it back to its origin—and then ask yourself if you want to keep carrying it.

5. Create a New Belief (Rewriting Exercise)

Pick one belief you're ready to release.
Then, re-write it in your own words—as your body would say it, as your spirit would say it, as your truth knows it now.

Example:
Old Belief: "Rest is laziness."
New Belief: "Rest is my birthright. It's how I heal, listen, and return to myself."
Tape it to your mirror. Speak it out loud. Let this become your new agreement.

Chapter 2:

The Process of Unlearning — Dismantling the Invisible

"Until you make the unconscious conscious, it will direct your life and you will call it fate."
— Carl Jung

The Awakening Is Not Polite

Unlearning is not polite. It doesn't arrive gently or wait for the right moment. It doesn't knock softly on the door of your consciousness and offer you a comfortable path to transformation. No — it barges in, uninvited, and begins rearranging everything you thought you knew. It pulls the furniture of your identity out from under you. It flips on the lights and demands that you see what's been hiding in plain sight.

This isn't the kind of awakening that makes for a pretty Instagram quote or a poetic caption under a sunset photo. It's not curated or candlelit. It's not aesthetic. It's disruptive. It's the kind of awakening that grabs you by the collar, looks you in the eyes, and says: *"Wake up. This isn't who you really are."*

Unlearning is messy. It shakes the foundation you built your life on and makes you question everything — your choices, your relationships, your career, your faith, your values, your reflection in the mirror. It doesn't whisper. It howls. And once you've heard it, you can't unhear it. You can't go back to sleep.

It's terrifying at first. The institutions and ideas you once clung to for security — school, religion, family, culture, media — suddenly feel less like safety nets and more like cages. You begin to realize that the scripts you've been following weren't written with your freedom in mind. They were designed to keep you manageable. Predictable. Small. And part of you may still cling to them, even though they hurt — not because they're true, but because they're familiar.

But underneath the fear is a deeper truth. That ache you've carried for years — the subtle discontent, the restlessness, the sense that something was always a little bit off — that was your soul trying to get your attention. That was your body, in its wisdom, whispering: *"This isn't it."* That was the sacred part of you that refused to settle for a life built on suppression and survival.

When you finally start to listen — really listen — it can feel like your whole world is falling apart. And in many ways, it is. You may feel anger that it took this long to see. You may feel shame for how well you played the part. You may feel grief for the years spent silencing yourself just to be accepted.

This process is not clean or linear. It is not graceful. It will not always make sense to the people around you. Some may call you dramatic. Unstable. Rebellious. Ungrateful. Selfish. But they're only seeing the collapse. They're only witnessing the shedding. What they can't see is what's being born underneath.

Because unlearning is not just a breakdown. It's a breakthrough. It's the moment the box begins to crack — and through those cracks, your truest self starts to emerge. Not the version of you the world rewarded. Not the version of you who made everyone else comfortable. But the version of you that remembers. The version of you that knows.

This is not a crisis.
This is an awakening.
And no, it is not polite.

It is sacred.

The First Step: Awareness

And that's the catch, isn't it?

So much of what shapes our lives is invisible. It's the water we're swimming in, the air we're breathing, the script we didn't even realize we were handed. We think we're making choices — but more often, we're just following patterns. Patterns passed down. Patterns internalized. Patterns lived so many times, we started to believe they were our own.

This is why awareness is the first — and perhaps the most powerful — step in the unlearning process. It's the moment you pause, mid-thought or mid-habit, and ask yourself, *"Wait... whose voice is this?"*

Sometimes, awareness arrives as a whisper.

It's the wave of guilt that crashes over you the first time you say no.
It's the sharp judgment in your mind when you look in the mirror and realize — this disgust didn't start with you.
It's the unease that creeps in when you try to rest and your body interprets stillness as danger.
It's the hollow feeling when someone praises your productivity and you smile, but something inside feels empty.

That whisper?
That's the veil beginning to lift. That's the sacred crack where light starts to pour in.

Awareness isn't always graceful. In fact, it rarely is.
It's humbling to realize how many of your so-called "preferences" were rooted in fear.
How many of your daily habits were actually coping mechanisms.
How many of your beliefs were adopted out of survival, not truth.
And how many of the voices in your head are echoes — not your own.

But as uncomfortable as it can be, awareness is also the beginning of power.
Because once you *see* what's running the show, you get to decide whether it still belongs.

This step doesn't require you to fix anything. It's not asking for action, solution, or a new plan. It's only asking for your presence. To sit with what is. To witness yourself — honestly, gently, compassionately.

You begin to notice the internal dialogue, the programming that plays on repeat:

- *If I rest, I'm lazy.*
- *If I speak up, I'll be abandoned.*
- *If I gain weight, I won't be lovable.*
- *If I don't succeed, I'm worthless.*
- *If I stop being who they want me to be, I won't belong.*

And somewhere in that witnessing... you finally hear it.

That is *not* your voice.
That is programming.
That is conditioning.
That is survival talking — not truth.

And the moment you recognize it, something sacred happens:
You crack the code.

Because if you can hear it, there must be a you beneath it.
A wiser you.
A quieter you.
A you who is watching, listening, and slowly beginning to wake up.

Awareness doesn't always come with fireworks. Sometimes it's subtle. Slow. Soft. Sometimes it arrives like a jolt to the nervous system. But no matter how it enters, it is real. And it is sacred.

Let yourself notice.
Let yourself name what you've always accepted as "just the way it is."
Let yourself tell the truth about how those beliefs have

shaped your choices, your relationships, your self-image, your body.

And remember:
You don't have to have the answers yet.
You don't need to rush to action.
You just need to see.

Because *seeing* is the beginning of remembering.
And *remembering* is how you come home.

The Grief of Letting Go

Unlearning is often spoken about like it's all lightbulb moments and liberation. As if awareness alone will set you free — and from that moment forward, everything becomes lighter, clearer, easier.

But here's the truth most people don't tell you: unlearning is grief. Holy, sacred, heart-splitting grief.

Because when you begin to release the beliefs that shaped you, you're not just letting go of thoughts. You're saying goodbye to entire versions of yourself — the ones who carried you through the storm. The one who stayed silent to avoid conflict. The one who overachieved to feel worthy. The one who starved, smiled, pleased, or performed — all in the name of being lovable. The one who made themselves small so others wouldn't feel threatened. The one who held it all together because there was no other choice.

And these parts of you — they weren't wrong. They weren't failures. They were brilliant, intuitive strategies. They kept you safe. They helped you survive. They allowed you to belong in places that couldn't hold your fullness. And for that, they deserve gratitude, not shame.

But now, something is shifting. You're beginning to feel the friction. The old ways no longer fit. What once protected you now feels like a cage. What once earned you love now exhausts you. What once made you feel safe now keeps you stuck. And choosing to let go of those parts — even when they hurt you — is still a kind of death.

It's the death of a self you've known for so long, it almost became your skin. It's the unraveling of stories you held like lifelines. It's the laying down of roles you played so well that you forgot they were never who you truly were. It's mourning the masks that once made you feel seen — even though they only ever revealed fragments of you.

It's grieving the person you had to become... just to make it through.

And it hurts. Deeply.

This is the part of the journey where so many people turn back. Not because they don't want freedom — but because they didn't know that freedom would require mourning. They weren't prepared for the ache that comes with letting go of the familiar, even when the familiar was wounding.

You may find yourself crying for a childhood you never got to fully live. For the rest your nervous system never knew it was allowed to receive. For the love you gave that was never returned. For the relationships that couldn't survive your return to self. For the version of you that never got to be real.

You may feel disoriented, alone, or raw. You may wonder, *Who am I without these beliefs? Without these roles? Without these patterns?*

But that question isn't a problem — it's a portal. It's an opening. It's where your becoming begins.

And the only way through it is grace.
Radical, unapologetic grace.
Grace for the parts of you that still feel afraid.
Grace for the urge to run back to comfort.
Grace for the waves of grief that arrive without warning and knock the air out of your chest.

Let yourself cry. Let yourself rage. Let yourself forget, and then remember, and then forget again.

This is not regression.
This is release.
This is not failure.
This is shedding.

This is the sacred middle — the space between who you were and who you are becoming. The raw and holy ground of transformation.

So let me remind you of this:
Grieving the old you is not weakness.
It is reverence.
It is a deep bow to the self who carried you this far —
so that you could live long enough to become who you truly are.

So cry.
Scream.
Write letters to the parts of you that are fading.
Light candles for the masks you're laying down.
Place your hand on your heart and whisper:

Thank you for keeping me safe.
But I don't need you anymore.

Then rest.
Because rebirth takes everything you have.
And you, love, are doing holy work.

The Discomfort of the In-Between

No one tells you how hard the middle is.

We hear stories of before and after. Of rock bottoms and radiant rebirths. Of awakenings and arrivals. But what about the space in between? The aching, disorienting stretch between what was and what's not yet? The place where the old self no longer fits, but the new one hasn't fully arrived?

This is where most people feel the urge to quit. Not because they don't want healing. Not because they lack the strength. But because freedom comes with a cost — the death of certainty, the loss of identity, and the hollow ache of wondering, *"I don't even know who I am anymore."*

In the in-between, everything feels blurry. The old beliefs have begun to crumble, but the new ones haven't taken root. You catch yourself mid-thought: *"I'm not supposed to believe this anymore,*" yet it still lives in your nervous system. You recognize the old patterns, but they still show up before the new pathways are strong enough to take their place.

You feel unmoored. Unanchored. Unraveled. Untethered from who you used to be — and yet not fully connected to who you're becoming.

And that feels terrifying.

Because even if the old version of you was suffering, at least it was familiar. At least it had a script. A role to play. A story to cling to. But in this liminal space, there is no script. No clear identity. No road map. Just silence. Just questions. Just... you.

This is why so many crawl back into the box. Not out of weakness, but because the unknown feels like death. And in a way — it is. A death of certainty. A death of autopilot. A death of performance.

But let me be clear:
The discomfort of the in-between is not a problem to fix.
It is a passage to move through.

It's in this sacred stretch of not-knowing that your nervous system begins to rewire. Your body starts to speak more clearly than your programming. Your real voice — the one buried under years of "shoulds" and "not enoughs" — begins to whisper again.

This space may not be easy, but it is holy. Not because it feels good, but because it is real. Raw. Stripped down. Unpolished. Honest. You are face-to-face with the truth of yourself — not the version you curated for others, but the one who exists beneath the noise.

You may feel lost here. That's okay. Being lost is often how we begin to find our way.

You may feel like you're going backward. You're not. You're sitting still long enough to finally hear what you've been avoiding. This is the messy middle. The space between caterpillar and butterfly. Between breakdown and breakthrough. Between forgetting and remembering.

Let yourself be in it.

Let yourself not know.
Let yourself scream and ache and rest and question.
Let yourself unclench.

You don't have to rush toward becoming. You don't have to force clarity. You don't have to sculpt a new identity overnight. The new version of you — the one who is whole, aligned, rooted — they are already forming. But first, they need space. Space to rise. Space to breathe. Space to emerge without pressure or performance.

This part of the journey will ask everything of you. And it will give you everything in return.

So please remember:
The discomfort of the in-between is not a sign that you're lost.
It's the most sacred evidence that you are becoming.

The Fear of Social Pushback

One of the hardest parts of unlearning isn't the internal work. It's not the journaling, the reflecting, or even the grief. It's what happens when you stop playing by the rules that everyone around you is still living by.

When you start speaking up, saying no, setting boundaries, or walking away from roles that once made you feel safe, people notice. And not everyone is going to applaud your growth. Some will question you. Some will distance themselves. Some will call you selfish, rebellious, dramatic, too much, or not enough.

Because your freedom threatens their comfort.
Your change shines a light on where they're still stuck.
And that can feel deeply unsettling to those who have built their identity inside the same box you're breaking out of.

You'll hear the words, *"You've changed,"* and they won't always be said with admiration.
But they'll be right.
You *have* changed.
That's the point.

Because staying the same would've meant continuing to abandon yourself — and you've made a sacred decision to stop doing that.

Still, the fear of social pushback is real. It's wired into us. We are human, and humans are wired for connection. We want to be accepted. We want to belong. We want to be seen and loved. And when we begin to challenge the very beliefs and behaviors that once made us feel safe in relationships, it can feel like we're putting everything we care about at risk.

You will lose people.
You will grieve friendships, communities, and family dynamics that were built on your silence or compliance. That grief is real. That grief is valid.

But here is the deeper truth: you're not losing love — you're losing the illusion of love that required you to shrink. You're losing connection that depended on your obedience. You're losing relationships that couldn't hold the fullness of who you are becoming.

True love doesn't demand your self-abandonment. It doesn't ask you to dim your light or betray your truth in order to belong. It doesn't require you to pretend, to perform, or to stay silent just to keep the peace.

If your growth threatens the relationship, it means the relationship was never built on the real you — it was built on a version of you that was performing safety, not living in truth. That's not your fault. That's survival. You were doing what you needed to do to feel loved and accepted with the tools you had.

But now you know more. And with that knowing comes the invitation to choose differently.

It will feel lonely at times. There will be moments when you question everything — when you wonder if it would've been easier to stay quiet, keep the peace, or go back to who you used to be. But peace that costs your wholeness isn't peace. It's a performance. And you're done performing.

Your new boundaries will unsettle those who benefited from your boundarylessness.
Your truth will disrupt dynamics that were built on your silence.
Your softness will confuse people who only know hardness as strength.

Expect it. But don't internalize it.

Their discomfort does not define your worth. Their reactions are not your responsibility.
And just as they are entitled to their discomfort, you are entitled to your freedom.

Keep going. Keep choosing yourself. The people who can meet you in your wholeness — the ones who will honor your voice, your boundaries, and your becoming — will find you. They may come slowly. They may be few. But when they arrive, they will feel like home. Like oxygen.

And in the meantime, hold this truth close:

You are not broken.
You are not selfish.
You are not too much.
You are courageous.
And that will always be enough.

The Body as Your Compass

If there's one thing I've learned throughout the process of unlearning, it's this: the body always knows. Even when the mind is spinning, rationalizing, doubting, or clinging to what feels familiar, the body holds a deeper truth. While the mind can be shaped by fear, programming, or performance, the body remains honest. It remembers. It responds. It signals — often long before we have words.

And yet, most of us were never taught how to listen. We were taught to suppress, to override, to distrust the body's messages. We were taught to push through pain, to smile through discomfort, to say yes when everything inside screamed no. We learned that stillness was laziness, that emotion was weakness, that our gut instincts were irrational. We were raised in systems that rewarded disconnection — where productivity was valued over presence, and politeness was prized over truth.

But the body never stopped speaking. It recorded every moment we felt unsafe but silenced ourselves anyway. It held onto the tension when we betrayed our boundaries just to be accepted. It stored the ache of every abandoned need, every unspoken truth, every time we chose approval over authenticity. Not to punish us — but to protect us. The body has always been trying to get our attention.

Now, as we begin to remember what we were taught to forget, the body becomes one of our greatest allies. While systems, authorities, and experts may try to tell us what's best, the body tells us what's *true*. It speaks not through logic, but through sensation — through the tightness in your chest, the flutter in your stomach, the constriction in your throat, the fatigue that no amount of caffeine can fix, and the deep relief that follows a long-awaited boundary or truth finally spoken.

This is your compass. Not a checklist. Not a guru. Not even a perfectly laid plan. Your body — your inner knowing — is what guides you back to yourself. And learning to trust it again is a process. If you've spent years living from the neck up or outsourcing your authority to someone else, it might feel unfamiliar at first. You might feel numb. You might doubt. You might hesitate.

But underneath all of that is truth. Your body has always been on your side. It has been trying to guide you — to warn you, to care for you, to bring you back home. The work now is to slow down and listen. Not with your mind, but with your presence. To notice what arises in your body when you speak, when you move, when you make decisions. To ask: *Where do I feel this? What shifts when I say yes? What contracts when I say no?*

It's in that pause — that subtle, sacred moment of tuning in — that something powerful begins to happen. You stop betraying yourself. You start building trust with your instincts. You begin making decisions from a place of grounded truth, even when others don't understand. You start walking through life with a deeper sense of integrity — not the kind defined by perfection, but by alignment.

So the next time you feel lost, disconnected, or unsure — don't rush outside yourself for answers. Sit. Breathe. Ask your body. And wait. The answer might arrive in a sensation, a wordless knowing, a wave of emotion, or a simple exhale that says, *this is right*.

Whatever comes — honor it.

This is not just intuition. It's remembrance.
This is not just body awareness. It's homecoming.
This is how you begin to live in wholeness — again.

Unlearning is Coming Home

Unlearning is not about burning everything down. It's not a reckless rebellion, or a rejection of everything you've ever known. It's not about walking away from every belief you've ever held or scorning the path that brought you here. Unlearning is not destruction for the sake of drama — it is reclamation. It's about discernment. It's the slow, intentional, and tender peeling back of everything that was never truly yours to begin with.

It begins with the realization that so much of what shaped you — what you were taught to believe about your worth, your body, your voice, and your place in the world — was inherited. Absorbed. Conditioned. You were given stories about what it means to be good, to be lovable, to be successful, to be safe — and you carried them without question, because that's what we do when we're trying to belong. But beneath all of that conditioning, something true was always there. A quiet, steady knowing that lived in your body. That knowing was yours long before the world taught you to doubt it.

Unlearning is the sacred return to that knowing. It is a homecoming — not to a perfect version of yourself, but to a truer one. A version untouched by the performance, by the shame, by the fear. A version that existed before you learned to shrink. Before you believed you had to earn love. Before your voice was buried under politeness, productivity, or protection. It's not about rejecting the past, but about choosing what you carry forward, and what you finally lay down.

Coming home to yourself can feel disorienting at first. You've spent years — maybe decades — seeking answers outside of you. Asking for permission. Playing roles that kept you safe but kept you silent. So when you begin to listen inward instead — when you honor your body's signals, trust your intuition's whispers, and begin following your inner voice — it might feel unfamiliar. It might feel strange. It might even feel wrong.

But it's not wrong. It's just unpracticed.

This is where the real work begins. Not in mastering a new set of rules, but in remembering what's real. In reconnecting with who you were before the world told you who to be. With who you are when no one is watching. With who you've always been, deep in your bones — before you learned to hide, to hustle, to hold it all together.

And make no mistake: this is not the easy path. It will ask everything of you. It will require grief, courage, stillness, and truth-telling. It will challenge your patterns. It may disrupt your relationships. It will almost certainly dismantle the illusion of control.

But it will give you back your life.

Because the path of unlearning is the path of returning. Returning to your breath.

To your body.
To your boundaries.
To your joy.
To your purpose.
To your wholeness.

This path is not linear.
It is not always graceful.
But it is wild.
It is sacred.
It is yours.
And it is how you finally, fully, come home.

Exercises for Chapter 2: Integrating the Process of Unlearning

Unlearning is not a one-time epiphany—it's a daily invitation. A moment-to-moment practice of awareness, embodiment, and truth-telling. These exercises are designed to help you move from insight to integration. To not just think about unlearning—but to feel it, live it, and trust it. You don't have to do them all at once. Start where you are. Return when you're ready. There is no wrong way to begin.

1. The Programming Pause

When to Use This:
In moments of strong emotion—guilt, fear, shame, anxiety, defensiveness.

What to Do:
Pause. Breathe. Ask yourself:
- Whose voice is this?
- What belief is being activated right now?
- Is this mine, or was it handed to me?
- Does this belief serve my truth—or someone else's comfort?

Why This Matters:
This is how you begin to spot the inherited scripts that are quietly running the show. Awareness breaks the spell.

Journal Prompt:
Write down one belief that surfaced today that no longer feels true for you.
What would your life feel like without it?

2. Body as Compass Practice

When to Use This:
When you feel unsure about a decision, boundary, relationship, or belief.

What to Do:
Find a quiet space. Close your eyes. Bring to mind a belief or choice you're sitting with (e.g., "I should always say yes to others"). Then ask:
- Where does this live in my body?

- Is there tension? Tightness? Numbness? Heat?
- What is this sensation trying to tell me?

Let your body speak—through feeling, image, breath, memory.

Why This Matters:
Your body remembers. It tells the truth. It often speaks before the mind catches up.

Reflection:
What would it look like to trust your body as your guide, even when it goes against what you were taught?

3. The Messy Middle Journal

When to Use This:
When you're in that liminal space between old beliefs and new truths—the foggy, uncertain in-between.

What to Do:
Use this journal prompt daily or weekly:
- What old belief am I releasing today?
- What grief or discomfort is arising as I let it go?
- What new truth is whispering to me, even if it's faint?

Why This Matters:
Naming the in-between helps you stay present through the transformation. It affirms that uncertainty isn't failure—it's the passageway to truth.

4. The Permission Letter

When to Use This:
When self-doubt, pressure, or perfectionism creep in. When you forget that healing has no timeline.

What to Do:
Write a letter to yourself, granting permission to:
- Not have it all figured out
- Be messy, slow, unsure
- Grieve what no longer fits
- Trust your body over your mind
- Let go of roles or relationships that no longer align

Tip:
Keep this letter nearby. Re-read it when you feel like crawling back into the box.

5. Find the Others

When to Use This:
When you feel alone in your unlearning. When the people around you don't understand who you're becoming.

What to Do:
Make a list of:
- People, communities, books, podcasts, or mentors that make you feel seen, safe, and sovereign.
- Spaces where your questions are welcome, not punished.
- Voices that help you remember who you really are.

Commitment:
Choose one small way this week to connect with that

energy—listen to a podcast, read a page of a book, reach out to someone who "gets it," or simply spend time in nature, which always honors your becoming.

Gentle Reminder

Unlearning is not a straight path.
It spirals, circles back, pauses, and begins again.

Some days you'll feel like fire—rising, clear, untouchable.
Other days you'll feel like fog—formless, fragile, unraveling at the edges.

Both are sacred.
Both are part of becoming.

You are not behind.
You are not failing.
You are shedding what was never truly yours, layer by tender layer.

This is the holy work of returning.
Of unbecoming the noise so you can remember the sound of your own soul.

Let it be wild.
Let it be soft.
Let it be yours.

Chapter 3:

The Messy Middle — Navigating the Void Between Who You Were and Who You're Becoming

"The space between where you are and where you want to be is where the magic happens."
— Alix E. Harrow

The Space Between Stories

Nothing prepares you for this part.

We often hear about the pain of breaking down old beliefs — about the courage it takes to question everything and start over. And we're shown the clarity that comes on the other side — the glow of becoming, the triumph of healing, the joy of freedom. But this middle place? This stretch of space between who you used to be and who you're still becoming? It's rarely spoken about. And yet, it's everything.

This is the space between stories.
The moment after the mask falls, but before your real face fully emerges.
The time when your old life has crumbled, but the new one hasn't taken shape.
Where you feel like a blank page — not the exciting kind, but the kind that feels exposed. Empty. Directionless.

It's a disorienting kind of quiet.
The stillness you didn't expect.
And if you're anything like I was, that stillness can feel like death.

For so long, I lived by scripts. I knew the roles I was expected to play — the good one, the overachiever, the helper, the strong one. Those roles were tight and confining, yes, but they also gave me structure. They gave me something to point to and say, *"See? I'm doing it right. I matter."* They earned me love. They gave me a sense of identity.

So when those roles began to unravel, I expected to feel free — and in some ways, I did. But I didn't anticipate the terror that came next. The quiet shock of waking up one morning and realizing... *I don't know who I am anymore.*

This is the wilderness.
The liminal space.
The void between stories.
There is no roadmap here. No milestones. No external validation that tells you you're doing it right. No one handing you a certificate that says, *"Congratulations, you're healing."*

Instead, it's just quiet. Sometimes too quiet. And in that silence, all the doubts and fears you've kept buried begin to rise to the surface. The thoughts you've outrun for years suddenly have room to echo. And they do.

I used to believe healing was linear. I thought that if I read the right books, followed the right practices, did enough of the right things, I would reach some kind of arrival point — a moment of clarity where everything made sense. But that's not how this works.

Before clarity, there is confusion.
Before becoming, there is undoing.
And the undoing is not neat. It's not pretty. It's not something you can package and share on social media. It's murky. It's maddening. It's lonely.

I remember sitting in my car one day, crying because I didn't know what I believed anymore — not about the world, not about myself, not even about God. The beliefs I used to cling to for meaning no longer felt true. But I didn't yet have anything new to stand on. I was untethered. Floating. Fractured. And yet, beneath the chaos, something in me whispered: *This matters.*

Because I wasn't broken.
I was in between.

This middle space isn't a mistake. It's not a sign of failure. It's not something to rush through or escape. It is sacred. It is the cocoon — the quiet space where transformation brews in the dark before anything visible begins to bloom. It's the soil where new roots begin to form, long before they break the surface.

But most people fear this space so deeply, they rush to fill it. They grasp for the next identity, the next belief system, the next label — anything to escape the discomfort of being undefined. I know that desperation. I've done it. I've reached for something, anything, to hold onto.

But here's what I've learned:
Unlearning is not about swapping one script for another.

It's about learning to live inside the question.
To sit in the darkness without reaching for the light switch.
To trust that something holy is happening — even when you can't yet name it.

This space between stories may feel like the place where everything is falling apart.
But it's not where you get lost.

It's where you get found.

The Urge to Fill the Void

The moment the old scaffolding begins to fall — the roles, the beliefs, the identities that once gave you structure — something primal inside of you starts to panic. The urge to build something, *anything*, in its place can feel almost unbearable. The silence is too loud. The stillness is too much. The blank space where your identity used to live begins to itch like a healing wound. And without warning, your nervous system kicks into overdrive, scrambling to make sense of the void.

You find yourself reaching for old patterns. Not because they feel good, but because they feel familiar. You catch yourself considering the job that once burned you out. The relationship that made you shrink. The belief system that kept you small. You think, *At least those things gave me a role to play. At least they gave me a name, a purpose, something solid to hold onto.*

I've done it. I've sat in the thick of the uncertainty and nearly convinced myself that I had overreacted. That maybe I had been too sensitive. That maybe healing had taken me too far. I've come dangerously close to returning to people, places, and systems that once harmed me — not because I forgot the pain, but because the ache of *not knowing who I was anymore* felt even more unbearable than the pain of pretending.

That's how powerful the void is.

We are wired for safety. We crave certainty. Our brains are designed to seek out narratives with clear beginnings, middles, and ends. So when you find yourself living in a chapter without a title — when nothing makes sense, and no role feels right — your body interprets it as a threat. It responds with urgency: *Just figure it out. Just go back to what you know.*

You begin filling in the blanks, trying to regain control:
Maybe I was overreacting.
Maybe I just need to try harder.
Maybe healing isn't worth the mess it's made.
Maybe if I find the "right" path this time, it won't hurt so much.
Maybe I'm the problem.

But here's what I've learned — painfully, humbly, and over time:
The void is not the problem.
The urge to escape it is.

Because the void — the blankness, the not-knowing — is not empty.
It is fertile.
It is sacred.

It is the dark, rich soil where new roots begin to grow before anything breaks the surface.

When we rush to fill the void, we miss the invitation it holds. The invitation to pause. To breathe. To meet ourselves beneath the noise. To feel what we've been avoiding. To listen for what's real — not what's familiar.

I had to learn that the discomfort wasn't a sign to turn back. It was a sign I was finally in the space where real transformation happens. Not the kind of transformation that comes with a step-by-step guide or a curated breakthrough — but the kind that rewires your nervous system, softens your edges, and clears space for truth to finally take root.

Now, when I feel the familiar urgency rise — the need to fix, to define, to escape — I stop and ask myself:
What am I trying not to feel?
What part of me is afraid of being seen without a mask?
What might happen if I stayed a little longer in the silence?

There is nothing wrong with craving clarity. But sometimes clarity doesn't come from searching. It comes from *staying*. From not filling the space too quickly. From trusting that the void is not a punishment, but a passage.

You are not broken for feeling lost.
You are not failing for needing time.
You are becoming.
And becoming — by its very nature — always begins in the void.

The Discomfort of Not Knowing

There's a peculiar kind of ache that lives in the space between clarity and confusion. Not quite lost, but not yet found. Not drowning, but not quite swimming either. It's the suspended moment — the in-between — where everything feels both too quiet and too loud at the same time. Where you are no longer who you were, but not yet who you're becoming. This is the discomfort of not knowing.

No one really prepares you for this part. They speak of breakdowns and breakthroughs, of dark nights of the soul and moments of clarity. But this? This floating space, where your old roles have been shed like skin but your new self hasn't yet taken form — this is something else entirely.

You no longer want the life you once had. But you don't yet know what to build in its place. You've released the identities that kept you small, but you haven't fully stepped into the truth of who you are. There is no script to follow. No guidebook to lean on. Just silence. Stillness. And questions without answers.

I've been there. I've sat in that quiet room — both metaphorically and literally — feeling like I had walked off the edge of a cliff and was suspended in midair. No ground beneath me, no sky above. Just the vast unknown. And it was terrifying. Not because something bad was happening, but because *nothing* was. And when you're used to a life of chronic doing, fixing, pleasing, and performing, that nothingness can feel like failure.

But here's the truth I want you to hear: the void is not failure. The silence is not a mistake. The fog is not proof that something is wrong. In fact, it's often the clearest sign that something is finally, beautifully, beginning to shift.

This is what it looks like when you stop abandoning yourself. When you stop numbing your truth with productivity or pretending. When your nervous system begins to recalibrate after years of living in fight, flight, or freeze. When your old coping mechanisms stop working — and your new ones haven't yet arrived.

It's the space where the pain you used to outrun finally catches up to you. Where the body begins to speak louder than the mind. Where the questions become more valuable than the answers.

And yes — it's deeply uncomfortable. Because we live in a culture that glorifies certainty. A culture that tells you to know your purpose, name your five-year plan, hustle harder, be productive, be sure. But healing doesn't happen in bullet points. Becoming doesn't arrive on a schedule.

I had to learn that being in the dark doesn't mean I've lost my way. Sometimes, it simply means I've finally stepped out of the fluorescent glare of conditioning and into the softer, quieter moonlight of my own becoming.

So if you're in the fog right now — if you're untethered, if you're unraveling, if you feel like everything familiar is slipping through your fingers — know this:

You are not failing. You are *feeling*.
You are not broken. You are *becoming*.
You are not behind. You are *right on time*.

The discomfort of not knowing is not the end of the story. It's the place where the deepest truths begin to grow.

Let them.

Letting Go of Who You Were

Letting go isn't just about walking away from the obvious things — jobs, relationships, titles, roles. It's not only about shedding external structures or changing your environment. True letting go is internal. It's about releasing the version of you who believed those things were necessary for survival. The one who built a life around coping strategies, not because they wanted to, but because they had to.

It's the you who hustled for love because they didn't yet know that worthiness could exist without proving. The you who said yes to everything because the fear of being left behind felt unbearable. The you who shape-shifted into whatever others needed — not because they lacked identity, but because no one ever paused to ask who they really were.

When I found myself standing in this space — the messy, raw middle of becoming — I thought I was ready for transformation. I had read the books. Done the work. Made the choice. But what I didn't expect was how much of transformation begins with mourning. Not the loud, dramatic kind. The quiet, aching kind. The kind that creeps in at 2 a.m. or shows up while folding laundry. The kind that catches you off guard with tears you didn't know you were still carrying.

I cried for the version of me who equated burnout with value.
I grieved the one who stayed in places that hurt just to feel wanted.
I wept for every younger self who endured what they never should have had to — without support, without clarity, without knowing they deserved better.

And that grief was complicated. Because those versions of me didn't fail. They saved me. They kept me afloat when I didn't yet know how to swim. They made choices rooted in survival, not shame. And that's what makes it so hard. You don't release these parts of yourself because they were weak — you release them because they did their job. They brought you here. To the edge. To the threshold. To the very moment where something new, something more honest and whole, is waiting to be born.

But as much as you honor them, you can't carry them with you into the life you're building now.
You can't wear the old armor into a new war.
You can't climb into your becoming while dragging the weight of your survival self behind you.

So instead, you pause.
You honor them.
You write them a letter.
You name what they carried, what they protected, what they endured on your behalf.
You thank them for their grit, their resilience, their unwavering fight to keep you safe — even if it cost you joy.
And then, with reverence, not rejection, you let them go.

This is the sacred grief of becoming.
Not because you're erasing your past — but because you're

finally making room for your future.
Letting go doesn't mean forgetting. It means integrating. It means choosing to no longer live from the wound, but to live with the wisdom that came from it.

As someone once said, *"Sometimes the hardest part isn't letting go of what hurt you. It's letting go of the version of you who tolerated it."*

You are allowed to grieve them and still move forward.
You are allowed to love them and still outgrow them.
You are allowed to thank them with a full heart and still release them with a soul that is ready for more.

Because this — this tender, courageous shedding — is what it truly means to become.

You Will Feel Lost (This Is Good News)

There will come a moment in this process — maybe many — when you feel like you're freefalling. No map. No anchor. No clearly defined identity to cling to. Everything that once gave you structure is dissolving, and you're left suspended in the unknown. And in that moment, every part of you might scream: *Something must be wrong.*

But what if it's not?
What if feeling lost isn't a sign you've failed — but the clearest evidence that you're waking up?

Because here's what's true: you're no longer numbing.
You're no longer moving through life on autopilot,

performing roles that never quite fit.
You're no longer pretending the box you were handed is big enough to hold your truth.
Of course you feel lost — you've stopped navigating with someone else's compass.

You've stepped off the well-worn path paved with expectations and "shoulds."
You've turned your back on the roles that once earned you belonging at the cost of your authenticity.
And now... you're in the wilderness.

It's terrifying — yes.
But also miraculous.

Because in this space, you are no longer choosing safety over truth. You are no longer chasing certainty at the cost of your soul. You are letting yourself *be* — before knowing who you are becoming. And that is not weakness. That is courage.

We live in a world obsessed with clarity. We are taught to define ourselves, to brand ourselves, to always know our next step. We're expected to have a five-year plan, a clear purpose, an identity that fits neatly on a resume or Instagram bio. But real healing, real transformation, doesn't follow that kind of script.

There is sacredness in the not-knowing.
There is holiness in the space where you loosen your grip on control, and life begins to move through you — not because you forced it, but because you made room.

I remember sitting on my kitchen floor during one of the deepest parts of my unraveling, whispering to myself, *"I don't know who I am anymore."* And somewhere, deep within, a softer voice responded: *"Good. Now we can begin."*

That is what this moment is. It's not punishment. It's purification.
It's the undoing of what was never yours.
It's the sacred clearing.
The shedding of false identities, of survival strategies, of roles that kept you safe but small.

You don't need to rush to fill the space. You don't need to grasp for a new identity or force a new narrative. This isn't a problem to solve — it's a space to honor. All you need to do is stay. Breathe. Keep going.

So if you feel lost right now — disoriented, unanchored, unsure — I want you to know this:

You are not broken.
You are not going backward.
You are not failing.

You are becoming.

Let this part be enough.
Let it be sacred.
Let it be exactly what it is:
The chrysalis before the wings.

The Gifts of the Messy Middle

The messy middle doesn't feel like a gift. It feels like confusion. Like grief. Like standing in an empty hallway between who you were and who you're becoming—no doors open, no lights on, no guide in sight. It's not glamorous. It doesn't make for pretty soundbites or neat timelines. It's raw. It's uncertain. It's often so quiet that the noise of your old life still rings in your ears, even though the life that awaits you hasn't yet begun to speak.

And yet... if you stay—if you resist the urge to numb, to run, to rebuild too quickly—something begins to stir.

Because this space, this aching, unclear, uncomfortable space, is sacred ground. It is the pause before the breakthrough. The silence before the truth. The stillness where your old patterns begin to unravel, not with a bang, but with a slow and steady softening. It is here, in this holy discomfort, that the real gifts begin to emerge—not flashy or fast, but deep and lasting.

The first gift is this: **You become your own authority.** When the outside noise begins to fade—when you stop outsourcing your identity to family, religion, society, algorithms—you begin to hear your own voice. Not the voice of fear. Not the voice shaped by performance, perfectionism, or the need to be good. But the quiet, steady voice of your inner knowing. The one that was always there, waiting beneath the layers. And from that place, you begin to make choices—not to please, not to prove, but to align. You no longer need approval to feel valid. You no longer need permission to exist fully as yourself. That alone is a revolution.

The second gift: **You learn to sit in discomfort.**
You stop running from the hard feelings. You stop reaching for the old coping mechanisms that once shielded you from pain, but also from truth. And instead... you stay. You breathe. You feel. At first, it's excruciating. But with time, you begin to build something that no external system can give you—capacity. The capacity to sit with the unknown without needing to fix it. To hold space for your humanity without abandoning it. You start to trust your own nervous system. You start to realize: *I can be with myself, even here.* And that becomes your quiet power.

The third gift: **You discover new truths.**
Once the noise dies down, once the conditioning begins to dissolve, a new frequency emerges—truth. Not the kind you absorb from books or experts. Not the kind packaged for mass consumption. But the kind that bubbles up from the marrow of your being. These truths don't shout. They don't perform. They feel like stillness. Like a deep exhale. Like clarity that was always waiting for you beneath the chaos. Sometimes it comes while walking in nature. Sometimes it finds you in the middle of a breakdown. But when it arrives, it doesn't grip—it frees.

The messy middle will humble you. It will stretch you. It will strip away everything that was built on fear, performance, or survival. It will challenge your old ways of measuring worth. But if you let it—if you allow the unraveling to do its holy work—it will return something far greater than a new identity.

It will return *you*.

Not the you that performs.
Not the you that pleases.

Not the you the world tried to shape into something more palatable.

But the you that is whole. Clear. Free.

You don't get to bypass this part.
But you can learn to bless it.

Let it shape you.
Let it teach you.
Let it strip away what was never yours to carry.

And when you emerge on the other side, it won't just be with a new story to tell.
It will be with a new relationship to truth—one rooted not in certainty, but in integrity.

A New Way of Being Emerges

There comes a moment—quiet, almost unnoticeable—when something begins to shift. Not because you forced it. Not because you finally "figured it out" or checked every box on the healing checklist. But because you stayed. You waited. You softened. You let the old unravel. You resisted the urge to rebuild too fast. You honored the void. You honored the questions. You honored the sacred pause between who you were and who you're becoming.

And somewhere inside that liminal space, a new way of being begins to rise.

It doesn't arrive with fanfare. It doesn't come with a to-do list or a step-by-step plan. It won't offer the kind of clarity that satisfies the mind's craving for control. Instead, it comes softly—like breath, like a whisper, like a tug in the chest you can't quite explain. It rises not from effort, but from surrender. Not from strategy, but from stillness.

It might show up in the smallest of ways—ways you barely recognize as transformation at first.

You say "no" when your body says no, even if your mind urges you to be polite.
You rest even when the old voice says you haven't earned it yet.
You show up without a mask, allowing yourself to be seen without performance.
You make choices that prioritize peace over proving.
You begin to move from alignment, not fear.

At first, it feels unfamiliar. Not like the "old you." But not quite like someone else either. It feels... more true. Because for the first time in a long time, your actions begin to rise from the inside out—not to gain approval or avoid rejection, but simply because they feel honest.

You're no longer reaching for identities that fit the mold. You're not constructing a self that pleases the crowd. You're not polishing yourself into someone the world will find acceptable. Instead, you begin living from your root— not your role. From your knowing—not your conditioning.

It feels quieter.
Simpler.
Almost anticlimactic.

And yet, in that quiet simplicity, there's something unmistakably sacred.

Because this isn't you shrinking. This is you arriving.
Not at a destination, but at a deeper relationship with yourself.
One that honors your capacity.
One that trusts your truth.
One that refuses to abandon what's real for what's expected.

Here's what's wild:
You didn't create this "new you."
You remembered them.
You unburied them.

This emergence isn't a reinvention—it's a reunion.

A reunion with your integrity.
With your intuition.
With your sacred inner authority.

There's no need for a polished brand or a flawless plan.
This version of you doesn't need to be flashy.
It just needs to be real.

And once you taste that kind of truth—
raw, rooted, and unmistakably yours—
you'll never want to go back to pretending again.

The Sacred Truth of the In-Between

The messy middle isn't a mistake. It's not a detour or a delay, and it's certainly not a punishment for getting something wrong. As much as it may feel disorienting or unglamorous, this liminal space—the in-between—is the path itself.

It's the part of your journey that rarely gets celebrated. There are no highlight reels, no before-and-after snapshots to showcase. There is only the quiet hum of uncertainty and the sobering stillness that arrives when you're no longer who you used to be, but not yet who you're becoming. It's the hallway between stories, the space where nothing seems to fit, where familiar structures crumble and the ground beneath you shifts in ways you can't control.

And yet, beneath all the discomfort and confusion, something sacred is unfolding.

This is the place where what is false begins to fall away—not because you've failed, but because you're finally ready to live in truth. It's where the masks you wore for acceptance begin to crack, and the roles you performed for approval start to feel too tight to keep wearing. Here, in this raw space, you're not being asked to fix yourself, but to meet yourself. Not to strive, but to soften.

In the in-between, you begin to see clearly what was never really yours to carry. The armor that once kept you safe now feels unbearably heavy. The habits that once helped you survive start to lose their grip. You feel the weight of old expectations slip off your shoulders, and for the first time, you notice how much lighter you are without them.

But this unraveling doesn't come with clear instructions. There's grief here—grief for the versions of yourself you've outgrown, for the identities you worked so hard to maintain, for the certainty you once clung to like a lifeline. There's also fear, because without the old labels, who are you now?

The answer doesn't arrive all at once. It comes slowly, softly, through moments of honesty that take your breath away. It comes in the pause before the rebuild, in the ache that teaches you how much capacity you actually hold. It comes in your willingness to stay—not to fix, not to perform—but to be with what is.

This is the sacred unbecoming. It's not glamorous, but it's deeply holy. It's the threshold between surviving and truly living. And once you begin to taste the freedom of not having to be anyone but yourself, you can't go back to the old performance—not because you're angry, but because it no longer feels true.

The in-between asks everything of you. It strips away the noise and hands you back your heartbeat. It teaches you to trust what's rising in the silence. It reminds you that healing was never about returning to who you were—it was always about becoming who you really are.

So if you're here, in the in-between, don't rush it. Don't shame it. Let it stretch you. Let it strip you. Let it shape you into someone who no longer needs to be defined by survival.

Because this middle isn't where your story ends.
It's where it begins

Chapter 3 Exercises: Embracing the Messy Middle

This chapter isn't meant to simply be read—
it's meant to be experienced, embodied, and lived.

The practices that follow are not prescriptions.
They are invitations—tender guides to help you root into
the discomfort of the in-between,
to honor what is dissolving,
and to make space for what is quietly, courageously
becoming beneath the surface.

This is not about fixing yourself.
It's about meeting yourself.
Again and again.

Not with urgency, but with reverence.
Not with control, but with curiosity.
Each step, a homecoming.

Exercise 1: The Identity Shedding Ritual

Create space. Light a candle. Turn off distractions. Breathe.

On a piece of paper, begin listing the roles, labels, and
identities you've carried—consciously or unconsciously—
that no longer fit who you are becoming.
- The caretaker.
- The fixer.
- The achiever.
- The martyr.

- The one who always says yes.

Write them all down.
Sit with each one.
Notice how it feels in your body.

Now, for each one, write a short thank-you:
"Thank you for keeping me safe."
"Thank you for helping me feel needed."
"Thank you for getting me through what I didn't yet know how to handle."

Then, write the cost:
"What did this identity steal from me?"
"What did I have to abandon to keep this mask on?"
When you're ready, bury it, burn it, rip it up—whatever feels most honoring and final. Let it go as a symbol of your release.

Reflection Prompt:
What do you feel in your body as you let these roles go?
What space opens up inside you when you no longer have to perform?

Exercise 2: The Body Trust Scan

The messy middle often triggers our desire to "figure it out."

When you feel yourself scrambling for control or trying to make sense of the unknown, pause and return to your body.
1. Sit in stillness. Close your eyes.
2. Ask: "Where do I feel the need to fix, rush, or control?"
3. Place a hand on that part of your body.

4. Inhale slowly through the nose for a count of 4.
5. Exhale slowly through the mouth for a count of 8.
6. Whisper to yourself: It's okay not to know yet. I trust what is becoming.

Repeat this as often as needed.
You don't need all the answers—
just enough trust to stay present with yourself.

Exercise 3: The Messy Middle Journal Prompts

These prompts are for the days when everything feels blurry and uncertain.

They're not about fixing anything.

They're about feeling, witnessing, and anchoring yourself in the present.

- What old beliefs or behaviors am I grieving today?
- Where in my life am I most uncomfortable not knowing?
- What would happen if I gave myself permission to be in the unknown without solving it?
- What am I learning about myself in this season of transition?
- What would I say to the version of me who wants to give up?

Use these prompts weekly—or daily, if needed—
to stay grounded and honest with yourself.

Exercise 4: Cultivating Nervous System Capacity

The ability to stay in the unknown without shutting down is not a mindset—it's a nervous system skill.

This daily practice helps you build capacity and regulate yourself through the emotional waves of the messy middle.

Daily Breath Practice:
- Inhale through your nose for a count of 4
- Hold gently for a count of 4
- Exhale slowly through your mouth for a count of 8
- Place a hand on your chest or belly
- Repeat for at least 5 minutes

Affirmation:
I am safe in the unknown.
I am supported by my breath.
I trust the unfolding.

Do this first thing in the morning or anytime you feel overwhelmed.
Your breath is your anchor.

Exercise 5: Gathering Evidence of Becoming

Healing often feels invisible while it's happening.

That's why you need to start tracking your becoming.

This is not a journal of perfection.
It's a log of the tiny, sacred shifts that signal transformation.

Start a "Becoming Log." Each day, write one moment where you noticed:

- You paused instead of reacting.
- You let yourself feel instead of numbing.
- You said no when it felt right.
- You trusted your own voice over others.
- You rested instead of pushing.

These moments are proof that you are becoming—
even if the outside hasn't caught up yet.

Reminder:
Healing isn't always loud.
Sometimes, it's as quiet as choosing peace over performance.

Part Two:

Rebuilding from Within

After you've broken free from the box, the initial silence can feel almost unbearable. You expected liberation to bring lightness, maybe even celebration—but instead, there's a strange, unfamiliar ache. Not the ache of harm or injury, but of exposure. It's the tenderness of standing in the open after years spent hidden, like a soul blinking against sunlight after living in the shadows.

And in that light, things begin to stir.

You start to feel emotions you hadn't realized you'd numbed—anger that rises in waves, desire you thought had long gone dormant, a grief so quiet and vast it has no language. Your body, once silenced, begins to speak again. Your intuition, once tucked away neatly behind politeness, becomes less willing to whisper. You cry without warning. You rage at things you once swallowed. You start waking up with questions pressing against your ribcage like seeds ready to sprout: Why did I accept that? Who was I protecting? What have I been running from?

Everything you once took as truth begins to wobble under closer inspection. You look at the life you've carefully constructed and whisper to yourself, *Whose life is this, really?* You peel back the layers of performance, of striving, of belonging at any cost, and you begin to see how many parts of yourself were quietly traded away—for safety, for love, for some semblance of stability.

And then, there you are. No longer hidden, no longer pretending. Just standing—trembling, maybe—but finally whole enough to wonder: *Now what?*

This is the turning point. Because while unlearning is its own revolution, it's only half the journey. What comes next is the slow and sacred art of rebuilding. Not louder. Not faster. Not flashier. But deeper. Truer. More honest.

This isn't about becoming someone brand new. It's about remembering the version of you that existed before the world began its editing. Before you learned to be palatable. Before worth was measured and love was earned. It's a return to the roots beneath all the roles—a return to the self that always existed, quietly waiting for permission to rise.

Rebuilding isn't glamorous. It doesn't come with milestones or external praise. It happens in kitchens while the coffee brews. In bedrooms where you finally allow yourself to rest. In bathrooms where the tears fall fast and silent. In parked cars where you exhale after holding it together all day. In fleeting moments where you choose your truth, even when no one else sees it.

It's in these moments that you begin to rewrite the rhythm of your life. You choose nourishment over numbing. Rest over rushing. Presence over perfection. It's not always clean or confident. Sometimes it looks like saying "no" through trembling lips. Sometimes it means saying "yes" to something that defies logic but feels like home in your bones.

You will falter. You'll forget. There will be days when the old patterns call you back with seductive familiarity. You'll question yourself, wonder if you're making it all up, and ache for someone to validate your path. You'll feel isolated in your truth, longing to be understood.

That doesn't mean you're lost. That doesn't mean you've failed. It means you've stopped abandoning yourself for approval. It means you're choosing the slow, courageous work of healing—work that often makes you feel alone before it makes you feel free.

To rebuild from within is not about fixing something broken. It's about unearthing what was never truly gone. That inner knowing. That quiet wisdom. The voice that's been whispering all along in dreams, in stillness, in moments of collapse and clarity alike: *There is more. There has always been more.*

Rebuilding is not a destination. It's a homecoming. A steady return to breath, to body, to the beat of your own becoming. It's the moment you begin laying a new foundation—not because you have all the answers, but because you're ready to stop betraying yourself.

This is where the real story begins.
And it begins right here.

Chapter 4:

Tools for Unlearning — Rebuilding Trust in Your Body, Intuition, and Inner Compass

"You were never broken. You were taught to believe you were."
— Nayyirah Waheed

The Tools Were Always Inside You

We're raised to believe that healing is something we must chase—something that lives just beyond the horizon. We think it hides in prescriptions or in perfectly curated wellness programs. We search for it in people with letters after their names, in systems that promise certainty if we just follow the rules.

Somewhere along the way, we learned to look outward for answers and to silence the quiet intelligence within us. We began to doubt the whisper that said, *This doesn't feel right.* We stopped listening to our body's cues, stopped trusting that soft inner voice that once spoke so clearly.

But the deeper truth—the one that breaks open the illusion—is this:

You were never missing anything.

The tools have always lived inside you. You didn't need to earn them. You didn't need to qualify for them. You were born with them. You just forgot where to look.

This unlearning, this sacred return, isn't only about shedding the false beliefs that were handed to you. It's about remembering what your body has always known. It's about reclaiming a language that was once your first tongue: the wisdom of breath, of sensation, of instinct.

Before someone told you your feelings were too much, you knew how to cry when you were sad.
Before someone told you to "be nice" at all costs, you knew how to say no.
Before someone made you believe hunger was shameful, you knew how to nourish yourself.
Before someone labeled your intuition irrational, you followed it like a compass.

None of this is new.
It's not radical.
It's ancient.
It's primal.
It's yours.

We forget, not because we're flawed, but because disconnection is profitable. A society that convinces you to distrust your body can sell you something to fix it. A culture that disconnects you from your needs can keep you striving, producing, proving.

But you were never broken. You were broken *away* from yourself.

And the path back isn't dramatic. It doesn't require perfection or performance. It's not found in shouting affirmations or chasing another version of self-improvement.

It's quiet.
Simple.
Soft.

It happens in the in-between spaces—the moments when you pause before reacting, when you ask yourself what you need before pushing through, when you finally allow your body to exhale.

This is the work:
To return to your own rhythm.
To rebuild trust with your inner knowing.
To listen—to really listen—to the voice that says, *You can trust me. I never left.*

You are not a project.
You are not an emergency.
You are a homecoming.

This chapter isn't here to hand you strategies to master or steps to perfect. It's here to remind you of what's already inside. The wisdom. The tools. The truth.

You've always had what you needed.

And now—it's time to remember.

The Body: Your First Tool for Truth

Your body was your first home, your first teacher, your first truth-teller. Long before you had language or logic, before you could explain or defend yourself, you *felt*. You instinctively knew what safety felt like—softness, warmth, attunement. You also knew what danger felt like—tightness, stillness, separation. You responded with your whole being, not because you were taught to, but because your body was already fluent in the language of aliveness.

In those earliest years, you reached for connection, flinched from what hurt, cried when you were hungry, clung when you needed comfort. There was no second-guessing. Your body and your truth were one.

But as you grew, something changed. The world—well-meaning or not—began to teach you another language. One that prioritized control over curiosity, performance over presence. You were told to stop crying. To sit still. To be good. You learned to override the ache in your belly, the lump in your throat, the flutter of anxiety in your chest. Slowly, you were praised not for listening to your body, but for silencing it.

Messages came from all directions. Doctors dismissed symptoms that had no clear cause. Teachers demanded stillness when your body needed movement. Caregivers scolded your tears or asked you to "toughen up." Religion may have told you that the body was something to discipline, even distrust. Over time, you internalized a deeper message: *You can't trust yourself.*

And so you adapted. Like all of us do. You moved into your head, into reason and logic and external approval. You became skilled at ignoring your needs, at pushing through, at showing up even when every cell inside you begged for rest. You disconnected—not because you were broken, but because it felt safer that way.

Still, your body never stopped speaking.

It whispered to you through tension, through fatigue, through the subtle unease that followed every yes you didn't mean. It flared with anxiety when you crossed your own boundaries, even if no one else noticed. It tightened when you stayed silent, when you smiled through pain, when you ignored your inner no.

These weren't betrayals. They were attempts to protect you. Your body wasn't trying to ruin your life—it was trying to *save* it. But without a map to decode its signals, you may have felt frustrated, even at war with yourself.

Now, as you begin to unlearn the beliefs that pulled you away from yourself, this is where the return begins: not in theory or concept, but in the body. The body is the place where truth first lived and where it still lives now, waiting for you to notice.

Returning to the body is not always comfortable. It asks you to slow down. To feel what you've avoided. To listen without rushing to fix or explain. But it also invites you into a more honest, embodied way of living. A life where you don't need to check in with the world before honoring your needs. A life where your no is valid without explanation, and your yes is guided by something deeper than fear.

To come home to your body is to begin again—not as a project to fix, but as a relationship to restore. Your body doesn't need to be controlled. It needs to be heard. It doesn't need to be punished. It needs to be trusted.

This is not about mastering some perfect new routine. It's about remembering an ancient knowing already inside you. A wisdom that was never lost—only buried.

When you stop treating your body like an enemy and begin listening like it's your oldest friend, something powerful happens. You realize you've had the compass all along.

And from that place—curious, grounded, and alive—you begin to move forward, not with certainty, but with a deep, steady trust in yourself.

Tool 1: Body Tracking and Felt Sense Awareness

For a long time, I lived almost entirely in my head. Thoughts ruled everything. If I couldn't explain it, I didn't trust it. If I couldn't analyze it, I didn't feel safe with it. My body became something I managed—something to push through, ignore, criticize, or fix depending on the day. I didn't realize I was disconnected; I just thought being exhausted, anxious, and reactive was how everyone lived.

It wasn't until I began practicing something called body tracking that I started to come home to myself in a way that no amount of thinking ever could.

Body tracking isn't about understanding anatomy or memorizing what each sensation might mean. It's not clinical. It's relational. It's about tuning in and listening to the subtle signals of your body with the same presence and care you'd offer a dear friend. You begin by asking the simplest question: *What's happening in me right now?*

At first, the answers come in whispers—tightness in your shoulders, a flutter in your stomach, heat in your face, heaviness in your chest. These are not meaningless. They're messages. They're the body's first language—expressing what your thinking mind may not be ready to admit. A dull ache behind the eyes may speak of grief. A tension in the jaw may hold unspoken boundaries. A fluttering heartbeat might not be danger, but anticipation or longing.

The first time I allowed myself to stay with a sensation rather than distract or dismiss it, I cried. Not out of pain, but because I finally felt heard. That moment cracked something open in me. It was as if my body had been waiting years for me to stop managing it and start listening.

As I practiced, I began to discover something deeper than just sensation. This is what somatic practitioners call *felt sense awareness*—the ability to attune not just to the physical, but to the emotional truth held inside those sensations. Instead of trying to decode or diagnose what I felt, I began to gently ask: *What might this part of me be trying to say? What is living underneath this tension? What does this feeling need from me right now?*

There wasn't always an answer. Sometimes, the body speaks slowly. Sometimes, it speaks in metaphors, or images, or silence. But over time, I began to recognize certain patterns. I could feel my body's "no" as a sinking in my stomach, a closing of the chest. I could feel my "yes" as a softening, an opening, a quiet confidence rising in my bones. I began to recognize that what I used to call anxiety was often just misalignment—my body alerting me that I was about to abandon myself again.

The more I practiced, the more I realized: my body had never lied to me. It had always been telling the truth. I had just been too busy, too conditioned, too disconnected to hear it.

Now, body tracking is part of my daily rhythm. It's simple, but sacred:

- I pause—especially when I feel off, tense, or unsure—and ask, *What am I feeling in my body right now?*
- I name it without judgment. Heat. Buzzing. Numbness. Tightness. Tingling. There's no need to fix it—just witness it.
- I place a hand on the area that feels activated and breathe gently into that space.
- I ask, *What do you need from me?*
- And then, I wait. I listen. Sometimes I journal. Sometimes I cry. Sometimes I simply sit and breathe.

This small practice changes everything. It becomes a compass that helps you discern what's truly right for you. It shows you where you're shrinking to stay safe, where you're pushing past your needs, where you're living out of habit instead of alignment. And maybe most importantly, it teaches you how to stay with yourself.

Not in your thoughts.
Not in your stories.
But in your body—where healing actually happens.

Because healing doesn't begin when we figure things out. It begins when we finally feel what's real.

"The body never lies. The body always speaks truth—even when the mind can't yet understand it."
— Dr. Peter Levine

Tool 2: Rebuilding Trust in Your Intuition

For most of my life, I didn't realize I even had intuition.

I thought it was something reserved for other people— people who were more "in tune," more spiritual, more rested, more whole. I was too busy surviving, too busy scanning my environment for danger, too busy trying to be who everyone needed me to be. Gut feelings? I couldn't even feel my own body half the time, let alone trust something so intangible.

But intuition isn't something only a lucky few are gifted. It's not reserved for mystics or sages or people with quiet morning rituals and sage sticks.

It's something we're all born with.

A biological, emotional, and spiritual compass—always available, always whispering, even when we've forgotten how to listen.

The problem is, we're taught to stop listening. We're taught that logic is reliable and emotion is weak. That facts are valid and feelings are flimsy. That "gut instinct" is irresponsible unless you can back it up with a spreadsheet or a citation.

I absorbed those messages like gospel. If something couldn't be explained, it wasn't real. If I couldn't justify it, I dismissed it. And so, like many of us, I began to make decisions from fear, performance, and practicality—ignoring the quiet hum of truth that lived inside me.

Looking back, I can trace every moment I abandoned myself to that silence. I knew the relationship wasn't safe, but I stayed. I knew the job would suffocate me, but I said yes. I knew the friend didn't truly see me, but I kept showing up.

Each time I ignored my body's wisdom, it chipped away at something sacred—my self-trust.

Rebuilding that trust didn't happen in a single breakthrough moment. It happened slowly, gently, through practice. I didn't try to "master" intuition. I just started listening again.

At first, I created space for quiet—just five minutes a day without noise, without input, without expectation. Not to find answers, but to find myself.

I began checking in with my body before checking in with anyone else. When faced with a choice, I would pause and ask, *Does this feel like a yes, a no, or a not yet?* I noticed what happened in my body. Did I feel open or closed? Grounded or shaky? Light or heavy? The sensations didn't always give me clarity right away, but they always gave me information.

I started tracking what I call "intuitive hits"—those gut feelings, those inner nudges—and watching what happened when I followed them... or didn't. I kept a journal of these moments, and what I found over time was undeniable: even when it didn't make logical sense, my body had always been trying to steer me toward alignment.

The more I honored those whispers, the more my intuition grew louder.

One of the biggest shifts came when I stopped explaining or justifying my "no." I didn't need a spreadsheet or an excuse. If something felt wrong, that was enough. At first, it was terrifying—especially for someone who had learned to earn love through compliance and caretaking. But each time I chose self-trust over people-pleasing, I felt more solid in myself. More rooted. More whole.

And that's the thing about intuition—it's a relationship.

If you ignore it, it grows quiet. Not out of punishment, but out of protection. But when you listen, when you respond, when you act even in small ways... it begins to trust you, too. It speaks more clearly. It shows up more consistently. And you stop needing so much external confirmation.

You begin making choices that don't require consensus.
You stop outsourcing your wisdom to people who don't live in your body.
You start living from your inner truth—not someone else's expectations.

And one day, without even realizing it, you notice you're walking through life differently.

Not always confidently, but with clarity.

Not always perfectly, but with integrity.

Because you're no longer asking the world for permission.

You're asking yourself.

And the answer, more often than not, has been there all along.

And that, my friend, changes everything.

Tool 3: Nervous System Regulation as Unlearning

You cannot unlearn from a place of survival.

No matter how badly you want to think differently, act differently, or live differently—if your nervous system is stuck in a stress response, your body will choose survival over transformation every time.

When we're locked in fight, flight, freeze, or fawn, the world narrows. Everything becomes about managing threat, even if that threat isn't obvious. You may want to pause, reflect, or respond with presence, but if your body doesn't feel safe, those options aren't accessible. You aren't weak or broken for struggling—your system is doing what it was designed to do: protect you.

This is why nervous system regulation is not optional on the path of unlearning. It's essential.

But let's be clear—regulation isn't about being calm all the time.

It's not about breathing through every hard moment or keeping your composure when chaos erupts. It's about building the capacity to move through activation without losing connection to yourself. It's about being with what arises in your body—without judgment, without urgency, and without abandoning yourself.

Regulation means remembering what safety feels like—not just as a concept, but as a lived experience in your body. And then slowly, gently, expanding your ability to return to that felt sense of safety even after you've been activated or triggered.

Because healing doesn't mean never getting dysregulated. It means knowing how to come back.

This is the foundation of unlearning.

You cannot rewrite old patterns, choose new ways of being, or open to deeper truths if your body doesn't believe it's safe enough to do so.

The Language of the Nervous System

Your nervous system is always listening. Not just through your ears, but through every cell. It listens through the pace of your breath, the tension in your shoulders, the tone of someone's voice, the softness or sharpness in their eyes, the space—or lack of it—in a room.

It's constantly scanning for cues: *Am I safe here? Am I seen? Am I allowed to be?*

And it doesn't care what your mind says—if your body feels threatened, it will protect you first and ask questions later.

The problem is, many of us were raised in environments where our nervous system's signals had to be ignored just to survive. We learned to normalize chaos. To downplay discomfort. To override the internal alarms that told us something wasn't right. We smiled when we were scared. We stayed quiet when we were violated. We performed when we were crumbling.

Over time, those protective responses became automatic. Familiar. Expected.

And even now, in safe environments, our systems can still respond as if the danger is present. Because they never learned how to come down. They never learned what safety really feels like.

This is the work now.

Not to "fix" the nervous system, but to rebuild the relationship with it.

To become fluent again in its language.

To notice the subtle signs: the tight jaw, the shallow breath, the buzzing in your limbs, the disconnection in your chest. To slow down enough to ask, *What are you trying to tell me?* and *What would help you feel safe right now?*

Sometimes the answer is movement. Sometimes it's stillness. Sometimes it's breath, or sound, or grounding your feet on the earth. Sometimes it's placing a hand on your heart and whispering, *I'm here.*

These small acts of regulation—repeated consistently—become a lifeline.

They remind your body that it's no longer trapped in the past.

They create space for choice, for presence, for possibility.

And slowly, gently, you begin to unlearn not just with your mind, but with your entire being.

Because when your body feels safe enough to stay—you stop reacting from old wounds and start responding from your true self.

And that, right there, is where everything changes.

Practices for Nervous System Regulation

These are not quick fixes. These are invitations to return.

1. Breath as Anchor

Slow, intentional breathing tells your body that it is safe. One of the most effective patterns is to exhale longer than you inhale.

Try:
- Inhale for 4 counts
- Hold gently for 2
- Exhale for 6-8 counts
  This activates the parasympathetic system—your body's rest and digest mode—and helps you shift out of urgency and into presence.

2. Grounding Touch
Place a hand on your heart, your belly, or your thighs.
Press gently. Feel the contact.
Remind your body:
I am here.
I am now.
I am safe.

This kind of physical connection sends calming signals to your brain and interrupts dissociation or spiraling thoughts.

3. Orienting to Safety
Look around the room you are in.
Name five colors.
Notice where the light is.
Listen for a sound that feels neutral or pleasant.

This simple practice helps the brain shift from threat-scanning into present-moment awareness.

4. Nature as Co-Regulator
When you are overwhelmed, go outside.
Even if only for five minutes.
Sit with a tree,
feel the earth beneath your feet,
listen to the wind.

Nature does not ask anything from you. It simply offers its stability. Let it hold you.

5. Vocalizing for Vagal Toning
Your nervous system responds to sound.
Try humming, sighing, chanting, or singing softly.

These practices stimulate the vagus nerve, your body's built-in brake pedal.
They invite softness, slow your heart rate, and calm the inner storm.

Remember:

Your ability to unlearn depends on your ability to regulate.

Not to master it.
Not to get it right every time.
But to come back—again and again—to presence.

Regulation isn't about achieving a state of eternal calm.
It's about cultivating the capacity to stay connected to yourself, even when things get hard.
It's about choosing presence over performance, gentleness over judgment.

Every time you return to your body—even for a breath, a moment, a soft whisper of awareness—you are practicing a new way of being.
You're teaching your system that safety is possible.
That you no longer have to armor up just to exist.
That you don't have to flee or freeze or fawn in order to be loved.

It's a slow, sacred reconditioning.
And with each return, it gets a little easier.

The more you show up with compassion instead of criticism,
the more you listen instead of override,
the more you pause instead of push—

the more your nervous system begins to trust that it's safe to be here.

And when safety returns, so does curiosity.

Curiosity opens the door to choice.

Suddenly, you're not trapped in the old pattern.
You're not reacting from the wound.
You're standing at a new threshold—one where awareness meets possibility.

This is where unlearning becomes embodied.
Not just a concept or a conversation,
but a felt shift in your internal landscape.

This is where your body begins to believe:
I don't have to live the old story anymore.

Not because someone gave you permission.
Not because the world changed.
But because *you* chose to come back to yourself.

And that return is the revolution.

Tool 4: Somatic Practices for Unlearning

Some patterns can't be unraveled by thinking harder.
Because they weren't formed in the mind to begin with.

Many of the beliefs you carry—about your worth, your role, your limits—weren't created through logic. They were

shaped in moments when your body had to adapt in order to survive.
Moments when the nervous system encoded protection as posture, tone, muscle tension, stillness, or shutdown.

And so, while insight is helpful, and language can offer clarity,
true healing asks more of us.
It asks that we return to the place where the pain lives—not just in memory, but in sensation.

This is where somatic work becomes essential.

I didn't understand this at first.
I thought if I could just talk it out, write it out, analyze it enough, I'd be free.
But no matter how much I processed with words, certain patterns kept resurfacing.
Reactions I couldn't explain. Emotions I couldn't name.
Exhaustion that no amount of rest could fix.

Then I began to notice something:
My body wasn't resisting me.
It was revealing something I hadn't yet been ready to face.

Through somatic work, I began to see my body not as the enemy,
but as the protector.
The witness.
The one who held the truth when words fell short.

Somatic practices aren't about performing a technique.
They're about slowing down enough to meet your body where it is—without agenda, without judgment.

They invite you to *feel* your way through, rather than think your way out.
To bring awareness into sensation, to name what's happening internally, and to create space for those sensations to move.

I began with simple practices:
Laying on the ground and noticing the support beneath me.
Following the path of my breath without trying to change it.
Letting my hands move in whatever way felt true in the moment.
Sounding. Shaking. Sighing. Pausing.

Each time, something subtle shifted.

Not in a dramatic, life-altering way—but in a quiet, foundational one.
My body began to soften.
My nervous system started to trust me.
And patterns that once felt immovable started to loosen their grip.

This is the power of somatic unlearning.

It bypasses the need for explanation and offers something deeper:
Integration.
Wholeness.
A return to yourself—not just in theory, but in sensation, breath, and presence.

And it begins with the simple choice to stop fighting your body
and start listening to it instead.

Somatic Practices That Changed Everything

These are the practices that helped me return to my body with compassion, regulation, and trust.

They are not about fixing—they are about feeling.
They are about learning to stay with yourself through discomfort, not escape it.

1. Orienting to Safety

This is where I started.
It sounds simple, but it changed everything.

I would slowly turn my head and let my eyes land on something neutral or pleasing—
a tree outside,
the corner of the room,
a plant,
a color I liked.

I noticed textures, light, shapes.

My breath softened.
My shoulders lowered.

My system learned:
It's safe to be here.

This practice gently signals to the brain and body:
"We are not in danger right now."

2. Titration and Pendulation

Instead of diving headfirst into trauma or overwhelming emotions,
I learned to move between discomfort and safety—
back and forth like a wave.

I would bring attention to a tight or heavy place in my body,
then shift to a more neutral or pleasant sensation.

This taught my nervous system that it could hold both
without shutting down.

Small doses.
Gentle swings.
Building capacity.
This is how real healing happens.

3. Spontaneous Movement and Shaking

There were days I couldn't speak the pain I was in—
but my body could move it.

Shaking, swaying, rocking, stretching—
letting my body lead without choreography.

I would let out tension through movement without judgment.

Sometimes I cried.
Sometimes I felt relief.
Sometimes I just felt real.

Like wild animals that shake after trauma,

this movement discharged the stuck survival energy I didn't know I was still holding.

4. Vagal Toning Through Sound

Soft humming.
Deep sighs.
Low, open-vowel chanting.

These became daily rituals.

They activated my parasympathetic nervous system and helped me re-enter a state of calm.

The sound vibrated through my chest and throat—
the same places I had silenced for years.

This wasn't just nervous system work.

It was reclaiming my voice—
without needing words.

5. Fascia Release and Micro-Movement

Trauma lives in the fascia—
those thin sheets of connective tissue that wrap our muscles and bones.

Through gentle touch, slow stretching, and self-massage, I began to unwind the frozen tension I had carried for decades.

Yin yoga and intuitive movement helped too—
not to "exercise," but to soften.
To listen.

To feel.

These slow, intentional movements told my body,
"You no longer have to brace.
You are safe now."

Let the Body Lead

The most profound shifts in my healing journey didn't come
through words.
They didn't arrive during long conversations or carefully
crafted insights.
They emerged in the silence—
in the pause between breaths,
in the tremble before release,
in the stillness that followed surrender.

It was never about finding the perfect explanation.
It was about allowing myself to feel—fully, honestly, without
performance.

What somatic work taught me was that healing doesn't
need to be forced.
The body isn't asking for control—it's asking to be trusted.
And when we stop trying to lead with our minds and start
following the wisdom of our bodies, something sacred
begins to unfold.

This is the difference between performing healing and
embodying it.
Performing asks, "Am I doing this right?"
Embodiment whispers, "Can I stay with what's real?"

Somatic practices aren't about getting somewhere fast.
They're about arriving—over and over—into presence.
And from that place, the old stories begin to loosen.
Not because we push them out,
but because we finally create enough safety for them to
soften.

This is how we unlearn—not just conceptually, but cellularly.
This is how we peel back the layers we were taught to wear,
and remember the version of ourselves that never needed
fixing.

Letting the body lead doesn't mean giving up.
It means giving in—to truth, to wisdom, to the part of you
that always knew the way back home.

Tool 5: Rhythmic and Bilateral Stimulation

There's a reason rhythm soothes us.
It reaches a place words can't—
a place older than logic, older than language.
It speaks directly to the nervous system in a dialect it never forgot.

Before I understood the science, I felt the truth of it in my bones.
The way walking calmed my racing thoughts.
The way rocking myself quietly brought relief on nights I couldn't sleep.
The way a steady beat made my chest loosen, just a little.

For most of my life, I didn't know I was dysregulated.
I thought it was normal to always feel "on."
To be exhausted but unable to rest.
To live with a constant undercurrent of urgency that I couldn't name or explain.
I had adapted to it, shaped my life around it, called it ambition, responsibility, survival.

But underneath that hustle was a body that didn't feel safe.

When I was introduced to the concept of bilateral stimulation—simple, rhythmic, left-right movement—it felt almost too easy to be powerful.
But that's the thing about the body: it doesn't need complexity.
It needs consistency.
It needs rhythm.
It needs something predictable to anchor into.

Walking.
Tapping.
Swaying.
Rocking side to side.
Even holding a warm mug with both hands and alternating gentle pressure.

These aren't just motions.
They're messages.
They tell your nervous system, "You're okay. You're here. You're safe."

The beauty of rhythmic movement is that it mirrors what our bodies already know.
The rhythm of a heartbeat.
The rise and fall of breath.
The left-right cadence of crawling as infants, or walking as adults.

Bilateral stimulation taps into that primal wiring.
It invites regulation not by force, but by familiarity.

Some days, my practice is as simple as a slow walk with deliberate steps.
Other days, it's tapping alternately on my knees while breathing deeply.
There's no perfect way to do it.
The key is presence—repetition with gentle attention.

And slowly, the edge begins to soften.
The overwhelm begins to ease.
The body, once bracing for the next invisible blow, starts to feel held.
Supported.
Safe.

This is how we create safety without needing anyone else to provide it.
This is how we remind our nervous system that peace is possible.
Not through words.
Through rhythm.

And in rhythm, the body remembers:
I don't have to fight anymore.
I don't have to run.
I can just be.

Why Rhythm Regulates

When the body is overwhelmed, it forgets its own rhythm.
Breath shortens into the chest.
Muscles grip and brace.
Movements either become frantic—or they stop altogether.

It's not a flaw.
It's biology.
Your nervous system, sensing danger, begins to reorganize everything around survival.
In that state, rhythm disappears. Flow becomes fragmentation.

But the body craves rhythm.
It's how we were designed—beating hearts, cyclical breaths, the cadence of footsteps, the rise and fall of our emotional waves.
We are rhythmic beings by nature.

And when those rhythms are disrupted, regulation becomes difficult.

That's why predictable, bilateral, patterned input can be so powerful.
It gives the body something to hold onto—something steady.
A reminder that not everything is chaotic. That not everything is a threat.

It doesn't have to be complicated.
It might be the simple repetition of walking or drumming fingers on your thighs.
It might be rocking gently in a chair, humming a melody, or even tapping your feet beneath your desk.

What matters isn't the technique.
What matters is the repetition—the message it sends.

With each steady movement, the body begins to organize again.
The breath deepens.
Muscles loosen.
Thoughts slow.
Presence returns.

The system no longer needs to scan for danger.
It has a rhythm now.
And rhythm signals safety.

These are the tools that helped me rebuild that internal beat—
one steady step, one small sway, one gentle breath at a time.

This is how I remembered what peace feels like in the body.
Not through control or discipline,
but through the quiet wisdom of rhythm.

Practices for Rhythmic and Bilateral Regulation

1. Walking in Nature (or Anywhere)
I began with slow, mindful walks.
Each step—left, right, left, right—became a metronome for
my nervous system.

The fresh air, the sway of my arms, the sound of gravel or
grass beneath my feet—
this was meditation. This was therapy.

And it never asked me to perform.
Just to be.

Walking is one of the simplest forms of bilateral
stimulation—
and one of the most powerful when done with presence.

2. Self-Tapping (Bilateral or EFT-Style)

I would tap one side of my body, then the other—gently,
rhythmically.
Thighs. Upper arms. Shoulders.

Sometimes I used EFT-style tapping on specific acupoints
when emotions surfaced.
It gave me something to focus on,
a pattern to follow,

a rhythm to ground into.

It wasn't about "fixing" the emotion.
It was about letting my body know: *you're not alone in this.*

3. Rocking, Swaying, and Repetitive Motion

I'd sit on the floor or curl up on the couch and gently rock
my body.
Front to back. Side to side.

Like an infant being held.

Some days, I would sway standing with my eyes closed,
feeling the earth beneath me.
Other times, I danced—slow and instinctual, like my body
was speaking without words.

These movements didn't need choreography—
they just needed *compassion*.

4. Rhythmic Sound and Music

There were days when all I could do was sit and listen.
Drumming tracks,
steady ambient beats,
even a heartbeat rhythm on repeat.

They gave me something to anchor to.
A pulse that said,
"You're here. You're safe. You can soften."

Sound doesn't just travel through your ears—
it travels through your whole being.

5. Bilateral Drawing or Tracing

Sometimes I'd take a pen in each hand and draw figure eights or mirror shapes on paper.
Other times, I'd trace lines along my arms or legs—left, right, left, right.

It sounds small, but the brain loves this.
It says:
"Something familiar is happening. You're allowed to rest."

When Logic Fails, Rhythm Speaks

There comes a point in healing when logic no longer helps.
You've read the books.
You've named the patterns.
You understand the why.

And still, your body trembles.
Still, your breath shortens.
Still, you freeze, or flare, or flee—despite everything you *know*.

That's because regulation isn't a mental process.
It's a sensory one.
And rhythm speaks the language the nervous system understands.

You don't need to analyze your way out of dysregulation.
You need to feel your way back into rhythm.

These practices are not dramatic.
They are quiet.

Almost invisible from the outside.
A hand drumming on your leg.
A slow rock back and forth.
A repeated tap, a sway, a hum.

To someone watching, it might look like nothing.
But on the inside—something powerful is happening.

The body is reorganizing.
The system is returning to a pattern it can trust.
You're no longer just surviving—you're syncing.

This is not performance.
This is presence.
This is how the body relearns safety—not because you told
it to feel safe,
but because you gave it the experience of safety through
rhythm.

It's subtle.
It's sacred.
And it works.

This is nervous system healing through rhythm.
This is unlearning through patterned safety.
This is coming home—again and again—
to the beat of your own becoming.

Tool 6: Rewriting Your Internal Dialogue

The voices in your head didn't start with you.
They were shaped in rooms where you weren't allowed to speak.
They were formed in moments when you needed comfort but received criticism.
They were handed down like heirlooms—sometimes lovingly, often unconsciously.

"You're too much."
"You're not enough."
"You should be over this by now."

These weren't truths.
They were someone else's wounds, echoed through you.
And when you heard them enough times—especially when you were young—you believed them.
Not because they felt right, but because they felt familiar.

That's the thing about early imprinting:
It doesn't ask for your consent.
It just embeds itself in your nervous system, in your sense of self, in the way you narrate your life.

And for a while, that narration helps you survive.
You perform to stay loved.
You shrink to stay safe.
You silence yourself to stay connected.

But eventually, survival becomes suffocating.
And the story that once protected you becomes the very thing that's holding you back.

This is where the unlearning begins.
Not by waging war against your inner critic,
but by meeting it with curiosity.

Whose voice is this?
Where did I first hear it?
What was happening in my life when I started believing it?

The goal isn't to silence the inner dialogue.
It's to shift the tone.
To rewrite the script from one of judgment to one of
compassion.
From shame to understanding.
From criticism to care.

Because every harsh thought you've internalized began as a
coping mechanism.
And now, with presence and intention, you get to choose
something new.

You get to speak to yourself the way you always needed
someone to speak to you.
Not with blame, but with gentleness.
Not with pressure, but with permission.

Permission to feel.
Permission to be messy.
Permission to still be learning.

This isn't just mindset work—it's nervous system work.
Because your body listens to how you speak to yourself.
It softens or tightens depending on your tone.

So the next time you hear that old voice rise up, pause.
Breathe.

And choose a new one.
One rooted in truth.
One rooted in care.
One that says, "I see you. I hear you. I'm with you."

This is how you begin to feel safe inside your own mind again.
This is how you come home to yourself—one word, one thought, one gentle rewrite at a time.

Internal Dialogue is a Survival Strategy

One of the most transformative shifts in my healing journey was realizing that my inner critic wasn't my enemy.
It wasn't cruel just to be cruel.
It wasn't broken or evil.

It was protective.

That voice—the one that nitpicks, doubts, shames, and pushes—was born from fear.
Not the irrational kind, but the kind that once made sense.
The kind that kept me safe in environments where being fully myself didn't feel welcome.

Fear of being rejected.
Fear of being humiliated.
Fear of being punished for taking up too much space.
Fear of being abandoned for being too sensitive, too loud, too needy, too real.

So I internalized the world's gaze.
I learned to scan for what might be "wrong" with me before anyone else could.
To criticize myself before anyone else had the chance.
To hustle for acceptance, perform for connection, and perfect my way into safety.

And it worked—until it didn't.

Because what begins as a strategy for survival eventually becomes a prison.
The voice that once kept you out of harm's way starts keeping you from your own life.
From your joy.
From your voice.
From your softness.

Unlearning this voice isn't about erasing it.
It's about meeting it where it began.

It's about hearing the fear underneath the criticism.
It's about noticing the moment that voice kicks in and pausing long enough to say,
"I see you. I know why you're here. And I'm not going to abandon myself this time."

This is tender work.
You won't always get it right.
Some days, the old voice will still be louder than the new one.

But over time, with gentleness and practice, you begin to create space.
Space for a new voice—one rooted in truth, not trauma.
One that reflects your present, not your past.

And in that space, healing happens.
Not because you've silenced the critic,
but because you've outgrown the need for it.

This is the slow, sacred work of coming home to yourself—
not by force, but by compassion.
Not by denying your history, but by rewriting your
relationship to it.

You don't need to shame the part of you that developed
this voice.
You just need to remind it that you're safe now.
That the danger has passed.
That there's room for a gentler guide.

And that guide?
It's already within you—waiting to speak.

Practices to Rewrite the Script

1. Identify the Script

Start by noticing the repetitive thoughts that show up when you feel stressed, ashamed, or uncertain.
They often begin with:

- "I should have..."
- "I'm always..."
- "I'll never be..."

These are *clues*.
They aren't *truths*.
They are *scripts*.
And they can be changed.

Try This:
Write out a belief that surfaced today. Ask yourself:

- Who does this sound like?
- When did I first start believing this?
- What emotion lives underneath it?

2. Bring in the Body

Sit with the belief.
Say it out loud.
Notice what happens in your body.

Is there tightness?
A drop in your belly?
Shallow breath?

Let your body tell you how it feels to hold that story.

Then, offer your body a *new* story.
A truth that feels more kind, more real, more whole.
Even if you're not sure you believe it yet—let your body feel it.

Example:
Old Script: "I'm a burden."
New Truth: "My needs matter. I am worthy of care."

How does your body respond to the shift?

3. Anchor in the New Truth

Once you find a new phrase or truth that resonates, anchor it in ritual.

Repeat it each morning with your hand over your heart.
Whisper it when the critic comes online.
Write it on sticky notes, on mirrors, in journals.

Not to force it—
but to remind yourself that you have a choice.

Healing doesn't mean the old voices never show up.
It means you don't have to believe them anymore.

4. Let the Inner Child Speak

Often, these old beliefs were formed when we were young—
before we had the words or power to advocate for ourselves.

Try this:

- Write a letter to your younger self.
- Let them share what they needed to hear back then.
- Then respond, as your adult self, with compassion and truth.

This dialogue can be one of the most healing practices I've ever experienced.
It bridges the parts of you that have long been disconnected.

A Practice for Daily Rewriting

Each evening, reflect on a moment where your internal dialogue became self-critical or fear based.

Then:
- Write the old belief.
    - *(e.g., "I'm lazy because I rested today.")*
- Write the new truth.
    - *(e.g., "Rest is not laziness. It's part of how I care for myself.")*

Repeat the new truth out loud.
Gently.
As if speaking to someone you love.

Because you are.

You Are the Author Now

For most of your life, the world handed you a script.

It came from your family—well-meaning or not.
From your religion—structured, moral, often rigid.
From your trauma—wordless, invisible, powerful.

It was written in moments you didn't choose:
The way someone looked at you with disappointment.
The silence after you cried.
The praise you received when you abandoned your own needs to please others.

You internalized these stories—not because you were weak, but because you were human.
Because we all seek belonging, and sometimes, the cost of belonging is the loss of self.

But here's the beautiful, quiet, revolutionary truth:
You don't have to keep living by that script.

You get to pause.
You get to question the lines you've memorized.
You get to pick up the pen and write something new.

This is the heart of rewriting your internal dialogue—not with forced affirmations or blind positivity, but with rooted truth. With compassion. With presence.

You get to choose a voice that sounds like safety, not scrutiny.
A voice that reflects who you are becoming—not who you had to be to survive.

A voice that softens your edges instead of sharpening your shame.

This isn't about pretending everything is fine.
It's about being honest with yourself in a way that heals, not harms.
It's about telling the truth with tenderness.
It's about becoming the voice you always needed—the one that says,
"I see you. I'm with you. You're doing just fine."

Your inner dialogue will either build a cage or open a door.
It will either repeat the old stories or help you write new ones.

And the choice?
It's yours now.

You are the author.
And the pen has always been in your hand.

Unlearning as a Daily Ritual

We live in a world that glorifies arrival.
It praises the finish line, the certificate, the transformation post.
It tells us that if we just work hard enough, heal fast enough, get it "right," we'll eventually be done.

But real healing—true unlearning—isn't about getting to some final destination where everything clicks and stays perfect.

It's not about mastering your nervous system, silencing your inner critic forever, or never falling back into old patterns. This work—this coming home to yourself—is a lifelong devotion.
It's not a box to check. It's not a course you graduate from.

Unlearning is a ritual. A practice.
A daily, sometimes moment-by-moment, return to the truth of who you are beneath the conditioning.

Some days, it flows with ease.
You'll notice the pattern before it hijacks your nervous system.
You'll soften your tone with yourself instead of slipping into self-judgment.
You'll make choices rooted in authenticity, not approval.

And on other days, it won't be so smooth.
You'll catch yourself people-pleasing before you even realize why.
You'll feel the old impulse to overwork, to prove your worth through productivity.
You might shut down, numb out, or react in ways that feel like setbacks.

But those moments don't mean you've failed.
They mean you're human.
They mean you're in the process.

Because healing is not a straight path—it's a spiral.
You will revisit old wounds in new ways.
You'll encounter familiar patterns with new awareness.
Each time you choose to pause, to soften, to listen again—you root yourself more deeply in truth.
And slowly, gently, the return becomes easier.

This is the sacred rhythm of unlearning: not arrival, but return.
Not perfection, but presence.
Not doing it right, but doing it with love.

Practice, Not Perfection

Unlearning doesn't ask for perfection—it asks for presence.
It's not made of grand gestures or breakthrough moments.
It's made of small, sacred choices repeated over time.
Tiny rituals that seem simple on the surface but carry the power to change your relationship with yourself from the inside out.

It looks like pausing before you react, just long enough to notice what's really happening inside you.
It looks like asking your body what it needs instead of pushing through with what you think it should do.
It's catching yourself in a moment of performance and gently choosing presence instead.
It's saying "no" and staying with the discomfort, rather than rescuing others from your boundaries.
It's saying "yes" to rest, to stillness, to the things that don't earn praise but restore your wholeness.

This kind of practice isn't glamorous.
It doesn't come with applause or instant transformation.
No one will hand you a certificate for choosing your truth in the middle of a hard day.

But your body will know.
You'll feel it in the ease of your breath.

In the softness of your relationships.
In the way your inner voice shifts—from harsh to honest,
from critical to curious.

These small moments are not insignificant.
They are the scaffolding of change.
They are the way you become more *you* with every breath,
every boundary, every act of gentle return.

You Will Forget. That's Okay.

There will be days when the old programming creeps back
in.
Not because you're failing—but because it's familiar.
You spent years—maybe decades—learning to override your
needs, abandon your truth, and measure your worth by
someone else's standards. That doesn't disappear overnight.

You'll catch yourself people-pleasing, shrinking,
overanalyzing, or numbing—sometimes without even
realizing it at first.
But the difference now is that you *can* realize it.
You have the awareness to pause.
To notice.
To choose something different.

This is the muscle you're building—not perfection, but
presence.
Not rigid control, but tender recognition.
You're not trying to become someone who never forgets
herself.
You're becoming someone who knows how to come home.

And the more often you practice this return,
the shorter the detours will be.
The softer the recovery.
The quicker your body will trust that it's safe to land.

Forgetting isn't failure.
It's part of the rhythm.
And every return plants your truth a little deeper.

This Is a Life's Work

There is no final destination on this path. No perfect version
of you waiting at the end of some healing timeline. The idea
that we're meant to "arrive"—to be fully healed, fully whole,
never triggered again—is a myth. A story sold to us by
industries built on our insecurity. A lie that keeps us
endlessly chasing and never resting.

But the truth is quieter.
It doesn't shout or sparkle.
It whispers: *You are already whole.*
You are already home.
Not someday. Not when you've finally figured it all out. But
now—beneath the layers you've had to wear to survive.

The work of unlearning isn't about becoming someone new.
It's about returning to who you've always been.
It's about peeling back the noise, the armor, the
expectations that never belonged to you in the first place.

So you return.
Day after day.

Sometimes with ease. Sometimes through tears. Sometimes with resistance.
But still—you come back.

You return to your body.
To your breath.
To your boundaries.
To your becoming.

You make a ritual of remembering.
A sacred devotion to truth, even when it's uncomfortable.
A gentle choosing of presence, even when patterns pull hard.

Because this isn't about mastery.
It's about practice.
And the practice *is* the point.
This is your life's work—not to fix yourself, but to remember yourself.
To keep coming home.

Chapter 4 Exercises: Coming Back to the Body, Intuition, and Inner Compass

These practices aren't about striving or achieving.
They're about remembering—what's always been within you.

Let them meet you exactly where you are—no performance, no pressure.
Let them be soft enough to soothe,
spacious enough to hold all of you,
and sacred enough to guide you home.

Let them draw you inward.
To your breath.
To your body.
To the quiet knowing that was never lost—only waiting to be heard.

Exercise 1: Body Tracking as a Daily Devotion

When to Practice:
Morning and/or evening (or anytime you feel disconnected)

What You'll Need:
A quiet space, a journal, and your presence

Step-by-Step:

1. Sit or lie down in a comfortable position. Close your eyes.
2. Begin to slowly scan your body from head to toe.
3. As you move through each area, pause and notice what sensations are present.
   - Is there tightness in your jaw?
   - Warmth in your belly?
   - Tingling in your hands?
   - A sense of numbness or blankness somewhere?
4. Try not to judge, change, or analyze. Just notice.
5. If a sensation feels strong, breathe gently into it.
6. When you finish the scan, open your eyes and journal what you noticed.

Journal Prompt:
What did I feel in my body today that I might have ignored in the past?
What might these sensations be trying to tell me?

Exercise 2: Rebuilding Intuition — The Inner Yes & No

When to Practice:
Throughout your day during moments of choice

What You'll Need:
Just your attention and willingness to pause

Step-by-Step:

1. Before making a decision (big or small), take a breath.

2. Close your eyes and ask your body:
   - Is this a yes, no, or maybe?
3. Notice what arises. Don't force. Just feel.
   - A yes might feel like openness, expansion, warmth, excitement.
   - A no might feel like contraction, tightness, resistance, dread.
   - A maybe might feel unclear, foggy, or disconnected.
4. Track where in your body you feel this knowing: gut, chest, neck, throat, womb?
5. Honor what comes up, even if your mind disagrees.

Reflection Prompt:
When did I trust my body's "yes" or "no" today?
What happened when I honored it? What happened when I didn't?

Exercise 3: Nervous System Grounding Ritual

When to Practice:
When overwhelmed, anxious, or activated

What You'll Need:
A quiet space, your breath, your hands

Step-by-Step:

1. Place one hand on your chest and one on your belly or thighs.
2. Take a long inhale through your nose. Exhale slowly through your mouth—twice as long.

3. Repeat this breath for at least 10 rounds.
4. Add a soft hum, sigh, or low "mmm" sound as you exhale to tone the vagus nerve.
5. Gently rock or sway your body side to side if it feels good.

Optional Affirmation (repeat out loud or silently):
I am safe to be here. I am safe to feel. I am safe to slow down.

Exercise 4: Somatic Pendulation Practice

When to Practice:
When sitting with emotional discomfort

What You'll Need:
A safe space to sit or lie down

Step-by-Step:

1. Bring awareness to a part of your body that feels activated, tense, or uncomfortable.
2. Just sit with it for a moment. Name it. Feel it. Breathe into it.
3. Now, gently shift awareness to a part of your body that feels neutral, calm, or safe.
4. Let yourself rest there for a moment—notice any warmth, softness, spaciousness.
5. Move slowly between the two sensations (discomfort and safety) a few times.

6. This back-and-forth builds capacity in your nervous system to hold both without becoming overwhelmed.

Reflection Prompt:
How did my body respond to this practice?
What surprised me? What softened?

Exercise 5: Rewrite the Script

When to Practice:
Daily, preferably in the morning or before bed

What You'll Need:
A journal and a quiet space

Step-by-Step:

1. Reflect on your day. What belief came up that didn't feel like you?
   o Example: "I should be doing more."
2. Gently rewrite it in your voice, your truth.
   o New truth: "I am allowed to rest. My worth is not measured by productivity."
3. Place your hand on your heart and read it out loud.
4. Let your body feel this new truth. Repeat it softly, like a lullaby.

Optional Practice:
Create a running list of these rewritten truths. Revisit them often. Let them become your new sacred script.

Gentle Reminder for Chapter 4 Practices

You don't have to do every exercise every day.
Let them meet you where you are.

Return to them like touchstones,
not homework.

Let them support you—
not shame you.

This is not about doing more.
It's about doing less with more presence.

Let this be a lifelong conversation with your body,
your spirit,
your truth.

You are safe to trust yourself now.
You always were.

Chapter 5:

The Day You Decide to Trust Yourself Again — Reclaiming Sovereignty and Inner Authority

"There comes a day when you realize that no one is coming to save you, and no one can give you the answers. That day is terrifying—and it is holy."
— Naomi Shihab Nye

The Threshold of Sovereignty

There comes a moment in the healing journey that arrives without fanfare. It doesn't come with applause or clarity or anyone else noticing. It's not something you can post about or describe easily. In fact, it often slips in quietly, without warning—a stillness that settles over everything and yet changes everything.

It's the moment you stop looking outside yourself for the rescue.

You stop waiting for someone else to make it better— whether it's a doctor, a therapist, a partner, a plan. You stop clinging to the belief that healing will arrive in a neatly wrapped solution, handed to you by someone with credentials or authority. And instead, something ancient inside you stirs. Something tired of being patient. Something ready to rise.

For me, that moment happened in a parking lot.

I had just left yet another appointment where my symptoms were minimized, where the prescription was handed out like a consolation prize, where the deeper questions were left unanswered. The doctor didn't mean harm. He just didn't see me. Not really. And I realized in that instant—I was done being unseen. Done being managed. Done being told to tolerate what my soul was screaming to heal.

That was the moment I stopped outsourcing my power. Not with rebellion, but with reverence. I didn't yell. I didn't fight. I just *knew*. Something shifted so deeply it could never unshift. I didn't want to manage my life anymore. I wanted to *live* it—on my terms, in my rhythm, with my own voice leading the way.

This is what it means to cross the threshold of sovereignty. It's not a single dramatic leap. It's a choice you make quietly, often alone, and then continue making again and again. A soft but fierce decision to trust your own body, your own intuition, your own sense of what is right—even when no one else understands it. Especially then.

The first time you say, "I trust myself more than I trust the noise," it feels like holy ground. Not because you feel invincible. But because, for the first time, you are choosing *you*—without apology, without approval, without waiting for permission.

And what rises in that moment is not a roar. It's a hum. A steady, quiet frequency of truth that moves through your bones. It vibrates in your blood. It echoes in the silence you once tried to avoid. It is power—not loud, but unshakable.

This is not the kind of power that seeks to control others. It's the kind that reclaims yourself. It's not about dominance. It's about devotion. A return to the truth that you belong to yourself—not in theory, but in practice.

And yes, it's terrifying.

You will grieve the years you spent waiting for someone else to define you. You'll feel the hollow ache of walking alone through your own wilderness. You'll doubt your steps. You'll second-guess your choices. You'll question if you're strong enough to carry the weight of your own becoming.

But then—something steadier will rise beneath the fear.

A breath.
A knowing.
A sense of solid ground beneath your feet that wasn't there before.

And you'll realize, you're not lost. You're not broken. You're just no longer willing to be led by someone else's map.

This is where the real journey begins.

Not when you're finally fixed.
Not when you've become fearless.

But when you say yes to being your own compass.
When you trust the voice inside that says, "This time, I lead."

No One Is Coming to Save You

There are truths that crack you open so completely, you're never quite the same after hearing them. This was one of them for me.

For most of my life, I had been quietly—desperately—waiting to be rescued. I didn't call it that, of course. I called it being hopeful. Being persistent. Doing the work. I convinced myself that if I just kept showing up, kept striving, kept being the "good patient," the "capable woman," the "strong one"—someone would eventually see me. Someone would swoop in with the right answers, the right energy, the right capacity to finally say, *"I've got you. You can rest now."*

And for a while, that belief gave me something to hold onto. I pinned my hope on the next doctor, the next relationship, the next opportunity that might finally lighten the weight I was carrying. I told myself I just had to work harder. Be more patient. Be more palatable. Someone would come.

But no one did. And not because people didn't care—but because it was never their role to carry what was mine to reclaim.

I remember one night in particular. I had just experienced a seizure. My body was wrecked. My spirit even more so. I lay in bed, disoriented, swollen-faced from crying, hollowed out by grief that spanned more than a decade. I wasn't just mourning the seizure—I was mourning everything I had lost along the way: the health I thought I'd never regain, the years spent in systems that never truly saw me, the parts of myself I'd abandoned just to survive.

And as I stared blankly at the ceiling, something in me gave way—not with drama, but with quiet, undeniable clarity.

No one is coming.

Not to fix it.
Not to carry it.
Not to make it make sense.

And strangely, that realization didn't destroy me. It released me.

Because in that moment, I stopped waiting. I stopped outsourcing my worth to people who didn't even know what I needed. I stopped postponing my healing for the day someone else gave me permission to begin. That night, through the wreckage and the weariness, I became the one I had been waiting for.

Now, let me be clear—this isn't about adopting some hyper-independent, lone-wolf mindset. This isn't the kind of self-reliance that cuts you off from love or help or softness. This isn't "I don't need anyone" in the way we've been taught as a defense mechanism. This is deeper. This is sacred self-responsibility. The kind that honors your humanity while also reclaiming your power.

It's about realizing that no one else can live in your body. No one else can decode its messages, respond to its needs, or honor its rhythms the way you can. And while you *can* and *should* ask for help, that act itself must still come from you. It's you who opens the door. It's you who allows the leaning. It's you who says, *"I am ready to be held now."*

And yes—it's terrifying. It means the safety you long for is no longer someone else's to give. It's yours to build. And that can feel like too much at first. But what rises in its place is something no external savior could ever provide: *inner ground that does not shake.*

Because once you stop searching for rescue, you start hearing your own voice again. You begin to trust your own instincts. You stop gaslighting your body in the name of someone else's protocol. You stop abandoning your truth to maintain connection or please the crowd. You stop reaching for a map that was never drawn for your terrain.

And instead—you return to the one inside you.

You begin to live from alignment instead of fear. From presence instead of performance. From design, not default.

Not because someone came to save you—
but because you remembered how to save yourself.

The Fear of Trusting Yourself

No one really talks about how terrifying it is to trust yourself again—especially after life has handed you evidence that maybe you shouldn't. When your mind has betrayed you, when your body has become unfamiliar terrain, when memory loss or trauma has made your own instincts feel like unreliable narrators—it's not just difficult to trust yourself. It feels dangerous.

After my stroke, that danger lived in every moment. Entire seasons of my life were missing, as if they had been swallowed by some invisible void. I would look at old photos and feel like I was staring at a stranger. I didn't remember her stories. I didn't recognize her voice. Her history felt like someone else's past.

Even my reflection felt foreign.

The result was a deep and constant disorientation. I would walk into a room and forget why I was there. I'd catch myself staring at the stove, unable to remember whether I had just turned it off or never turned it on at all. Simple conversations became riddled with hesitation, as I second-guessed every word before it left my mouth. My brain glitched, my body didn't feel like home, and perhaps most painful of all—my inner knowing, once so sharp and intuitive, was now buried under thick static.

The fear that followed was not abstract—it was embodied. Every decision, no matter how small, felt like it carried the potential to spiral me back into chaos. I didn't just doubt myself. I feared myself. My nervous system was raw, exposed, and on constant high alert. I longed for someone else to step in. To hand me the script. To make the choices. To give me rules to follow so I could stop feeling like every moment was a trap.

I remember thinking: *What if I get it wrong again? What if I hurt someone? What if I forget something critical and pay for it?*

And in the depths of that fear, I learned something essential: **Trust isn't a switch you flip. It's a slow and sacred rebuilding.**

It didn't come back with one decision. It came in glimmers. It came in the tiniest of moments—the first time I made a choice without crowd-sourcing validation from five other people. The time I chose to rest without feeling guilty. The quiet victory of listening to a body cue and actually honoring it. No drama. Just a slow, careful return.

At first, I didn't think I was allowed to trust myself. I hadn't earned it. I wasn't "recovered" enough. The past whispered lies that made me think trust was something reserved for people who had it all together—who never forgot, who never wavered, who never broke.

But the truth is, **self-trust isn't something you earn through perfection—it's something you rebuild through compassion.**

I had to stop comparing myself to the version of me that once was. She was gone. And in her place was someone new—still worthy, still wise, but in need of gentleness, not judgment. I had to anchor myself in the present, in what I *could* feel, in what I *could* know, one breath at a time. Safety didn't live in certainty. It lived in permission.

There are still days I feel the pull to ask someone else what to do. To outsource my answers. To run from the discomfort of choosing. But I've learned to pause. To check in. To place my hand on my heart, breathe into my belly, and ask: *Is this fear... or is this conditioning?*

Because fear will always tell us to flee. But so often, it's just the echo of a story that used to keep us small. A story that no longer fits.

Now, when I choose to stay with myself—to breathe through the shakiness, to move slowly, to trust the quiet signal inside—I'm not just surviving. I'm rewriting the story of my own sovereignty.

So if you're afraid to trust yourself, you're not alone. And you're not broken. You're healing.

And with every micro-moment you choose to believe your body again, believe your voice again, believe your worth again—you're inscribing a new rhythm into your nervous system.

You're not just remembering who you are.
You're becoming someone new—rooted, steady, and finally safe to lead yourself home.

Reclaiming Sovereignty Is a Daily Choice

Sovereignty doesn't crash into your life like a bolt of lightning or arrive wrapped in a moment of grand revelation. It doesn't show up with fanfare or announce itself on the mountaintop. It unfolds slowly, intimately—like a whisper you almost miss. It is found in the mundane, often invisible choices that only you can feel: the quiet "no" you honor without guilt, the deep breath you take before reacting, the softness you extend toward yourself instead of self-punishment.

For me, it started in the smallest, most ordinary moments. Moments where I felt the familiar urge to override my body's cues—but didn't. Moments where I let my nervous system take the lead instead of pushing it to perform. Saying no to plans when I didn't have the capacity. Eating something that felt nourishing, not punishing. Staying with my emotions long enough to hear what they were trying to tell me, even when I didn't fully understand them.

Some days, reclaiming sovereignty looked like choosing rest without explanation. Other days, it meant asking for help—not because I was incapable, but because I was worthy of support. It meant noticing when I was falling back into performance and gently choosing presence instead. It meant releasing the need to justify my yes or my no to anyone outside of me.

What I've learned is that sovereignty is not a one-time declaration. It's not a title you receive when you've done enough work. It's a daily devotion—a sacred practice of choosing yourself over and over, especially on the days when it would be easier not to. Especially on the days when the pull of old patterns—people-pleasing, over-giving, second-guessing—feels louder than your truth.

For a long time, I believed I had to earn my own authority. That someone wiser, more credentialed, more healed, would one day affirm that I was finally ready to lead my own life. But the deeper truth is this: sovereignty isn't something anyone else can give you. It isn't granted by a therapist or a partner, a parent or a system. It must be claimed.

And that claiming happens in the unglamorous moments. When you choose to trust your inner voice above the noise. When you stand by your truth without needing to be understood. When you stay with yourself—even in the discomfort, even in the doubt—because leaving would cost you too much.

Sovereignty is not about controlling everything. It's not about never needing support. It's about being in right relationship with yourself. It's about holding your own hand through the mess. It's about remembering that your body, your intuition, your lived experience—they are valid sources of wisdom.

And as you choose this path—day by day, breath by breath—you begin to dismantle the internalized systems that taught you not to trust yourself. You begin to build something new. Not just beliefs, but embodied pathways: of presence, of inner leadership, of quiet power that doesn't need to prove anything. Power that simply honors what is real.

So no, it won't always be loud or obvious. And no, it won't always feel easy. But each time you return to your own side, each time you refuse to abandon yourself, you are living a revolution.

And that is sovereignty.

What It Means to Live as Your Own Authority

Living as your own authority isn't about becoming impenetrable or perfect. It's not about always knowing what to do or never making mistakes. It's certainly not about being the loudest or most certain voice in the room. Rather, it's about learning to listen inwardly first—quietly, consistently, and with reverence. It's about honoring your own body, your intuition, and your felt sense as sacred sources of wisdom, even when the world insists on logic, credentials, or permission slips.

For me, this kind of authority didn't arrive in a flash of confidence or a grand declaration. It came in pieces. Slowly, ungracefully. Especially after my stroke, when everything I thought I knew about myself was suddenly gone. My memory fractured into silence, whole chapters of my life wiped clean. And in that void, I couldn't rely on the past to define me. I couldn't borrow certainty from other people's stories about who I had been. Their memories felt foreign, like watching someone else's life on a screen I couldn't touch.

So I had to begin again—not by trying to rebuild what was lost, but by learning how to be present with what remained. I had to feel my way forward in real time. And at first, that meant noticing the small things: when my stomach clenched in warning versus when my chest softened in curiosity. When a decision felt tight and constricted versus when it left space for my breath. I began to tune into the whispers of my own body, not as an inconvenience to override, but as a compass to trust.

This kind of authority showed up in unexpected places. In giving myself permission to say no, even when I didn't have a polished explanation. In choosing rest not because I had earned it, but because I needed it. In allowing myself to pause, to check in, and to change my mind when something no longer felt aligned. These weren't big, dramatic acts—but they were revolutionary for someone who had spent a lifetime seeking approval, performing for acceptance, and shape-shifting to be palatable.

Living from your own authority means releasing the compulsion to chase validation. It means you no longer need to earn your worth through over-functioning or contorting yourself to fit someone else's expectations. You stop measuring your decisions against other people's comfort. You stop abandoning yourself in exchange for being liked. And most importantly, you begin to trust that even when you get it wrong, you will meet yourself there—with presence, with tenderness, with responsibility.

It's not about always getting it right. It's about building the kind of self-trust that says, "Even if I fall, I'll be the one who catches me." That's the muscle. That's the foundation. You become the elder you needed. The anchor you longed for. The protector and nurturer you once searched for in others.

And maybe the most radical shift of all? You stop outsourcing your worth. You stop waiting for someone to crown you enough. You decide—fully and finally—that you already are.

Living from your own authority isn't about making declarations or demanding recognition. It's a quiet steadiness that lives in your chest. A knowing that doesn't flinch when met with disapproval. A clarity that allows you to say, "This is who I am," even when no one else understands. It's the ability to walk away from what dishonors you, not in anger or defensiveness, but in sovereignty.

This isn't arrogance. It's not rebellion for the sake of rebellion. It's devotion. A deep, reverent commitment to your truth, your healing, your becoming. And when you live that way—when you root yourself so deeply in your own authority—you give others permission to do the same. Not by preaching. But by being.

Because the most powerful thing you can offer this world is a person who has returned to themselves—fully, unapologetically, and with love.

Living in Partnership with Your Body and Intuition

There's a profound shift that happens when you stop viewing your body as a problem to solve or a machine to control—and begin relating to it as a partner. A co-navigator. A living, breathing ally in your journey. The same shift applies to your intuition. These aren't lofty spiritual concepts or abstract ideals; they are real-time, moment-by-moment guides. They speak in the quietest tones—through tension, breath, discomfort, goosebumps, a racing heart. They speak before your brain has time to translate, if you're willing to listen.

After my stroke and the amnesia that followed, I didn't just lose memory—I lost access to my internal compass. My body felt like a stranger I had to reintroduce myself to. My intuition, once something I could lean on instinctively, felt like it had gone completely silent. I was left questioning everything: was this fear, or was it insight? Was my body alerting me to danger, or simply reacting from old trauma? There were moments I would freeze, my chest tight, unsure whether the feeling meant "this is wrong" or "this is healing."

In those early days, I learned not to chase answers, but to get curious. That curiosity became my saving grace. Instead of rushing to find the right choice, I slowed down enough to ask better questions: What is my body trying to say right now? Where do I feel constriction? What does a no feel like in my gut? What does a yes feel like in my chest? I stopped demanding certainty and started building relationship. Not control, but communion.

Living in partnership with your body and intuition means creating space before the override. It means checking in before you check out. It doesn't mean you ignore advice or reject support—but it means you sit with yourself first. You become your own counsel. You ask, "Is this aligned with my truth?" before you ask anyone else, "What would you do?" And when you do reach out for guidance, you're not abandoning your knowing—you're holding it alongside someone else's perspective.

That is sovereignty—not isolation, but discernment. It's not about rejecting others; it's about not rejecting yourself in the process. You learn to recognize when your body is whispering, "Enough," before it screams. You make room for both instinct and fear, giving them both a seat at the table without letting either one take over the whole conversation.

You begin to treat your body and your intuition as worthy of your time, your tenderness, your trust.

Eventually, I realized that my intuition hadn't disappeared—it had been buried beneath years of override, masked by the noise of survival. And my body wasn't broken—it was exhausted from being dismissed. When I finally began to listen—not to fix, not to silence, but to truly listen—they both began to speak again. Softly at first, then more clearly. My yeses started to feel solid, grounded. My noes came with a quiet conviction, even when they were hard to say. I began to feel decisions in my bones—not always free of fear, but anchored in clarity.

Now, that's the practice I return to daily. I no longer expect certainty from every sensation. I don't wait for perfection or a complete lack of doubt. I wait for presence. That deep, steady inner attunement that says: "This may not be easy. But it's mine. And I'm listening."

Because in that listening, trust returns.

And in that trust, you begin again.

Signs You Are Reclaiming Your Inner Authority

Reclaiming your inner authority doesn't always announce itself with bold declarations or dramatic transformations. In fact, most of the time, it's so subtle, so deeply internal, that no one else even notices. But you do. You feel it. Not in words—but in the softening of your nervous system, the slowing of your breath, the quiet steadiness that returns when you choose yourself.

It often begins in the smallest of moments—pausing before you respond instead of defaulting to please. Noticing the tightness in your chest when you're about to say "yes" but mean "no." Catching yourself mid-pattern, mid-performance, and instead of going through the motions, you stop. You check in. You let your body speak before your brain takes over. And when it does, you listen.

These moments may seem inconsequential on the surface. But underneath, something monumental is happening. Your body starts to relax in your own presence. Your shoulders drop when you honor your no. Your stomach unclenches when you stop forcing your timeline. You begin to notice how much more at peace you feel—not because everything is perfect, but because you're no longer abandoning yourself.

You'll start to hear yourself saying things like, "Let me check in with myself first," before making decisions. You'll feel more grounded when you act in alignment with what *feels* right, not just what *looks* right. You'll stop explaining your boundaries, stop defending your healing pace, and instead, simply hold them. You'll trust your gut nudges, your weird hunches, the spontaneous shifts that make no sense but feel deeply true.

One of the most powerful signs you're reclaiming your inner authority is when you notice the moment—the exact moment—an old pattern tries to pull you in, and instead, you choose differently. Not because it's easy. But because it's yours. That moment is everything.

I remember the first time I said "no" without cushioning it with an explanation. My body trembled from the inside out, but the shaking wasn't fear—it was a kind of pride. A reclamation. A quiet voice inside whispering, "This is who we are now." It was the beginning of coming home to myself.

You may not realize it while it's happening. These shifts are quiet. But over time, they build. They rewire the old pathways of self-abandonment and carve new trails of self-respect. Each breath, each pause, each moment you choose your truth over someone else's comfort—it matters. It compounds.

Little by little, you become the wise elder you used to long for. You become the loving parent to your inner child, the fierce protector of your boundaries, the gentle guide through your own shadows. You stop waiting for permission to belong to yourself.

And while it doesn't necessarily get easier, *you* get stronger. More rooted. More steady. More sovereign.

This is the power of inner authority. Not the kind that needs to be proven or performed. But the kind that lives quietly in your bones. It doesn't shout. It hums.

And in that hum, you begin to trust yourself again.

You Become the One You Were Waiting For

There's a unique kind of ache that settles in when you realize no one is coming to save you. It doesn't just sting—it unravels you. Like waking up in the ashes of a life you barely recognize, standing barefoot in the rubble with no map, no direction, and no familiar voice guiding you forward. The grief is real. The fear, suffocating. The disorientation, complete.

And yet... if you stay in that stillness long enough, something holy begins to stir beneath the wreckage.

You start to see what was always there—buried under the scripts, the striving, the survival. Not a rescuer. Not a savior. But a steady, sacred ember of you. You weren't meant to be saved. You were meant to remember.

And in that remembering, you become the very thing you've spent your life searching for.

For years, I looked outward, hoping someone would come along who could make it all better. Especially after the stroke—when my memories vanished and the narrative of my life slipped through my fingers—I felt untethered, erased. I didn't just feel broken. I felt gone. Like my soul had been wiped clean of its story.

In that emptiness, I reached for certainty in others. Doctors. Therapists. Voices that sounded confident, composed, assured. Because I didn't trust the silence inside me. I didn't trust myself. How could I, when I didn't even know who I was anymore?

But healing doesn't hand you your identity back wrapped in a neat little bow. It hands you a shovel and says, "Dig." And that's what I did. Slowly. Tenderly. Not to recover the woman I once was—but to meet the woman who had been buried underneath the performance, the pleasing, the pain.

Piece by piece, I found her. Not the version who had perfected her mask. Not the one who measured her worth by how needed she was. But the one who knew how to listen, how to feel, how to rise. The one who had always been there, waiting for my return.

You become the one you were waiting for the moment you stop chasing rescue and start cultivating relationship—with your body, your breath, your truth. The moment you realize you don't need someone else to validate your enough-ness. You don't need fixing. You need space. You don't need direction. You need to remember you've known the way all along.

It's not some epic transformation. It's not a clean, Instagrammable breakthrough. It's a slow, sometimes awkward, often unglamorous return. One brave, shaky choice at a time. Choosing to stay instead of flee. Choosing to listen instead of numb. Choosing to trust what's real, even when it scares you.

And then one day, you catch yourself doing something radical—something like honoring your own no without explanation. Saying yes to joy without guilt. Making a decision that honors your energy, even if no one claps for it. And in that moment, you realize: *You're the one holding yourself now.*

You become the nurturer you once craved.
The protector you longed for.
The guide you waited on.
You become your own steady hand.

You begin crafting a life that reflects who you truly are—not who you had to be to survive. Your rhythm becomes your compass. Your truth becomes your map. Your self-trust becomes your anchor.

And maybe the most breathtaking realization of all?

The life you thought someone else would build for you... was always yours to create.

You didn't need saving.
You needed space to remember.
And now that you have, you are no longer waiting.
You have arrived.

Chapter 5 Exercises: The Daily Practices of Self-Trust

Self-trust isn't something you either have or don't.
It's a muscle—quietly built over time through presence, patience, and compassion.
Not through perfection. Not through performance.

Each of these exercises isn't asking you to fix or improve yourself.
They are invitations to return.
To remember who you were before the world taught you to doubt your knowing.

This is the slow, sacred work of choosing yourself—
not all at once, but in small, powerful ways
that whisper:
I am worth coming home to.

Exercise 1: The Self-Trust Body Check-In

When you're faced with a decision, a moment of self-doubt, or an emotional wave:
- Pause.
- Place your hand on your heart, your belly, or anywhere that feels grounding.
- Close your eyes.
- Ask yourself:
  - "What does my body say about this?"
  - "Is there a yes, a no, or a maybe?"

- o "Where do I feel it—in my chest, gut, jaw, shoulders, or somewhere else?"

Let the first sensation, image, or word arise.
Trust it, even if your mind wants to override it.

Journal Prompt:
What did my body say today that I might have missed before?
Did I honor that wisdom, or did I ignore it? Why?

Exercise 2: The Sovereignty Declaration

Write your own personal declaration of sovereignty—
an affirmation that reminds you of who you are
and who you are no longer outsourcing your life to.

Here's an example to get you started:
I am the authority of my life.
I trust my body, my pace, and my inner knowing.
I no longer abandon myself for comfort, approval, or certainty.
I do not owe the world an explanation.
I choose me—today and every day.

Daily Practice Tip:
Read your declaration out loud each morning, with a hand on your heart or your gut. Let your voice hear your truth.

Exercise 3: Self-Authority Reflection Journal

At the end of each day, reflect gently:
- Where did I act from my own authority today?
- Where did I feel tempted to give my power away?
- What did it feel like to choose myself—even in small ways?
- What do I want to celebrate about my choices today?

Remember:
Reclaiming your authority is not about doing it perfectly. It's about noticing, returning, and choosing again.

Exercise 4: Somatic Anchoring — The Sovereignty Seat

This daily somatic practice helps you embody your inner authority and ground into your truth.
1. Sit or stand comfortably with your feet planted.
2. Close your eyes and slow your breath.
3. Imagine a throne, seat, or sacred anchor point inside your body—a space that belongs only to you.
4. With each breath, feel yourself seated more deeply in this place.
5. Repeat to yourself:
   - I am seated in my authority.
   - I trust myself.
   - I am home in me.

Use this before important conversations, choices, or anytime you feel like you're giving your power away.

Exercise 5: The "No" Practice

Self-trust often starts with one powerful word: No.

Today, practice saying no to something small:
- A request that drains you
- A task that doesn't align
- A thought that says you should do more to be worthy

Say no. Even if it's just in your head. Even if it's just to yourself.

Reflection:
How did it feel in your body to honor your no?
What resistance came up?
What freedom?

Returning to You: A Gentle Path to Self-Trust

These practices aren't meant to be rigid or performed.
They are invitations—soft, sacred openings—to remember yourself.

You don't have to do all of them, and you don't have to do them perfectly.
You just have to keep coming back.

Because self-trust isn't forged in grand declarations or flawless routines.
It's built in the quiet.
In the pause.

In the moment you choose yourself, even when it's hard.
Even when no one's watching.

Every small act of self-honoring is a thread in the fabric of trust.
And the more you trust yourself,
the more life begins to trust you back.

Chapter 6:

Living the New Way — Choosing Wholeness Over Perfection

"Healing is not about becoming perfect. It's about becoming whole."
— Parker J. Palmer

The Myth of Arrival

If I'm being honest, there were countless moments on my healing path when I believed wholeness was a destination. A place I could finally get to—if I just tried hard enough. If I healed deeply enough. If I became good enough. It felt like the ultimate finish line. The proof that all the pain had been worth it.

I told myself that if I ate the right foods, meditated every day, stuck to every protocol, uncovered every trauma, and stayed relentlessly devoted to the "work," I would earn peace. I'd wake up one day and *feel it*—that deep exhale of finally being healed, finally being safe, finally being done.

That day never came.

What came instead were softer moments. Moments that didn't announce themselves or prove anything. Flickers of peace in the middle of chaos. Little whispers of clarity, presence, and grounded-ness—often when I least expected them.

Not because I had done it all perfectly.

But because I had finally stopped trying to become someone else.

I had stopped running toward an illusion.

You see, wholeness isn't something you earn. It's something you remember. It's not the top of a mountain you conquer—it's the ground beneath your feet you forgot was holding you all along.

It lives inside the ordinary.

In the breath you didn't abandon.
In the moment you chose grace over self-judgment.
In the time you let your heart crack open instead of hardening again.

And yet, even with this knowing, the forgetting still happens.

You forget you're whole.
You forget you're safe.
You forget that healing isn't linear, that it doesn't make you immune to pain or relapse or grief.

And then—you remember.

And then you forget again.

And then, on a quiet afternoon or a sleepless night, you remember once more.

This is the truth behind the myth of arrival: there is no endpoint.

No final version of you who will never struggle, never ache, never get triggered again.

There's just this sacred unfolding.

This practice of coming back to yourself—not because you failed, but because you're human.

Because life will shake you sometimes.
Because even healed hearts get bruised.
Because forgetting is part of remembering.

Real healing doesn't erase your humanity—it deepens it.

It gives you the tools to meet your messiness with presence.
To hold space for your fear without collapsing.
To choose love in the middle of the unknown.

And when you stop chasing the finish line and start honoring the return, everything changes.

You begin to live *here*—not in the imagined future where you've finally earned your peace, but in the truth of this moment.

In the heartbeat of now.

That's where your wholeness lives.

Not in perfection.
Not in completion.
But in your willingness to come back, again and again.

You are already whole.
And you are still becoming.

Both can be true.
Both *are* true.

Always.

Wholeness Over Perfection

For much of my life, I was caught in the exhausting pursuit of getting it all right—striving to be the perfect mother, the perfect partner, the perfect patient, the perfect survivor, even the perfect healer. I wore perfection like a badge of honor, believing that if I could meet everyone's expectations, I'd finally feel safe, worthy, and loved.

I became a master of shaping myself into what others needed, bending my truth to fit the room, quieting my needs so I wouldn't be too much. Productivity became my protection, and self-sacrifice became the measure of my value. I convinced myself that the more I carried, the more indispensable I was. But behind that polished exterior, I was quietly unraveling.

The more I tried to be perfect, the more disconnected I became—from my body, from my emotions, and from any honest sense of self. I didn't realize it at the time, but in trying so hard to be everything for everyone else, I was slowly abandoning myself.

My breaking point didn't come with a gentle realization. It came with a crash. Years of pushing past my limits led to medical diagnoses that forced me to stop, culminating in a stroke that stripped away my illusion of control and erased parts of my memory. In the wake of that loss, perfection no longer seemed noble—it felt hollow. What had once been my armor now lay in pieces at my feet.

That's when I began to understand something deeper. Perfection was never the goal. It was the barrier.

Wholeness, I discovered, had nothing to do with being flawless. It wasn't about checking all the boxes, saying all the right things, or healing in a straight line. Wholeness was raw and honest. It was the willingness to be seen fully, without performance. It was about embracing the parts of myself I had spent years trying to hide—the messy parts, the tender parts, the parts still in process.

Wholeness made room for all of me: the part that was still afraid and the part that longed to break free, the grief and the joy, the clarity and the confusion. It allowed me to exist in contradiction and still be enough.

I learned that I didn't need to fix my body before I deserved rest, or master my emotions before I could feel peace. I didn't need to reach some mythical milestone before I could live with intention, love, or presence.

Wholeness invited me to belong to myself again—not as an ideal version, but as I was. It asked me to stop performing and start listening. To stop striving and start honoring. It whispered, *you are allowed to be fully human here.*

This shift changed everything. I no longer needed to earn love through perfection. I could show up as real. As becoming. As deeply, imperfectly human.

And that's the way I live now. Not perfectly. But honestly.

The new way isn't about curating your life for acceptance. It's about bringing your whole self to the table—your sacred, scarred, radiant, unfinished self—and knowing that you still belong.

Because when you stop chasing perfection, you make space for presence. And presence is where healing actually begins.

This is what I choose now. Not the impossible standard of getting it right, but the deeper, more liberating truth of being whole—just as I am.

Integration Is the Work

There's a part of the healing journey that rarely gets spoken about—not because it's unimportant, but because it's not flashy. It doesn't offer the kind of transformation that makes for a compelling before-and-after photo. It's not the breakthrough moment on the therapist's couch or the life-altering realization that comes during a weekend retreat. Integration isn't glamorous, and it doesn't always feel profound. It's quiet. Uncelebrated. Often invisible to anyone but you.

Integration is what happens after the big shift. After the awakening, the release, the sacred unraveling. It's how you live in the aftermath—not in collapse, but in continuity. It's brushing your teeth while remembering to unclench your jaw. It's choosing to eat when your body signals hunger, even if your calendar says you're too busy. It's pausing at the threshold of an old pattern and—maybe for the first time—choosing differently. These moments may look small from the outside, but they carry the weight of your entire transformation.

This is the part of healing that asks if you're willing to show up without an audience. It doesn't care how articulate you are about your trauma or how eloquently you describe your growth. It cares how you treat yourself when no one is watching. It wants to know if you can remain present when life gets messy, when the old version of you tries to take the wheel again. It asks if you can hold steady in the quiet, not because anyone is asking you to—but because you know it matters.

There were many times I thought I had already healed, only to find myself slipping back into familiar cycles—over-giving, overworking, overriding my own limits. I used to think that meant I had failed. That all my effort had unraveled. But now I understand that falling back isn't the failure. The difference is that I notice it sooner. I feel the dissonance in my body. And I know how to return. That is integration—not perfection, but presence. Not flawless execution, but embodied awareness.

Healing doesn't transform your life in sweeping, cinematic moments. It changes you in micro-movements, in repeated choices where your new awareness meets your old life. And sometimes, yes, you'll forget. You'll fall into comparison, urgency, or shame. But with each return to yourself, you build resilience. You teach your nervous system that this new way is safe. That you don't have to abandon yourself to survive. That you can soften, even here.

The truth is, integration is not a one-time event. It's a lifelong rhythm. A daily devotion to remembering what you've reclaimed. And over time, that devotion becomes less about trying to prove your healing and more about living it. Not perfectly. Not performatively. But honestly. Quietly. Rootedly.

You don't have to have it all together to be integrated. You just have to keep choosing the version of you that honors your truth—again and again. That's the sacred repetition. That's the work no one claps for. And that's what brings you home.

Living from Wholeness

Living from wholeness is not about reinventing yourself or striving to become someone new. It's about remembering who you've always been beneath the conditioning, the performance, the survival strategies. It's the return—not to an idealized version of you, but to the honest, raw, complex self that existed before the world told you who you needed to be.

This way of living isn't loud or performative. It doesn't demand applause or require constant validation. In fact, it's often quiet. Rooted. Almost invisible to the outside world. But inside, it feels like truth. Like home.

For a long time, I mistook wholeness for perfection. I thought it meant having it all together—being regulated at all times, eating cleanly, never raising my voice, never needing help. I believed that if I could just embody the "healed" version of myself all the time, then I'd be enough. But that wasn't wholeness. That was performance. It was a new kind of mask—one that wore spirituality as a costume but still demanded control.

The truth is, wholeness isn't neat. It isn't polished or curated. It doesn't promise you'll never wobble again. It simply means that when you do, you don't make it mean you've failed. You no longer exile the messy parts. Instead, you let them be part of the whole. The grief, the doubt, the fear, the desire, the uncertainty—they all get to be here. They all belong.

To live from wholeness is to stop waiting until you've cleaned yourself up to show up. It's to stop dividing yourself into acceptable and unacceptable pieces. It's allowing the still-in-process parts to have a seat at the table, not just the parts you've learned to present. It's the shift from trying to control your life to being in relationship with it.

When I first started practicing this, I wasn't sure it was safe. I questioned whether I could really say no, really show up this undone, really let myself be seen in the fullness of my humanity and still be held with love. But each time I took the risk—each time I showed up without the mask—I learned something new. Wholeness doesn't repel connection. It deepens it. Because real connection doesn't come from being perfect. It comes from being real.

Living from wholeness allowed me to stop managing everyone else's perception of me and start tending to my own truth. I stopped trying to fix things that were never broken. I stopped editing myself to be more palatable. I stopped waiting for the perfect body, the perfect plan, the perfect moment to arrive. And instead, I began asking better questions—gentler ones.

What does my wholeness need today?
What parts of me are asking to be seen, heard, or held?
How can I live fully—even if it's messy, even if it's tender?

Living from wholeness isn't about being unshakeable. It's about being rooted, even when the ground beneath you trembles. It's dancing with fear rather than banishing it. It's letting your voice tremble if it has to, and speaking anyway. It's choosing compassion over correction—again and again.

And slowly, it becomes your new baseline. Not a practice you perform, but a way you relate to yourself. You no longer need to abandon parts of yourself to belong. You don't need external proof to validate your knowing. You don't have to perform. You simply get to present—your full, unfiltered, unedited self.

That is what it means to live from wholeness. Not as something you achieve, but as something you return to. A birthright. A homecoming. A way of being that was always yours.

The Lifelong Practice of Becoming

There's a tender kind of grief that comes with realizing healing isn't something you arrive at. Not because healing is a myth, but because we've been taught to believe it ends in a destination—a point of completion where the pain dissolves, the work is done, and we finally become the version of ourselves we've been striving toward. That version comes with promises: peace, stability, certainty. It's comforting to imagine that if we just do enough—heal enough, grow enough, prove ourselves enough—we'll land in a place where nothing can shake us.

But the truth is, when you choose to live a life rooted in wholeness, in truth, in the wisdom of your body and intuition, you learn that becoming isn't a checkpoint. It's not a phase you move through and graduate from. It's a relationship. Ongoing. Evolving. Alive. And just like any relationship worth keeping, it asks for your presence—not your perfection.

There are no gold stars for how aware you are. No grades for how well you've regulated your nervous system. No moment when you get to close the book on your growth and say, "That's it. I've arrived." Instead, you find rhythm. You move through seasons—of clarity and confusion, of forward motion and gentle stillness. You forget and remember and forget again. And with each cycle, you deepen.

You'll still slip into old habits—because they're familiar. You'll find yourself second-guessing what you once knew in your bones. You'll notice old patterns knocking at your door: the people-pleasing, the self-abandonment, the pull toward performance. And some days, you'll answer. Not because you failed, but because those pathways were well-worn, and on the hard days, familiarity can feel safer than freedom.

I've had months where I questioned if I'd lost all the progress I'd made. Times when my nervous system shook like it had in the beginning, and I wondered if I was starting over. Times when the grief hit harder than expected, or when the old longing for someone else to take the pain away rose up like a wave. And for a while, I believed that meant I had somehow undone everything I had built.

But now I understand: falling doesn't erase the rising. Doubt doesn't cancel your truth. And tenderness in those moments isn't weakness—it's strength. It means you're still open. Still here. Still becoming.

Becoming is not about accumulating more knowledge or adding more tools to your kit. It's about deepening into yourself. It's about asking again and again: What is true for me now? Because what was true six months ago might not be anymore. Because each version of you—the one who was surviving, the one who is healing, the one who is still unsure—deserves compassion. All of you gets to belong here.

This is the lifelong work. To keep choosing yourself even when it's hard. To keep listening even when the world is loud. To hold your contradictions not as proof of failure but as evidence of your humanity. You will forget who you are. You will remember again. And with every return, the roots grow deeper.

That's not regression. That's practice. That's integration. That's what it means to live awake. Not flawless. Not finished. But fully alive.

Wholeness Is Your Birthright

You were never broken. That may be hard to believe after years of being told you needed fixing—by systems, by relationships, by culture itself. But at your core, before the world layered on expectations and shame, you were whole. Not perfect, not polished, but whole. Your essence— untamed, deeply feeling, sensitive, wild, intuitive—was never too much. It was exactly as it was meant to be.

The idea that you had to earn your worth came later. That was the programming, the learned behavior, the conditioning that taught you to perform in order to belong. You learned to measure yourself against impossible standards, to shrink when you wanted to expand, to quiet your emotions in exchange for acceptance. You learned to survive by abandoning yourself.

But before all of that—before the pressure to be palatable or pleasing—you knew who you were. You came into this world fluent in wholeness. You laughed before you ever understood why. You moved with freedom, without shame. You expressed hunger, fatigue, curiosity, and frustration without hesitation. You knew what you felt and didn't apologize for it. That wasn't taught. It was instinct.

That knowing, that clarity, came from within. From the breath in your lungs. From the rhythm of your heartbeat.

From something ancient and primal that never needed permission to exist.

And even if it's quiet now—even if it feels distant or buried—it's still there. Your wholeness never left you. It may be layered beneath trauma, silenced by years of disconnection, or dulled by chronic self-doubt, but it is not gone. It is not lost. It is not something you need to hustle for or prove you deserve.

Wholeness is not a prize at the end of a spiritual race. It's not a badge you earn for surviving your hardest seasons. It is your origin. Your home frequency. It lives underneath the noise, waiting for you to remember.

You are allowed to be whole in your mess. In your breakdowns. In your softness and stillness. You don't need to be high-functioning to be valid. You don't need to be emotionally regulated 100% of the time to be worthy. You don't need to have it all figured out to belong.

Even when your voice trembles, even when your boundaries bend, even when you revisit the same wounds you thought you had already healed—your wholeness remains. It holds space for your humanity, not despite it.

The way forward is not through becoming some flawless, curated version of yourself. It's through returning—over and over—to the raw, rooted truth that has always lived inside of you. The you that existed before the world taught you to perform. The you that knew rest, joy, anger, hunger, and truth without shame.

You don't need to be perfect to be powerful. You don't need to be fixed to be free. You don't need to arrive to finally be enough.

You already are.

This is your birthright. This is your truth. And this—this return to your unshakable, unedited self—is what it means to come home.

Chapter 6 Exercises: Living the New Way

These practices aren't about fixing yourself.
They're not about getting it right or reaching some final destination.

They're about remembering—
and choosing, moment by moment,
to return to the truth of who you are.

Each exercise is here to meet you in the middle of the mess, not to rescue you from it,
but to remind you that even here, you are whole.

Take what speaks to your soul.
Leave what doesn't.
And trust that whatever you choose is already enough.

Exercise 1: Wholeness Check-In

At some point in your day—morning, lunch break, bedtime—pause and ask:
- What part of me needs attention today?
- Where am I chasing perfection instead of honoring my wholeness?
- How can I hold space for both my fear and my courage?

Journal Prompt:
Write about one part of yourself you've been neglecting, avoiding, or shaming.
How can you welcome them home today, without fixing or changing them?

Exercise 2: The Micro-Moment Integration Practice

Healing doesn't happen in the big moments.
It happens in the tiny ones you think don't matter.

Each night, reflect on:
- Where did I honor my truth in small ways today?
- Where did I override or abandon myself?
- What's one small act I can choose tomorrow that supports my wholeness?

Examples:
- Taking a 10-minute rest instead of pushing through.
- Letting yourself cry without rushing to stop it.
- Saying "no" when your body said no—even if your brain said yes.

Exercise 3: The Both/And Body Practice

Sit or lie down somewhere quiet.
Place one hand on your heart, one on your belly.
Breathe in through your nose, and exhale slowly through your mouth.

Say softly, aloud or in your mind:
I make space for both my grief and my joy.
I make space for both my fear and my courage.
I make space for both who I was and who I am becoming.

Notice:
How does your body feel when you stop asking it to pick a side?
What softens? What opens?

Exercise 4: The Wholeness Ritual

Once a week—on Sunday night, Friday morning, or any time that feels sacred—create a ritual to honor your wholeness.

Try this:
- Light a candle.
- Sit quietly and write down:
    - What I'm proud of this week.
    - What I'm still grieving.
    - What I'm becoming.
- Speak them out loud.
- Thank your body for carrying you through.

This can be messy.
It can be quiet.
It can be whatever you need it to be.

The honoring is what matters—not the performance.

Exercise 5: Self-Compassion Mirror Practice

Each morning or night, stand in front of a mirror.
Look into your own eyes—not to judge, not to fix.
Just to witness.

Say to yourself:

I am already whole.
I do not need to be perfect to be worthy of rest, joy, or love.
I belong as I am—right here, right now.

This will feel very uncomfortable at first.
That's okay.

It's not about feeling instant peace.
It's about practicing presence.

Part Three:

Living Outside the Box

Leaving the box is a pivotal act of courage. But learning how to live without it—that's where the real work begins. At first, freedom doesn't feel like open skies and expanded possibilities. It feels like standing in the wreckage of everything you used to cling to, with no rulebook, no roadmap, and no familiar signs pointing the way forward.

The scaffolding that once propped up your identity—your roles, your routines, your shoulds—has collapsed. And though it may have been confining, it was familiar. Predictable. Within it, you knew the rules, even if they never truly served you. Outside of it, there is only space. Space that can feel exhilarating and terrifying at the same time.

There's no checklist telling you how to build this new life. No applause waiting for you at the edges of your breakthroughs. No one to validate that you're doing it right. Just you—raw, real, and unfiltered. And for the first time, you're not performing. You're not bending to keep the peace or pretending to be okay to make others comfortable. You're not hustling for approval or shrinking yourself to fit into boxes you've outgrown. You're just here. Present. Listening.

And what you begin to hear is sacred—the voice of the wild self. The parts of you that were once silenced, shamed, or surgically removed to make you more palatable to others. These pieces rise in the quiet, asking to be felt, remembered, honored. It's not glamorous. It's not curated. It's deeply human.

Life outside the box doesn't guarantee ease. But it offers something better: truth. And from that truth, you begin to build—not from fear or force, but from a rooted sense of alignment. You stop manipulating your body into submission and start listening to it as a wise and ancient compass. You stop saying "yes" out of obligation and begin saying "no" from self-respect.

You start choosing relationships that nourish instead of drain, and redefining love—not as endless sacrifice, but as something mutual, honest, and anchored in self-honor. You let go of work that extracts and exhausts, and you begin pursuing work that expresses who you truly are, even if it doesn't make sense to the world.

You rewrite success, stripping it from hustle and proving, and grounding it in sustainability and joy. You create rhythms that restore rather than grind, allow yourself rest without guilt, and give yourself permission to play without needing to be productive. You slow down—not because you've failed to keep up, but because your soul demands a pace that's rooted in presence, not pressure.

Living outside the box isn't the absence of fear. It's the refusal to abandon yourself just to keep everyone else comfortable. It's choosing to walk with your truth, even when it's inconvenient. It's allowing yourself to be soft enough to feel and strong enough to act on what you know to be true.

And over time, you stop waiting for some future arrival point—the polished, perfected version of you that never wavers. You begin to understand: there is no finish line. No grand unveiling. Just this breath. This moment. This sacred unfolding.

That's when the real rebellion begins.

Not the kind you post about. Not the kind that wins you approval. But the quiet, sacred rebellion of coming home to yourself. Of reclaiming the parts of you that were once called too much or not enough. Of trusting the soil of your own becoming.

You didn't survive what you did to go back to smallness. You didn't come this far to perform someone else's version of a "good life." You came to remember. To rise. To root. To rebel.

And that rebellion? It starts now. And it starts within.

Chapter 7:

Staying Awake in a World That Wants You to Go Back to Sleep

"It is no measure of health to be well adjusted to a profoundly sick society."
— *Jiddu Krishnamurti*

The Pull to Return to the Box

Everyone talks about the awakening—those piercing moments of clarity when the fog lifts and something inside you shifts irrevocably. But what no one really prepares you for is what happens after. Staying awake? That's the hard part. That's the daily devotion. Because awakening isn't a one-time event—it's a lifelong reckoning with the truth. And truth, when lived fully, doesn't always feel liberating. Sometimes, it feels like loss.

In the beginning, the transformation feels bold, even exhilarating. You feel powerful in your new awareness, certain that there's no going back. But then come the quiet days. The ones that don't get celebrated. The ones where everything you thought you knew feels slippery again. The world you woke up from? It's still there. Unchanged. Operating by the same rules, echoing the same messages. And sometimes, it calls you back with an ache so familiar, it feels like comfort.

The pull to return to the box doesn't always come loudly. It starts in whispers. In soft, seductive thoughts that creep in when you're tired or tender: *Maybe I'm overreacting. Maybe life really was easier when I didn't ask so many questions. Maybe all this awareness is making it harder than it needs to be.* These whispers don't sound like fear—they sound like relief. Like rest. Like certainty.

After my stroke, when everything I knew about myself collapsed, I felt that pull more strongly than ever. I was lost in a sea of not knowing—my memories fractured, my body unfamiliar, my identity a blank page. In that raw and terrifying limbo, I longed for the safety of the old systems. The medical authorities I used to defer to. The cultural scripts I used to follow. The religious rules that once gave me a sense of control.

I wanted someone to hand me a guidebook. I wanted to feel held again. And that's when the box started calling—telling me it could offer me order, stability, belonging. It was so tempting. I hovered at the edge, flirted with the idea of going back. Maybe if I just complied this time, maybe if I didn't resist, maybe if I let them decide what was best for me... I could feel safe again.

But that's the illusion. The box doesn't offer true safety. It offers predictability disguised as peace. It rewards silence over truth, compliance over connection, performance over presence. And once you've tasted what it means to live from your truth—even if it's messy, even if it's uncertain— you can't go back to pretending.

That pull isn't just mental. It's embodied. It lives in your nervous system, in the parts of you wired for survival. It activates old trauma responses—fawning, freezing, pleasing—because for so long, those strategies kept you alive. The pull back to the box is really a pull back to perceived safety, to the familiar structure of who you used to be before you knew better.

But knowing better changes you. You can't unknow the cage once you've seen it. You can't unfeel the relief of being fully yourself. You can't shrink back into old identities without fracturing something sacred inside you.

So the question isn't: *How do I make the pull stop?* It's: *How do I hold myself when the pull comes?* Because it will come. In conversations with people still asleep in the system. In moments where your truth makes others uncomfortable. In relationships that only function if you keep shrinking. It will come when you're weary, when your progress feels invisible, when the weight of consciousness feels too heavy to bear.

And in those moments, you'll need to root. To ground back into your body, back into your breath, back into the truth of who you've become. You'll need to remind yourself: *I didn't come this far to go back to sleep. I didn't fight to reclaim my life just to perform someone else's version of who I should be.*

You will be tempted to go back. That's normal. But the fact that you can pause and question it—that you can feel the pull and still stay rooted—is the proof that you've already changed.

So when the old systems beckon, when the old roles seduce, when the box tries to lure you with its false promises of safety—pause. Breathe. Remember.

You are no longer who you were.

And you are not going back.

The Exhaustion of Staying Awake

No one really prepares you for how utterly exhausting it is to live fully awake in a world built for numbness. It's not the same kind of tired you feel after a long day or a sleepless night. This is deeper—an ache that settles in your bones, a kind of soul-weariness that comes from carrying truth in a culture that constantly hands you someone else's version of it.

Staying awake isn't about being hypervigilant or constantly "doing the work." It's about showing up—again and again—to your own aliveness. It's about being present with what's real, even when it's uncomfortable, inconvenient, or misunderstood. It's choosing to feel—grief, joy, rage, tenderness—without numbing, bypassing, or explaining it away. And in a society that rewards suppression, performance, and detachment, that kind of presence is radical... and often, it's exhausting.

There were days I wanted to go back. Not because I believed in the old systems anymore—but because I was tired. Tired of having to explain myself in spaces that didn't speak my language. Tired of holding boundaries that people saw as rejection. Tired of being labeled too much, too intense, too emotional—when all I was doing was being honest. Tired of pushing against a culture that glorifies burnout and calls it ambition.

After my stroke and the amnesia that followed, that exhaustion hit differently. I was alive—but raw. Awake—but disoriented. Every emotion felt like a flood. Every mask I once wore felt suffocating. I couldn't pretend anymore—not because I didn't want to, but because something inside me refused to. I had no tolerance left for the performance. The old roles no longer fit, and the new ones hadn't fully formed. I was between identities—awake, but unanchored.

That liminal space? It's not just uncomfortable—it's draining. And yet, it's also where the real work happens. Where the self that is emerging begins to take shape. It's where you begin to rebuild—slowly, honestly, from within.

Over time, I've come to understand something crucial: the exhaustion isn't a sign that you're failing. It's not weakness. It's not regression. It's simply what happens when you choose to stay present in a world that numbs. When you choose to feel in a world that avoids. When you choose to be fully human in a system that prefers you as a machine.

Of course you're tired. You're carrying awareness in a world that prefers autopilot. You're holding truth in a society that rewards performance. You're navigating conversations, relationships, and institutions that often make you feel like the problem for not fitting inside the mold. That kind of presence costs energy. That kind of embodiment asks for rest.

Which is why we can't do this alone.

Awakening might begin in solitude, but healing requires community. You need people who speak the language of truth. Who don't ask you to shrink or sugarcoat. Who don't flinch when you name what's real. Who remind you that your awareness isn't too much—it's sacred. That your exhaustion isn't a flaw—it's a sign you've been present. That your pauses are not failures—they're part of the rhythm.

Rest is not the opposite of healing. It is healing. You can be awake and still lay your body down. You can be conscious and still crumble. You can be deeply committed to your growth and still say, *"I can't carry it all today."*

Because this work isn't about being on all the time. It's about being honest with yourself. It's about honoring your humanity. It's about listening to your body, even when it asks you to slow down. Especially when it asks you to slow down.

So when the exhaustion sets in, let it. Don't fight it. Don't shame it. Let it soften you. Let it remind you that you're alive, that you're feeling, that you're awake in a world that wants you to sleepwalk through your life.

And remember—you're not doing it alone anymore.

The Power of Conscious Community

There comes a point on the path—especially after you've stepped outside the box, stopped performing, and begun living more awake—when the solitude gets loud. Not the nourishing kind of solitude, but the kind that feels like an echo. The kind that reminds you that while your truth may have set you free, it also set you apart.

You begin to notice it in everyday spaces. The old conversations no longer land. The masks you once wore feel impossible to put back on. You sit across from people you used to feel close to and wonder if they can still see you—this newer, fuller version of you who no longer fits neatly into the roles they remember. It's not that you've outgrown them in ego—it's that you've outgrown the performance. And that kind of shift doesn't always come with applause.

I remember that moment vividly. Sitting at a dinner table surrounded by laughter and familiar faces, yet feeling completely alone. The surface-level talk scraped against something tender in me. It wasn't that I no longer cared—it was that I could no longer pretend. I had changed. And pretending I hadn't would be a betrayal to the part of me that had worked so hard to come back to life.

That's when I began to understand: awakening isn't just about breaking free from systems and beliefs—it's about finding new ground to stand on. And for that, you need others. Not just anyone—but people who are also walking the path with open eyes and open hearts. You need conscious community.

This kind of community isn't built on convenience or social obligation. It's built on presence. On truth. On mutual reverence for the messy, beautiful, in-progress reality of being fully human. It's found in spaces where your pain is not pathologized, your sensitivity is not dismissed, and your joy is not dimmed. Where your truth doesn't require an apology or a disclaimer. Where your "no" isn't questioned and your "yes" isn't exploited.

For me, finding that kind of connection didn't happen overnight. It began slowly—through one honest conversation, one safe relationship, one brave step toward vulnerability. Sometimes it looked like a circle of women sharing stories under the moonlight. Sometimes it was a text from someone who simply understood without needing me to explain. Sometimes it was the steady presence of a mentor who could hold my process without needing to fix it.

And sometimes, it was the sacred grief of letting go. Letting go of the relationships that couldn't meet me where I was going. Letting go of the hope that everyone would understand. That grief wasn't cold or bitter—it was holy. It was a way of honoring the space I was clearing for what was next. It was a way of saying: I choose alignment over attachment. I choose truth over comfort.

You don't need a crowd. You need resonance. You need people who mirror your light back to you on the days you forget it's there. People who will hold space for your breakdowns without rushing you back to the highlight reel. People who let you show up exactly as you are—and stay.

That's what conscious community is. It's not about fixing each other. It's about witnessing each other. Sitting side by side in the fire, not with solutions, but with presence. Saying, "I see you. I'm here. You don't have to walk this alone."

If you haven't found those people yet, don't give up. Keep living in your truth. Keep trusting your path. The more you embody your authenticity, the more you naturally attract those who are doing the same. And when you find them? When your path intersects with another soul who's walking with intention, with tenderness, with presence—it feels like home. Not the one you left behind, but the one you've been creating all along.

Everyday Practices for Staying Awake

Staying awake isn't a singular moment of enlightenment. It's not the kind of decision you make once and never revisit. It's a devotion—a gentle, daily returning to yourself. It's the art of remembering who you are, especially in the quiet spaces where no one is watching and there's no one to applaud your choice.

So much of what we've been taught about awakening makes it sound like a dramatic transformation—an earth-shaking epiphany that changes everything overnight. And sometimes, sure, it arrives with intensity. But more often than not, awakening is made of micro-moments. Soft recognitions. Silent pivots. A breath taken instead of a reaction given. A truth spoken instead of swallowed.

It's you standing at your kitchen sink, catching yourself saying yes to something that doesn't feel right—and choosing, instead, to pause. It's you sitting in your car, realizing you're holding your breath and softening your jaw instead of bracing your way through the day. It's noticing the old inner critic rising up—asking, "Who do you think you are?"—and meeting it with tenderness instead of shame.

These are the moments that matter. Not the big, performative gestures. Not the perfectly curated healing routine. But the ordinary ones. The inconvenient ones. The ones that invite you, again and again, to live in alignment even when it would be easier not to.

In the early days of my own awakening, I thought I had to "stay on" all the time. Hyper-aware. Hyper-committed. Always scanning for signs that I was doing it right. But that only wore me out. It fed the same old pattern of striving. Of believing I had to earn my worth through effort. That staying awake meant being perfect at it.

But staying awake is not about performance—it's about presence. It's about honesty. It's about having the courage to admit when you've slipped back into old patterns, and the compassion to meet yourself there without judgment.

Some days, it means saying no when you'd rather avoid the discomfort. Other days, it means feeding yourself even when your nervous system feels frozen. It might look like holding a boundary. Or softening into your grief. Or calling a friend instead of isolating. It might look like dancing. Or lying on the floor. Or simply taking one conscious breath and whispering, "I'm still here."

Over time, I've discovered a handful of everyday practices that help anchor me when I start to drift:

- **Body check-ins before decisions.**
  I pause and ask, "What is my body saying right now?" It's not always convenient. But it's almost always honest.
- **Unlearning questions.**
  Before reacting, I gently ask: "Is this coming from my truth, or from a belief I never chose?" That one question has interrupted decades of conditioning.
- **Naming the urge.**
  When I feel the pull to override, appease, or shrink, I say it out loud: "This is people-pleasing." Not to shame it, but to make it conscious. Awareness is the first step toward choice.
- **Creating soft rituals.**
  Lighting a candle before journaling. Putting my bare

feet on the earth. Placing a hand on my heart before bed and saying, "I choose to return to myself." These rituals don't need to be grand. They just need to be sacred.

- **Letting rest be part of the practice.**
Awakening isn't about endless doing. It's about sustainable being. And being requires rest. Unapologetic, nervous-system-honoring rest.

These are not rules. They are invitations. Anchors. Reminders that staying awake doesn't mean being vigilant— it means being honest with yourself about what's real, what's true, and what's needed in this moment.

And yes, you will forget. You will fall asleep to your truth sometimes. That's not failure—it's part of the rhythm. What matters is not whether you drift, but how lovingly you come back. Again and again and again.

Because staying awake is not a destination. It's a devotion. And every time you choose presence over performance, truth over comfort, compassion over critique—you are practicing the very art of becoming.

You are not behind. You are not broken. You are not bad at this.

You are waking up—moment by moment, breath by breath—and that is enough.

The Courage to Keep Choosing Yourself

Choosing yourself isn't some grand, one-time declaration. It's not a single moment of bravery where everything suddenly changes. It's quieter than that. More subtle. Often more uncomfortable. It's a practice made up of countless small decisions—decisions that, in the moment, don't always feel powerful or profound. They often feel awkward. Inconvenient. Lonely. Even painful.

It's the slow, steady defiance of choosing to honor your own truth in a world that's been conditioned to reward your compliance. And let's be honest—doing that takes courage. Not the kind splashed across headlines or celebrated in movies. The kind that shakes. The kind that makes your palms sweat. The kind that feels like loss before it ever feels like freedom.

Because choosing yourself often means disappointing others. It means being misunderstood, mischaracterized, and mislabeled. It means hearing things like "You've changed" or "You're too much" or "Why can't you just go back to the way you were?" And the hardest part? Sitting in that discomfort without rushing to fix it. Without shrinking to fit someone else's version of acceptable.

This was one of the hardest lessons I had to learn after my stroke.

When I woke up in a body I didn't recognize, with nearly a decade of my memory gone, I didn't just feel lost—I felt erased. Every part of my life felt foreign. My routines, my relationships, even the sound of my own voice felt like someone else's story. I was a stranger to myself.

And when you've lost your sense of self, the temptation to reach for someone else's definition of who you should be is strong. It's easier, at first, to conform. To mirror back the version of you that makes people most comfortable. To become what they expect—because at least that feels known.

But then there came a moment. A raw, trembling, soul-baring moment—where I realized: if I didn't choose me, no one else would. Not the curated version. Not the easy version. Not the "palatable" one that played nice and kept the peace.

The real me. The messy, aching, rising-from-the-ashes version of me.

And that choice came with consequences. It cost me relationships. It cost me certainty. It cost me the illusion that I could bend myself into every shape needed to keep everyone else happy. But what I gained—what I *reclaimed*—was everything.

I found peace. Not the kind that comes from external validation or a perfectly balanced life. But the kind that settles deep in your bones when you know you are no longer betraying yourself to be loved.

I found wholeness. Not because I had reached some finish line of healing, but because I finally stopped pretending I needed to be fixed.

I found freedom. Not the kind that demands attention or makes bold declarations, but the quiet kind that whispers, "I belong to myself now."

And still, it's not easy. Because we live in a world that profits from your self-abandonment. Systems that thrive on your doubt. Cultures that celebrate your silence and call it grace. It takes fierce devotion to choose yourself within all that noise.

But every time you say no when your body says no—
Every time you pause before people-pleasing—
Every time you speak your truth, even when your voice quivers—
You are choosing a different way.

You are building safety inside your own skin.
You are breaking the pattern that says you must earn your place.
You are becoming the sanctuary you've always needed.

And yes, you'll forget sometimes. You'll fall back into the old patterns. You'll find yourself biting your tongue or betraying your gut just to make things smoother.

But the grace of this work is that you always get to begin again.

There is no "too late" here.
No final judgment.
No deadline for your return.

Only the ongoing, sacred invitation to come home to yourself—again and again and again.

You Were Never Meant to Go Back to Sleep

There will be days when the box—the old way of living—starts to look tempting again. Not because it was ever truly safe or aligned, but because it was familiar. Comfortable. Predictable. There will be moments when the weight of feeling everything becomes too much, and you'll find yourself craving the numbness of autopilot. Longing for the simplicity of not knowing. Not seeing. Not caring so deeply.

I've had those days. I still do.

After my stroke, when my world fell apart and I was forced to rebuild without a map, there were moments when I would have given anything to go back. Not just to the life I had, but to the way I used to be. The version of me that didn't question everything. That followed the rules. That nodded and smiled and blended in.

There's a strange comfort in conformity—especially when your nervous system is overwhelmed. I remember thinking, *Maybe it would be easier if I didn't feel so much. If I could just do what's expected. If I could stop caring, stop resisting, stop waking up every morning to a world that doesn't reflect my truth back to me.*

Because when you're awake—truly awake—there's no going through the motions. Everything requires presence. Everything demands truth. And sometimes, that can feel like too much.

But then I remember what it felt like before.

I remember what it cost me to live in that box.

How my soul felt caged.
How my body was constantly crying out, trying to get my attention.
How I had to keep shrinking, performing, silencing myself just to maintain a life that never truly fit.

I looked "fine" on the outside—but inside, I was withering.

Because even when that life was easier, it wasn't free.
Even when it was comfortable, it wasn't true.
Even when it was praised, it wasn't mine.

You will have moments—many of them—where you question this path.
Where the fire of your awakening burns too hot.
Where the grief of what you've outgrown feels heavier than what you've gained.
Where the loneliness of truth makes you wonder if it's worth it.

But hear this with your whole heart:

You didn't come this far to abandon yourself again.
You didn't break open just to tape the pieces back together for someone else's comfort.
You didn't do the sacred, brutal work of remembering who you are, only to forget again.

You were never meant to go back to sleep.

You were never meant to dim your light just because it makes someone else squint.
You were never meant to trade your truth for approval, or

your aliveness for acceptance.
You were never meant to disappear in order to belong.

You were born to rise.
To live fully awake, even when your voice trembles.
To speak, even when it would be easier to stay silent.
To rest, absolutely—but never to retreat into the false
safety of pretending again.

This path? It's not always pretty.
It's not always affirming.
It will break your heart open a hundred times.

But what it gives you in return is everything.

It gives you your breath—unrestricted, intentional, real.
It gives you your body—not something to manage, but
something to honor.
It gives you your sacred yes, your holy no, your voice, your
rhythm, your presence.

It gives you *you.*

And yes, you'll stumble.
You'll forget.
You'll ache.

But now, you know the way home.

And once you've tasted freedom—raw, embodied, sovereign
freedom—
you can't unknow it.

It lives in your bones.
It pulses in your belly.
It whispers in the quiet moments: *Come back.*

Because you were never meant to sleepwalk through this life.

You were meant to live it—fully, fiercely, awake.

Chapter 7 Exercises: Staying Awake

This chapter was never meant to push you to strive harder.
It was here to help you remember.

To remember that even when the world grows loud,
you are not lost.
Even when you forget,
you can still return.
And even when loneliness creeps in,
you are never truly alone.

These exercises are not demands for transformation—
they are gentle invitations.
To choose your truth.
To come home to yourself.
Daily. Softly. Bravely.

Exercise 1: The Awake Check-In

"Awareness is not the absence of chaos—it is the practice of choosing presence within it."

Use this daily reflection to gently return to yourself:
- What am I noticing in my body right now?
- Where today did I feel tempted to go back to sleep (numb out, override, perform, disconnect)?
- Where did I stay awake to my truth?
- How did it feel in my body—before, during, and after?

Journal Prompt:
What made me feel most alive, most awake, most connected to my truth today?
What tried to pull me away from that? What helped me return?

Exercise 2: The Social Inventory

"Staying awake isn't just about what you believe—it's about who you're surrounded by."

Make two lists:
- The people, communities, and environments that nourish your awake self
- The people, communities, and environments that subtly (or loudly) encourage you to stay small, quiet, or asleep

Reflection:
What boundaries need to be fortified?
What relationships feel like safe havens—and which feel like

cages?
What conversations are calling to be had, even if they're uncomfortable?

Reminder:
It's okay to grieve what can't come with you.
It's okay to protect what helps you stay awake.

Exercise 3: The Nervous System Replenishment Practice

"You don't have to burn out to prove you're awake."

When staying awake feels like too much:
- Find a quiet, safe space.
- Sit or lie down and place your hands on your body (your chest, belly, thighs—wherever feels most grounding).
- Take 10 slow, nourishing breaths. On the exhale, sigh out loud.
- With each exhale, whisper to yourself:
  It's safe to rest. I can stay awake and still rest. I don't have to carry it all at once.

Tip:
You were not built to live in fight-or-flight.
Rest is not regression—it is regulation.
It is how you stay awake.

Exercise 4: Staying Awake Ritual

"Honor the moments you chose yourself—even if no one else saw it."

At the end of each week:
- Reflect on one moment where you stayed awake when it would have been easier to fall back asleep.
- Honor it.
  o Write a note to yourself.
  o Light a candle and speak your truth aloud.
  o Dance, cry, walk barefoot in the grass—anything that anchors you in that courage.

Speak this out loud:
I honor the courage it takes to stay awake in a world that rewards sleepwalking. I chose myself. I choose myself again.

Exercise 5: Body Anchor Affirmations

"Your body remembers—even when your mind forgets."

Create a short list of body-based affirmations you can return to when you feel tempted to perform, please, or disappear:
- I can trust my body.
- I am safe to live fully awake.
- It's okay if others don't understand.
- I am not here to belong to the box—I am here to belong to myself.

Practice:
- Ground your feet.
- Place your hands over your heart, belly, or thighs.

- Repeat these affirmations slowly, with breath.
- Let them move from your head into your nervous system.

Final Reminder:

You will forget.
You will have days when staying awake feels heavy—
when presence feels like too much,
and old patterns call you back.

But forgetting isn't failure.
It's part of the rhythm.
Because every time you return,
you root deeper.
Every time you soften back into yourself,
you strengthen your becoming.

This isn't a weekend transformation.
This is the sacred unfolding of a lifetime.

Chapter 8:

Building a Life Outside the Box — Living, Relating, and Healing on Your Own Terms

"When you liberate yourself from the world's expectations, you finally begin to build the life that was always meant for you."
— Unknown

The Freedom to Rebuild

There comes a moment—quiet but certain—when you realize you're no longer waiting for permission. Not from your past. Not from the people around you. Not even from the version of yourself who once needed rules, structure, and approval just to feel safe in the world.

You've outgrown all of it.
And suddenly, without fanfare or anyone noticing but you, there it is: freedom.

They don't tell you that after the grief, the collapse, the chaos... something else gently takes root. Not a dramatic rebirth or a perfect resolution. But a soft, steady knowing. An internal whisper that says, *You can start now. Right here. As you are.*

You don't have to wait until you're fully healed.
You don't need all the answers.
You don't have to make it look like anyone else's version of success.

You are free to rebuild.

And not just rebuild the old life with fresh paint.
But to create something entirely new. Something that fits you now—after all the breaking and remembering. After all the unlearning and coming home.

This kind of freedom isn't loud. It doesn't shout.
It arrives quietly, often in moments no one else would notice—when you exhale without bracing, when you make a choice without overexplaining, when you stop performing and simply exist.

I remember that moment after the stroke, standing in the wreckage of everything I thought I knew. My memories were gone. My identity had unraveled. And yet, in that strange, stripped-down space, something inside me began to stir. I wasn't trying to fix what broke. I wasn't trying to recreate what had been lost.

I was free to build something different.
Something real.
Something mine.

At first, it was terrifying. I had no roadmap. No script. No one handing me the next step. But that blank slate became sacred. Because without all the noise, I could finally hear what I wanted. What my body needed. What my spirit craved.

And I didn't want the hustle.
I didn't want the performance.
I didn't want to mold myself into another "should."

I wanted peace.
I wanted truth.
I wanted to breathe inside the life I was creating.

This is the quiet revolution of rebuilding—
not from who you were,
but from who you are now.

It's not about big plans or timelines.
It's about building your life in a way that feels kind to your
nervous system and true to your soul.
It's about choosing alignment over approval, nourishment
over productivity, meaning over metrics.

Maybe you've never seen it modeled.
Maybe you don't have a blueprint.
But you don't need one.

You need honesty.
You need presence.
You need the willingness to let your life take a shape that
actually fits.

Because once you've stepped outside the box,
you realize just how many parts of your old life were built
for someone else's comfort, not your wholeness.

And now?
You get to choose something different.

You get to define success in a way that doesn't sacrifice
your well-being.
You get to create relationships that are rooted in mutual
respect, not obligation.

You get to shape your days in ways that allow space for joy, stillness, and authenticity.

Brick by brick.
Boundary by boundary.
Truth by truth.

This isn't about perfection.
It's about intention.

And no, it won't happen overnight.
But it *will* happen—if you keep choosing it.

That is the gift of freedom.
And this time, what you build will not be a performance or a survival strategy.

It will be a home.

A life you can actually live inside of.

Creating a New Definition of Success

Redefining success sounds beautiful in theory— empowering, liberating, a soulful return to what truly matters. But in practice? It's disorienting. Painful, even. Because when you've spent your entire life chasing a particular version of success, letting go of it can feel like you're unraveling the very threads of your identity.

The version we were taught wasn't just about external milestones. It was about belonging. Safety. Worth. We were raised on a script that said success looks like a stable paycheck, a tidy house, a polished marriage, a perfectly behaved family, and a life that looks good on paper—even if it feels hollow behind closed doors. We were told that if we just kept achieving, hustling, performing, producing— eventually we'd arrive. Eventually we'd be enough.

But the cost of that chase?
Was always ourselves.

So when you finally slow down and begin to question it— when that first whisper rises inside you and asks, *"What if this isn't working?"*—everything begins to shake. Because you're not just rethinking your goals; you're stepping outside a system that trained you to tie your worth to your output.

You'll feel lost at first. You might feel lazy or directionless or like you're falling behind everyone else. Social media will tempt you back into comparison. The people around you may not understand. And the old version of you—the one who thrived on checklists and external praise—will panic. She'll wonder who she is without her gold stars.

This part of the journey takes grit. It takes courage to sit in the in-between, where the old version of success has been stripped away but the new one hasn't fully formed. It takes strength to resist explaining your choices to people who don't see the world like you do. It takes trust—deep, bone-deep trust—to believe that your value isn't in what you achieve, but in who you are.

I remember this phase vividly. After my stroke, after my memory loss, after I lost the "me" I had been performing for so long, I couldn't go back to chasing. But I didn't know what to chase instead. I had no language for what I wanted—only the raw clarity that I couldn't survive another version of success that required me to abandon myself.

So I started small. I stopped asking what would impress people and started asking what would nourish me. I stopped trying to prove anything and began tuning in to how I actually felt. Some days, success looked like feeding myself. Other days, it looked like saying "no" without guilt. There were days when it was simply choosing rest over productivity—or allowing myself to cry and not labeling it as failure.

That's when I realized:
Success wasn't a performance anymore.
It was a practice of coming home.

Real success, the kind that resonates with your nervous system and honors your truth, has nothing to do with how it looks to others. It has everything to do with how it *feels* to you. It's not about being ahead of the curve. It's about being in alignment with yourself. It's not about accumulating more. It's about carrying less—less shame, less pressure, less pretending.

And it takes time. You don't just snap your fingers and suddenly feel liberated from a lifetime of programming. You'll slip. You'll find yourself measuring your worth by old standards again. You'll have to remind yourself, gently, that this is a process of peeling back—not perfection.

But eventually, something shifts.

One day, you'll catch yourself not explaining your choices.
You'll feel peace instead of panic in the pause.
You'll stop chasing and start living.

That's when you'll know:
You didn't just create a new definition of success.
You reclaimed it.

And this time, it belongs to *you*. Not your past. Not your parents. Not the algorithm. You.

Your breath will feel easier.
Your life will feel softer.
And you'll realize—you didn't lose your ambition.
You just rerouted it toward something that actually feels like freedom.

Building Rhythms Instead of Routines

The world conditioned us to live on autopilot.
We were taught to wake up, push through, get it done—regardless of how we felt. Eat when the clock said to. Work when the system told us to. Rest, but only if we earned it—and only if there was time left over.

That's not a life. That's survival masquerading as success.

Inside the box, we weren't just given routines—we were handed scripts that had nothing to do with our actual needs. We were told structure equals discipline, and discipline equals worthiness. But no one ever asked us if the structure itself might be the problem. No one ever gave us permission to ask, *"What if I'm not meant to live like this?"*

After my stroke, I didn't just lose memories—I lost the ability to operate on a system that ignored my body. I couldn't keep up with the tidy routines anymore, even if I wanted to. My brain was slower. My body was unpredictable. My energy moved in waves, not straight lines. And honestly, it always had—I had just spent decades forcing it to behave.

What I once called "discipline" was really disconnection. What I once called "structure" was often just self-abandonment with a gold star.

When my nervous system collapsed, the illusion of control went with it. And in its place, something softer emerged. I didn't need tighter routines—I needed rhythm. I needed a new way of living that was rooted in listening, not overriding. One that worked with my body, not against it. One that asked not, *"How can I do more?"* but *"What does my body need right now?"*

That's what building rhythms is about. It's not about chaos or laziness. It's not the absence of structure—it's the presence of relationship. It's a shift from rigid systems to responsive ones. A way of moving through your days that honors your energy, your cycles, your seasons, and your soul.

Rhythm invites you to pause and notice:

- When do I feel most alive, focused, or creative?
- When do I need quiet, slowness, or solitude?
- How does my energy shift with the seasons, my hormonal cycle, or my emotional waves?

Rather than bending yourself to fit into external expectations, you begin building a life that fits *you*.

In the early stages of my recovery, there were many mornings when I couldn't get out of bed until nearly noon. For a while, I hated myself for it. I carried shame like it was productive. But over time, I learned that shame doesn't create change—it creates paralysis. It silences the wisdom of your body. It keeps you trapped in loops of guilt and punishment instead of allowing you to listen, adjust, and grow.

So I stopped fighting myself.
I stopped forcing productivity.
And I started paying attention.

I noticed how winter made me want to slow down and go inward.
I noticed which foods, people, and environments nourished me—and which ones left me drained.
I noticed that my creativity pulsed in waves, and that those waves didn't care about my to-do list.

I began to build slowly.
Deliberately.
Rhythmically.

Living by rhythm didn't mean I threw out all structure. It meant I let the structure breathe. I created frameworks that allowed for flexibility, that responded to my actual life instead of some idealized version of it. And that shift changed everything.

Sometimes that looked like working in short, focused sprints instead of eight-hour marathons.

Sometimes it meant eating when I was hungry, not when the schedule said it was "time."
Sometimes it meant honoring the days when I needed more rest—during my luteal phase, after emotional triggers, or in seasons of grief or transformation.
And sometimes, it meant choosing joy over obligation— because I finally understood that pleasure is productive too.

Rhythm honors your capacity as a living being.
And the truth is—your rhythm will change. Again and again.

What worked for you in your twenties might not work after a trauma, a diagnosis, a breakup, a spiritual awakening, or a birth. And that's not regression. That's evolution. That's growth. That's *life*.

Building rhythms is a sacred act of rebellion in a world that wants to turn you into a machine. It's a declaration that says, *"I trust my body's intelligence more than I trust the system's demands."* And that kind of trust? It's revolutionary.

Because while the world runs on conveyor belts, deadlines, and metrics—
you are learning to move like a tide.
Alive.
Attuned.
Free.

Relating from Wholeness, Not Roles

When I started waking up—*really* waking up—I began to see just how much of my life had been shaped by roles I was never meant to carry. They weren't chosen consciously. They were handed to me before I even knew who I was: Be the good girl. Be polite. Don't talk back. Don't make a scene. Make others proud. Make yourself useful. And whatever you do, don't take up too much space.

At first, those roles felt like safety. They helped me navigate environments that couldn't hold my full humanity—family dynamics, cultural expectations, religious systems, and social settings that favored silence over truth. The roles became strategies. And for a while, they worked.

But eventually, those roles became cages. I could feel myself shrinking inside them—contorting to stay liked, compliant, useful. My spirit was aching for space, but the more I tried to express my real self, the more resistance I met—from the world, from others, and from within.

From the beginning, we're taught who we need to be in order to belong. We learn that worthiness is conditional. So we become who the system praises: the helper, the peacekeeper, the overachiever, the strong one. We become dependable, composed, emotionally low-maintenance. We adapt not because we're weak, but because it feels like the only way to survive.

And the world rewards it.
People compliment the mask. They call it strength, maturity, selflessness. But they don't see what it's costing us. They don't see the fatigue behind the performance, the pain

behind the smile, the longing behind the perfectly polished role.

When you begin the sacred work of returning to yourself—of unlearning the performance and reclaiming your truth—one of the hardest and most liberating things you'll come to realize is this: You were never meant to be a role. You were never meant to live inside someone else's idea of who you should be.

Relating from wholeness means stepping outside those old scripts. It means showing up with your full self—your feelings, your boundaries, your voice. It means saying, "This is who I am now," even when it disappoints the people who preferred the version of you that stayed small and agreeable.

This shift is not without cost. Some relationships won't know what to do with your truth. They'll miss the version of you that played along, made it easy, kept the peace. And when you stop performing, the entire dynamic shifts. Not everyone is willing—or ready—to meet you in that new space.

But this is the sacred cost of freedom.
The price of living honestly.

Relating from wholeness means no longer shape-shifting to avoid rejection. It means letting your "no" stand without explanation. It means speaking up even when your voice shakes and no longer rescuing others from their discomfort just to protect a fragile peace. It also means extending the same space to others—letting them be real without trying to fix or manage them.

And yes, it means grieving.

You'll grieve the relationships that depended on your silence to function.
You'll grieve the times you twisted yourself into someone else's ideal just to feel loved.
You'll grieve the seasons of your life when you thought being palatable was the same thing as being safe.

But grief is not the end. It's the doorway.

On the other side of grief is something real. A kind of connection that doesn't require you to shrink. Relationships built not on convenience or control—but on resonance. On truth. On choice.

When you relate from wholeness, you invite others into something deeper. You give them permission to be real, too. You create relationships rooted in presence, not performance. And that presence—that raw, unfiltered, embodied presence—is what makes love feel like home instead of labor.

You're not here to be easy to love.
You're here to be *fully you*.

And when you belong to yourself first, the connections that follow won't ask you to trade that belonging for proximity. They'll honor you there. They'll rise to meet you there.

That is the return.
That is the healing.
That is the truth.

Work That Nourishes Instead of Drains

Let's be honest—most of us weren't taught to choose work that nurtures our nervous system, our creativity, or our natural rhythms of rest and renewal. We were taught to survive. To find something stable. Respectable. Safe. We were told to climb the ladder, collect the benefits, and be grateful for the paycheck, no matter the cost to our bodies, our hearts, or our sense of purpose.

Work wasn't presented as something meant to fulfill you—it was something you did to prove your value. To earn your place. To keep the machine running. And if it drained you? If you burned out or collapsed beneath the weight of all that proving? The world simply told you to push harder. Take a long weekend. Come back smiling.

But what if work isn't supposed to be a place where you disappear?
What if it's not meant to extract your energy in exchange for validation?

What if work could be a sacred extension of your soul—an offering, not a sacrifice?

When you begin unlearning the rules of the box, this question becomes a turning point:
Not "What do I need to do to be successful?"
But "What am I here to create that actually aligns with my truth?"

That shift doesn't just change your job.
It changes your entire orientation toward work.

You stop striving to meet someone else's standards.
You begin listening to your body—really listening.
You pay attention to what expands you instead of just what earns approval.
You notice what energizes you, not just what sustains your income.
And you begin moving in ways that honor both your soul and your nervous system.

It's not about avoiding effort. It's about redefining what effort is *for*.

Sometimes, this shift will feel inconvenient. It may mean walking away from a job that looks good on paper but leaves you chronically depleted. It may mean pivoting careers, downsizing expectations, or starting something new without a clear path. You may feel the tension between security and soul for a while.

But once you taste the alignment of doing work that feeds you, you can't un-feel it.

Because now, your work serves you—not the other way around.

Work that nourishes doesn't mean you're never tired. But it *does* mean the tiredness feels different. It's not the kind of exhaustion that leaves you hollow. It's the kind that comes after a day of meaningful creation, of aligned effort, of being fully present with what you're building.

You get to decide what "enough" looks like for you.

Maybe enough means working fewer hours with more intention.

Maybe it means creating a work rhythm that honors your menstrual cycle, your seasons of grief or growth, your emotional bandwidth.
Maybe it means turning down high-paying opportunities that would cost you your peace.
Maybe it's walking away from the hustle culture altogether.

For some, nourishing work might look like writing, painting, or building something with your hands. For others, it's caregiving, community-building, or simply protecting your presence outside of work so you can actually *live* your life. It's not about what you do—it's about how what you do feels in your body.

This is your permission to choose differently.

To stop sacrificing your nervous system on the altar of productivity.
To stop proving your worth by how much you accomplish.
To stop measuring your value by output, income, or applause.

You were not put on this earth to produce until there's nothing left.
You were born to live.

And when your work supports that living—when it becomes a space of alignment, expression, and dignity—it stops being something that drains you. It becomes something that roots you.

Let it be meaningful.
Let it be honest.
Let it be enough.

Healing as a Way of Living

For most of my life, I believed healing was a destination. A place I would finally arrive if I could just find the right combination of answers. The right diagnosis. The right supplement. The right practitioner. I treated healing like a riddle to solve—something that existed outside of me, waiting to be unlocked if I just tried hard enough.

I poured myself into protocols, chased down lab results, followed expert advice, and kept thinking, *maybe this is it... maybe this will finally fix me.* But no matter how much I did, the cycle would eventually repeat—burnout, disappointment, and a familiar sense of failure. I had confused healing with achievement. With something to complete and conquer.

What I eventually learned—through the collapse of my body, the silence that followed my stroke, and the long, slow return to myself—was this:

Healing isn't a finish line.
It's a way of being.

It's not a one-time event. Not something you check off a to-do list. And it's not reserved for some special season of life labeled "recovery." True healing is how you choose to live—every day, in the small moments when no one is watching. In the choices you make when things feel tender. In how you meet yourself when life feels messy or uncertain.

Healing lives in the pause between the trigger and the reaction.
In the breath you take before speaking to yourself with

judgment.
In the moment you choose to soften instead of strive.

It's not found in the "perfect" diet or the right wellness routine—it's in the way you listen to your body's wisdom and respond with respect. It's how you feed yourself, not just what you eat. It's how you care for your nervous system, not just what you eliminate from your environment. It's how you let yourself *feel*, not just how you try to fix.

Outside the box, healing no longer means endlessly working on yourself as a project. It means relating to yourself with compassion and curiosity. Not because you're broken. But because you are worthy of care, exactly as you are.

That shift is everything.

You stop searching for a version of yourself who is finally "healed enough." And instead, you begin living in ways that bring healing to this moment. You start asking better questions:

What does my nervous system need today?
What would feel grounding—not just efficient?
Can I offer myself grace even if I don't have all the answers?

Healing becomes less about striving and more about inhabiting.

It shows up in how you choose food that nourishes instead of punishes.
In how you stretch to feel instead of to fix.
In how you take a break without needing to earn it.
In how you let tears fall without labeling them weakness.

This kind of healing doesn't come with applause. There are no shiny milestones. It's often quiet. Unseen. Deeply personal. But it's real.

It's in the way you open the windows for fresh air instead of numbing with distraction.
In the way you put your phone down and actually feel the sun.
In the way you ask for support instead of pretending you're okay.
In the way you let yourself be *here*, as you are.

You stop postponing your life until you're "better."
And instead, you begin to live in ways that *are* the medicine.

This is the kind of healing that endures—not because it's dramatic or perfect—but because it's integrated. Embodied. Sustainable.

Because it's not separate from your life.
It *is* your life.

And that, I believe, is what healing was always meant to be.

Designing a Life You Don't Need to Escape From

There was a time in my life when everything felt like a countdown—waiting for the next weekend, the next vacation, the next moment where I could finally exhale without everything feeling so heavy. I wasn't really living—I was enduring. When the days felt too tight, too loud, too much, I numbed with distractions: scrolling endlessly, eating past fullness, daydreaming about a different future that felt far away and almost unreachable. Back then, I believed I just needed more motivation or willpower. But the truth was simpler and deeper: I was exhausted—not from failure, but from living a life that didn't actually feel like mine.

Most of us weren't taught to design our lives. We were taught to survive them. From a young age, we're handed a blueprint: go to school, get the stable job, climb the ladder, buy the house, check the boxes, perform the script. And if you're lucky, maybe—just maybe—you'll earn a few years at the end to finally enjoy it all. But what no one tells you is that if the life you're living doesn't nourish you along the way, those years at the end won't feel like freedom. They'll feel like recovery from a life you were never meant to carry in the first place.

As I began to wake up from my own autopilot, I realized I didn't need to overhaul everything or abandon responsibility. I needed to ask better questions. Questions like: What would it feel like to create a life that doesn't require escape? What rhythms make me feel grounded and alive—not just productive? Who am I when I'm not performing for approval or hustling for worth? These questions didn't come with easy answers, but they became anchors as I began the slow, deliberate process of reclaiming my life from the inside out.

Designing a life you don't want to escape doesn't mean every day will be joyful or free of stress. It means your days are more aligned with what matters. It means choosing presence over perfection, ease over performance, truth over appearance. It means you stop making decisions based solely on logic, income, or optics—and begin letting your nervous system, your energy, and your soul be part of the conversation.

That might look like letting your mornings be slower and more intentional instead of rushed and resentful. It might mean saying no to things that drain you, even if they're expected or praised. It might mean choosing joy without guilt, rest without apology, and beauty without having to earn it. These aren't indulgences—they're foundations of a life that feels worth living *now*, not someday.

This kind of life requires courage. It asks you to trust yourself enough to live differently. You might feel resistance from others who don't understand your new pace, your new boundaries, your newfound clarity. But that discomfort is part of the process—because the life you're designing isn't built to impress others. It's built to sustain *you*.

You'll still face hardship. There will be bills, heartbreak, and unexpected detours. But the difference is, you'll meet those moments from a place of rootedness, not from burnout. You'll have rhythms that support you, values that guide you, and a self-trust that holds steady even when the world doesn't.

This is your reminder that you were never meant to live for weekends or to count the days until the next break. You were meant to build a life that feels like home within your own skin—one breath, one boundary, one brave decision at a time.

And that life? It's not out there waiting. It begins right here, where you choose yourself again and again.

Chapter 8 Exercises: Building a Life Outside the Box

This work isn't about mastering a perfect version of life.
It's about softening into what's real—
what feels true,
what feels aligned,
and what's actually sustainable for *you*.

These exercises aren't boxes to check.
They're doorways.
Invitations to pause,
to listen,
to come back to yourself with honesty and grace.

This is how we begin again—
by rebuilding a life that feels like home
in your body,
in your breath,
in your being.

Let's begin.

Exercise 1: Define Your Own Success

Instructions:
Find a quiet space. Breathe. Drop into your body. Then, ask yourself:
- What does success feel like—not just in my mind, but in my body?
- When in my life have I felt successful on my own terms?
- Where am I still chasing someone else's version of success?
- What internal or external metrics am I ready to release?

Journal Prompt:
Write your Success Manifesto.
What values anchor it?
What rhythms sustain it?
What does it look like in your relationships, health, creativity, work, and joy?
Let this be your compass—not a rigid plan, but a rooted intention.

Exercise 2: Create Your Daily/Seasonal Rhythms

Instructions:
Instead of forcing a routine, explore your natural rhythms. Take note over a few days or weeks:
- When do I feel most energized?
- When does my body crave rest, nourishment, or silence?
- What shifts with the seasons—emotionally, physically, spiritually?

Reflection:
Using your observations, design a gentle rhythm map.
Let it be fluid. Let it breathe.
- Morning rhythms
- Evening wind-downs
- Movement or stillness
- Creative or social windows
- Seasonal foods, rituals, and habits

You're not trying to get it "right."
You're trying to get it honest.

Exercise 3: Relationship Inventory — Relating from Wholeness

Instructions:
Draw two columns in your journal.

Column 1:
- Relationships where I feel free to be my whole self

Column 2:
- Relationships where I feel the need to perform, fix, or self-abandon

Reflection Questions:
- Where am I still living in a role, not my truth?
- What boundaries or conversations are needed?
- What relationships might be shifting—and how can I grieve that with love?

This isn't about blame.
It's about clarity.
You get to choose how you relate—

and what you are no longer willing to compromise.

Exercise 4: Work from Nourishment Reflection

Instructions:
Pause and check in with how work feels in your body.
- What aspects of my work bring me alive?
- What parts leave me drained or anxious?
- Where am I operating from fear, old programming, or external validation?
- What would work feel like if it were rooted in purpose, not pressure?

Journal Prompt:
Write a vision for Work That Nourishes You.
What does your ideal workday feel like—emotionally, energetically, practically?

Include your ideal schedule, environment, values, and the kind of impact you want to have.

This is your sacred blueprint.

Exercise 5: The Life That Feels Like Home Visioning

Instructions:
Close your eyes. Place a hand on your heart or belly.
Breathe deeply. Imagine:

- What kind of life would feel like coming home to myself?
- What sounds, sights, textures, and spaces would surround me?
- Who would be with me?
- What would I do each day—not for status, but for joy, connection, and truth?

Action:
- Write or sketch your vision.
- Don't worry about how realistic it seems. Start with what feels real in your body.
- Then ask: What is one small, courageous step I can take this week to embody one piece of this vision?

That's how it begins.

Brick by brick.
Truth by truth.
Moment by moment.

You don't need to build a perfect life.
You get to build a real one.

One that nourishes you,
reflects you, and holds you
with the tenderness
and power of the life

you were always meant to live.

Chapter 9:

The Forever Path — Embracing Unlearning, Relearning, and Becoming as a Lifelong Practice

"There is no finish line. There is only the next layer, the next remembering, the next becoming."
— Unknown

The Illusion of Done

We're raised in a world that celebrates the finish line. From an early age, we're taught to measure life in milestones: get the degree, land the job, check the box, heal the wound, fix the flaw, move on. Even in spaces that claim to honor healing, there's often a subtle pressure to "graduate" from our pain—to reach some polished summit where we can finally say we're whole, we're free, we're done.

But healing doesn't work like that. And the truth is, there *is* no summit.

Healing isn't a final destination—it's a way of being, a lifelong becoming. And while that may sound poetic, in real life it's anything but easy. I spent years believing that if I just worked hard enough—at therapy, at self-reflection, at spirituality—I would eventually arrive at a place where the pain would stop revisiting me. So when the old grief resurfaced, when the same emotional patterns circled back, I felt like I had failed. I questioned everything. *Didn't I already process this? Didn't I already cry these tears?*

What I didn't understand then—but do now—is that healing is not linear. It's not a straight path from broken to fixed. It's a spiral. A sacred, winding return. And every time you revisit a wound or a story, you're not starting over—you're starting deeper. You're meeting the same truth with new awareness, stronger boundaries, more embodied wisdom. You're not failing. You're evolving.

But the world rarely makes space for that kind of process. It celebrates quick turnarounds, tidy narratives, and stories that resolve by the final chapter. It doesn't always know what to do with the rawness of real healing—with its messy timelines, emotional spirals, or quiet seasons of undoing.

That's why this journey asks so much of you.

It asks you to release the shame of still feeling.
It asks you to trust yourself even when the path looks unfamiliar.
It asks you to stop measuring progress by how far you think you should be—and instead honor how fully you're showing up now.

True healing often doesn't look like healing at all. It looks like pausing when you want to push. It looks like crying over something you thought you were "past." It looks like saying "no" without justifying it. It looks like resting in the middle of your transformation, not after it's complete.

And somewhere in the midst of all that softness and surrender, something sacred happens: you return to yourself. Not to some polished version of who you think you're supposed to be—but to the real you. The one beneath the masks. The one who has always been whole, even in her unraveling.

That's what this path offers—not a neat resolution or a gold star, but a deeper relationship with yourself. One that doesn't depend on perfection. One that knows how to hold space for your humanity, again and again.

This is the forever path. And while it may never offer the certainty of a finish line, it offers something more enduring: the freedom to become. Not just once, but over and over again. Each time with more truth. More softness. More you.

Relearning Is Not Failure

There was a time in my healing when every step backward felt like defeat. The return of an old emotion, the reactivation of a wound I thought I had already worked through—it all felt like evidence that I wasn't as far along as I should be. That I had somehow faked my progress or failed the test of "healing right." That's how deeply the conditioning runs. We're taught to view healing as a straight staircase: move up, don't look back, and never repeat a step. We're taught that once we've learned the lesson, the pain should vanish—that if it returns, we must've done something wrong.

But that narrative is a lie. And it's a damaging one.

Because real healing—the kind that reshapes your nervous system, rewrites your inner scripts, and rebuilds your relationship with yourself—doesn't unfold in neat, linear steps. It spirals. It deepens. It returns, not to punish you, but to invite you into greater wholeness.

Relearning is not failure. It's actually a sign of wisdom. It's your body saying, *We're ready to feel this now. We're safe enough to go deeper.*

There have been so many moments when I thought I was "done" with a certain layer of my healing. I had found clarity. I had spoken my truth. I had practiced the tools and felt the release. And then—days or weeks later—I would find myself back in the same story, the same emotion, the same grief. And at first, it would crush me. I would spiral into shame, questioning whether I had made any progress at all.

But with time and gentleness, I came to see those moments not as failure—but as deepening. I wasn't circling back in the same way. I was returning with more self-awareness, more capacity, more tenderness. I had new eyes. A steadier nervous system. A softer heart. The old pain was meeting a new version of me—one who knew how to hold it differently.

That's the beauty of the spiral. You're not who you were the last time you touched that wound. You bring with you every tool you've earned, every ounce of self-trust you've built, every boundary you've practiced. You may still cry, but now those tears are wrapped in compassion instead of shame. You may still fall, but now you know how to rise—with slower breath, with softer expectations, with kinder language toward yourself.

Relearning is not regression—it's integration. It's a sacred reminder that healing isn't something you control; it's something you partner with. It's not about getting ahead. It's about staying present with what's here—again and again—with reverence for the fact that your body holds timelines your mind can't always comprehend.

Sometimes a trauma takes years to feel safe enough to fully process. Sometimes grief needs to be held in multiple seasons before it can move. Sometimes we revisit the same inner landscape not because we're failing, but because we're becoming more capable of honoring it.

You're not behind. You're becoming. And every time you relearn something with more gentleness than the last time— that's progress.

That's healing.

That's what it means to walk the forever path with grace.

The Practice of Staying Curious

If there's one thing that's kept me from giving up—on healing, on people, on myself—it hasn't been discipline or motivation. It hasn't even been hope, because there were seasons when hope felt too far away to grasp. What remained, like a quiet ember flickering in the dark, was curiosity. That small, persistent whisper inside asking, *What else might be true?*

Curiosity has saved me more times than I can count. When shame told me I was too broken to be loved, curiosity gently asked, *Who taught you that?* When fear tried to convince me I'd never feel safe in my body again, curiosity responded, *What if there's another way to live?* When grief felt too heavy to carry, curiosity wondered, *What would happen if you didn't carry it alone?*

In a world that often demands answers, quick fixes, and certainty, curiosity is the sacred pause that softens our edges. It doesn't force healing; it invites presence. It doesn't require you to solve anything—it simply creates enough space for your soul to breathe, for your nervous system to settle, for truth to reveal itself in its own time.

This isn't the kind of curiosity that pushes or analyzes from the mind. It's a deeper, embodied practice. It sounds like: *Why does this still hurt? Where did I learn this pattern? Is this belief even mine? What does my body need right now, if I were really listening?* These questions don't seek to shame or expose—they seek to understand. And in that understanding, something shifts. You begin to see your pain not as proof of failure, but as a doorway to deeper compassion.

When we forget who we are, curiosity becomes a bridge—back to our bodies, back to our needs, back to the parts of us that have been waiting patiently to be acknowledged. It slows us down. It interrupts the autopilot. It offers gentleness in moments when we're most tempted to self-abandon. Curiosity doesn't expect you to be perfect; it only asks you to stay present. Present to the discomfort, to the mystery, to the truth emerging beneath the surface.

And maybe that's the most courageous thing of all—staying in relationship with your own becoming. Not rushing to fix or label, but choosing to remain in the unfolding. It's a practice. A posture. A way of being with yourself that makes healing less about arriving somewhere, and more about allowing what is true right now to matter.

So the next time you feel stuck, lost, overwhelmed, or ashamed—pause. Don't reach for control. Don't shame yourself for not knowing. Instead, ask the quiet questions: *What's here for me in this moment? What truth wants to be felt, not fixed? What do I need that I've been too afraid to ask for?*

You don't need to have it all figured out. You just need to be willing to stay in the conversation with yourself.

That willingness—tender, imperfect, curious—is where everything begins again.

Living in the Questions

There was a time in my life when I believed the goal was to have all the answers. I thought that if I could just *figure it out*—the right healing protocol, the ideal daily routine, the correct belief system, the universal truth that made everything make sense—then maybe I'd finally feel safe. Safe in the world. Safe in my body. Safe in my own skin.

But the deeper I walked this path, the more I came to understand that answers were never the destination. Because just when I thought I had something "solved," life would shift. A new season would arrive, bringing unfamiliar questions. A new challenge would surface. A new version of myself would emerge—one I didn't yet know how to care for or love.

That's when I realized: there are no permanent answers. Only deeper, more honest questions.

And while that realization used to feel terrifying, over time it became a kind of freedom. The freedom to evolve. To change my mind. To not know and still be enough. Living in the questions stopped being something to fear and started becoming a lifeline—one that anchored me not to certainty, but to truth as it revealed itself moment by moment.

I stopped craving black-and-white rules and started embracing the sacred space of nuance. I made peace with contradiction. I began to see that life—this real, raw, beautifully imperfect life—wasn't a puzzle to be solved. It was a relationship to tend to. A process to surrender to.

And something remarkable happened when I stopped demanding answers from life. I made space for a different kind of wisdom—truth that couldn't be downloaded or intellectualized, but lived and felt. I learned that some of the most transformative questions aren't designed to fix us. They're meant to *meet us* exactly where we are.

Questions like:

- What is true for me now, in this body, in this season?
- What can I let go of today that no longer fits who I'm becoming?
- Where am I still performing when I'm longing to be seen?
- How can I honor both my grief and my gratitude, without needing to choose?
- What parts of me are waking up—slowly, painfully, beautifully?

These aren't questions that arrive with clean answers or perfect timing. They are portals—openings into new ways of being, seeing, and healing. They invite us to slow down, to listen inward, to move with reverence instead of rush.

The world may tell you that confidence means having all the answers. That success means certainty. That wisdom means arriving. But what I've learned is that the most powerful people I've met aren't the ones who know everything— they're the ones still willing to ask the right questions. The ones who remain soft in the discomfort of uncertainty, rooted not in knowing, but in curiosity and compassion.

So if you find yourself in a season where everything feels unclear—where the ground beneath you is shifting, and clarity refuses to come—don't force your way through. Don't abandon yourself in the search for certainty.

Stay present. Breathe into the fog. Ask one honest question. And then listen, gently, for what your body, your heart, or your spirit might whisper in response.

That whisper is enough. That question is the work. And that willingness to remain awake, even when you can't see the whole path—that is where transformation begins.

You Are the Guide Now

There comes a moment on the healing path—quiet, subtle, but undeniable—when you pause, look around, and realize: no one is coming to save you. No one is going to hand you the map. No one else has the answers you've been searching for. And while that realization might seem terrifying at first, it doesn't shatter you. It liberates you.

Because in that moment, something within you awakens. You begin to see what's been true all along: you are the guide now. The years you spent searching for permission, approval, and validation weren't wasted—they were the crucible that taught you how to listen. Not to others. But to yourself. To your body. To the deeper voice within that's been whispering the truth from the beginning.

You begin to understand that you don't need another checklist. You don't need to contort yourself into someone else's version of success, healing, womanhood, manhood, or worth. You don't have to walk paths that were never made for your feet. You were never meant to be a reflection of someone else's idea of "enough." You were meant to embody your own truth—fully, unapologetically, and with deep reverence for everything that got you here.

This is where your new life begins. Not with certainty, but with courage. Not with a perfect plan, but with a willingness to trust the next step. You begin writing your own map—not because the path is clear, but because you finally trust yourself to walk it.

And when you stop looking outward for the answers, you begin asking questions that truly matter: What feels aligned in my body? What does freedom look like for me? What kind of world do I want to help create? These are not small questions. They are revolutionary. Because when you answer them with your life, you don't just heal yourself— you change the narrative for everyone who comes after you.

You become the cycle breaker. The truth-teller. The one who roots so deeply into authenticity that no storm can uproot you. And you don't need a title, a degree, or a spiritual badge to validate that role. You've already earned your wisdom—in the fire of your own becoming.

You earned it on the nights you stayed awake with your pain, when silence was your only witness. You earned it in the moments you set boundaries even when it meant losing connection. You earned it every time you stood up when the world told you to shrink.

Now, you lead by living. You lead not by force or performance, but by presence—by being honest, by being whole, by letting your life be the message. You show others what's possible outside the box. And when they ask how you did it, you'll smile and say:

"I stopped trying to be who they wanted me to be. I started listening to who I already was."

"I stopped asking for directions. I started building the road."

And you'll mean it. Because you never stopped becoming.

You are the guide now. Not because you have every answer—but because you are brave enough to keep asking the questions. Because you stay when it's uncomfortable. Because you return to your truth again and again.

This isn't the conclusion of your journey—it's the threshold of your next becoming. You get to choose what this life looks like. You get to write the story. And no one else needs to understand it for it to matter.

You are living proof that it's possible to walk away from the noise—and come home to yourself.

So take the step. Then the next.
And know that every footprint you leave becomes a path
for someone else to find their way home, too.

The Forever Path Is the Most Human Path

We live in a world that worships the finish line. A world that measures success by completion, by how quickly you can tick off the boxes: the degree, the job, the healing, the transformation. And when you don't reach those milestones on time—or at all—you're told something is wrong with you. That you're falling behind, broken, not trying hard enough.

But I want to tell you something I didn't learn from books or polished programs. I learned it from crawling through the dark with scraped knees and a heart that refused to close: the real path—the healing path, the human path—is not linear, and it never truly ends.

There is no moment where you arrive fully healed, untouched by grief or fear or shame. There is only this moment. This breath. This choice to return to yourself, again and again. You don't outgrow your humanity; you grow deeper into it. You don't erase your past; you build a life tenderly alongside it.

The forever path isn't about striving for perfection or chasing enlightenment. It's about staying awake in a world that constantly tempts you to go numb. It's about remembering who you are beneath the noise, the roles, and the pressure to always be doing more, fixing more, achieving more.

It's about unlearning the idea that your worth is tied to productivity, perfection, or performance. It's about being in relationship with every part of yourself—especially the ones you were taught to hide. It's dancing in the kitchen with tears still on your cheeks. It's yelling into a pillow one hour and whispering "I'm okay" the next. It's contradiction. And it's all sacred.

You don't need to figure it all out. You don't need to get to a place where you never wobble, never regress, never feel like falling apart. That's not weakness. That's wisdom. That's what it means to be fully human.

You are allowed to change your mind. To grieve what could've been. To slow down when your body asks you to. You're allowed to grow at your own pace—not at the speed the world demands. And more than anything, you're allowed to do it without performing it for anyone else.

This path doesn't require a title, a certificate, or an external transformation to be valid. It asks only that you keep showing up—to your truth, your breath, your becoming. It invites your softness as much as your strength, your laughter as much as your sorrow, your rest as much as your action.

You weren't made to be a machine. You were made to feel deeply. To change and evolve. To fall and rise and fall again. You were made for depth—not speed. For presence—not perfection.

So if you've been waiting for the moment when you finally "arrive," let this be your reminder: you're already on the path. You've already begun. You're already enough. The evidence isn't in how much you've achieved—it's in your willingness to stay, to listen, to keep going.

This is the forever path.
It won't always be easy.
But it will always be yours.
And that, in the end, is the most human thing of all.

Chapter 9 Exercises: Embracing the Forever Path

This Work Doesn't End
It deepens.

These practices aren't tasks to finish.
They're invitations—
to return to yourself,
to honor your rhythm,
to step into who you're becoming.

They are not linear steps.
They are living portals.
Each time you revisit them,
you meet a new version of you.

Let them stretch and shift as you do.
Let them become what you need,
again and again.

Take your time.
This is not a race—
it's a return.

Exercise 1: The Spiral Reflection

Instructions:
Draw a spiral in your journal. At the outer edge, write an old belief, behavior, or pattern you once thought you were "done with."
Now, slowly move inward.
At each curve, jot down a version of yourself who met that pattern with more awareness, more tools, or more grace.

Maybe it looked like:
- The first time you set a boundary and your voice trembled.
- The moment you noticed the urge to people-please but paused instead.
- The day you cried and didn't shame yourself for it.

Reflection Questions:
- What is this pattern still teaching me?
- How can I meet this layer with more compassion, not criticism?
- What wisdom have I gained from revisiting it?

This is not you failing.
This is you spiraling upward.

Learning deeper.
Loving wider.

Exercise 2: Living in the Question Journal

Choose one question a day and sit with it—not to solve it, but to feel it in your body.
Let your intuition, not just your logic, respond.

- What is true for me today?
- What does my body want me to know?
- Where am I being invited to unlearn or remember?
- What truth is whispering beneath my discomfort?
- What would softness look like right now?

Tip:
Let your pen move slowly. Let silence be part of the answer. Let this be more about presence than productivity.

Exercise 3: The Curiosity Check

When you feel triggered, stuck, or disconnected:

1. Pause.
2. Breathe deep into your belly.
3. Ask yourself:
   - What else might be true here?
   - What is this reaction trying to protect me from?
   - Where might curiosity help me soften instead of defend?

Journal Prompt:
Write about a recent moment where curiosity shifted the way you viewed yourself or someone else.

Curiosity doesn't need immediate answers. It just needs space.

Exercise 4: The Forever Path Closing Ritual

Create your own sacred ritual to anchor your commitment to lifelong unlearning and becoming.
Options:
- Light a candle and place your hand on your heart.
- Sit outside under the sky and feel the earth beneath you.
- Write a letter to your future self.

Speak aloud or write:
I am on the forever path.
I release the illusion of arrival.
I trust the spiral.
I trust my body.
I trust the wisdom within me.
I am not broken. I am becoming.
Tip:
Return to this ritual any time you feel lost, stuck, or tempted to retreat into old stories. This is your grounding point.

Exercise 5: Becoming Your Own Guide Affirmation

Say these words daily. Say them especially when you feel unsure. Let them live in your body.
- I am the guide of my life.
- I trust my process, even when it's messy.

- I get to ask questions, change direction, and grow.
- I am not here to perform. I am here to live.
- I am becoming—and that is enough.

You don't need a map. You are the compass.

Closing Words — A Letter to the Reader

"And then the day came when the risk to remain tight in a bud was more painful than the risk it took to blossom."
— Anaïs Nin

If you've made it here, pause for a moment. Let yourself feel that. Not just intellectually, but in your body. Take a breath that fills your lungs, softens your belly, and gently anchors you into the truth: you made it. Through the unraveling. Through the remembering. Through every tender, gritty, uncomfortable space that asked you to stay with yourself when it would have been so much easier to disconnect. You didn't run. You didn't numb. You didn't abandon yourself. You kept going. You chose presence over performance. You chose courage over comfort. You chose you—and that alone is holy.

This book was never meant to be a manual or a map. It was never about checking off a list, fixing your flaws, or arriving at some idealized version of who you were told you had to become. It was a remembering—a quiet returning to what has always been true beneath the noise. A sacred hand on your back, whispering, "Come home." Not to perfection, but to presence. Not to a role, but to your essence. Not to someone else's timeline, but to the rhythm of your own breath, your own becoming.

Maybe no one told you that healing often looks like grief. That becoming can feel like being stripped bare. That choosing a life outside the box might sometimes feel isolating, but also more real, more alive, and more free than anything you've ever known. Maybe no one warned you that the price of truth is sometimes letting go of the stories, identities, and relationships that once felt like safety. Or that the path forward would ask you to sit still long enough to hear your own body speak. But here you are—braver than you know, stronger than you feel, and more whole than you've ever been told you're allowed to be.

This isn't about becoming someone new. It's about shedding everything you were never meant to carry. It's about honoring your softness, your pace, your truth. Rebuilding not with urgency or pressure, but with gentleness. Brick by brick. Boundary by boundary. Breath by breath.

I wrote these pages not from a place of mastery, but from the middle. From the trenches. From the nights I wasn't sure I'd make it. From the mornings I chose to rise anyway. From the quiet reclamation of joy and dignity that doesn't always look loud or triumphant—but is no less sacred. These words came from my body, my story, my lived truth. And now, they belong to you too.

So as you close this book, let this be your reminder: you're not behind. You're not broken. You're not too much, and you're not too late. You are right on time for your own life. You don't need a transformation to prove your worth. You don't need a perfect version of yourself to be lovable or free. You just need to keep showing up—imperfectly, courageously, and fully human.

Keep questioning what you were taught. Keep honoring the whispers of your intuition. Keep choosing rest over rush, truth over performance, softness over survival. Keep creating a life that feels like home in your body, even when the world tells you to hustle, shrink, or conform.

And when the world tries to pull you back into the box, into the old roles, the old masks—remember this: you've already tasted freedom. And once you've tasted it, you can't go back. Not without losing yourself again.

So choose you. Again and again. And if the path ever feels quiet... if you ever forget how far you've come... if you need to remember that someone else understands—come back here. To these words. To your truth. To this moment.

I'm not ahead of you. I'm beside you. Still learning. Still unlearning. Still becoming.

Right here, with you, on the forever path.

With deep truth, fierce compassion, and unwavering belief in you,

Cash
Your fellow traveler on this sacred journey we call life.

Acknowledgments

There are moments in life when words feel far too small to carry the weight of our gratitude. This is one of them.

To every person who stood beside me, who chose to stay when it would have been easier to walk away, who reminded me—through their presence, compassion, and fierce love—that I was not alone: thank you. You may never fully know the depth of your impact, but please hear this— your support saved me in ways I may never be able to articulate. You gave me something sacred in my darkest hours: the gift of being seen, held, and chosen. For that, I am forever grateful.

And yet, my deepest and most complete acknowledgment belongs to the Lord.

Without His love, His unwavering presence, and His relentless pursuit of my heart, I would not be here to thank anyone at all. My truth is simple and unshakable: no matter how many tools I tried, no matter how diligently I practiced the techniques, rewired the thoughts, broke away from the systems, and tried to live outside the box—none of it truly healed me until I surrendered. Until I laid it all at His feet.

I was broken beyond human repair. And the day everything changed was the day I stopped striving and simply gave it over to God. Every burden, every wound, every addiction, every sin—I handed it to Him. And He received it with grace. He took it all without hesitation and never once turned His face from me. Through every stumble, every relapse into old patterns, every moment I doubted my worth—He stayed. He reminded me that I was still loved. Still whole. Still His.

Having a relationship with God doesn't erase pain, but it transforms it. It gives it purpose. It strips away the fear. It replaces despair with hope—an unshakable hope that remains even when the world trembles. And when I stumble now, I know I won't fall far. Because He is there. Always.

From this day forward, I carry Him with me into every corner of my life. I no longer try to do it alone—because I've already tried that path. And I've failed, again and again. But He called me by name. He claimed me as His own. And I will spend the rest of my life here on this earth striving to live in a way that honors that calling. I know I will never be "worthy" by the world's standards—but in His eyes, I already am.

To God be the glory. Forever and always.

References & Gratitude to the Teachers

This book was born from lived experience—
but it is braided with the voices, teachings, and courageous work of those who walked before me, and beside me.

While the words are my own and shaped by the contours of my story, the truths held within them have been stirred, sharpened, and softened by the wisdom of many others.

To the teachers who cracked something open in me,
who offered language where I once had none—
thank you.
Your light lit the path I now walk.
And I carry it forward with reverence.

Influential Thinkers, Healers & Guides

- **YHWH (The King of Kings)** – Thank you for saving me, for restoring what was broken, for calling me back to wholeness when I had forgotten my worth. You lifted me from the dust, from what felt discarded and forgotten, and in Your mercy, made me whole — again and again. I am in awe of Your love, Your faithfulness, and the way You never let go.
- **Philip Anthony Mitchell (2819 Church)** – Thank you for faithfully stewarding the call of the Lord and boldly bringing His gospel to our people and this nation. Your obedience and dedication are a light in dark places, and your leadership carries the heart of

our Father. May you be blessed as you continue to lead with truth, love, and unwavering faith.

- **Dr. Stephen Porges** – For the gift of Polyvagal Theory, helping us understand safety, regulation, and how the body keeps the score long before we ever find the words.
- **Deb Dana** – For making Polyvagal Theory human, relational, and accessible, and for helping us bring curiosity and compassion to our states of being.
- **The Centre for Healing (Ryan Hassan, Melissa Hiemann & Matt Kay)** – For teaching the spiral nature of trauma recovery and for modeling integrity and depth in a world of quick-fix healing.
- **Dr. Peter Levine** – For showing us that trauma is a physiological wound, not a mental weakness, and that the body holds both the imprint and the key.
- **Irene Lyon** – For empowering thousands to become more attuned to their nervous systems and to heal in slow, sustainable, deeply embodied ways.
- **Francine Shapiro** – For developing EMDR and giving the world one of the most transformational tools for reprocessing trauma gently and effectively.
- **Dr. Gabor Maté** – For courageously connecting the dots between childhood trauma, chronic illness, addiction, and self-compassion.
- **Dr. Bessel van der Kolk** – For offering groundbreaking research and real-world language for how trauma shows up—and how we begin to heal.
- **Dr. Mark Hyman** – For leading a revolution in root-cause medicine and helping us reclaim agency over our health.
- **Dr. Casey Means** – For bringing functional medicine and metabolic health into the mainstream in a way that feels empowering, not overwhelming.

- **Barbara O'Neill** – For reminding us that the earth still provides, the body still remembers, and healing can be both simple and sacred.
- **Dr. Jordan Peterson** – For his unflinching challenge to cultural conformity and his call to individual responsibility, meaning, and depth.
- **Dr. Nicole LePera (The Holistic Psychologist)** – For making inner child work, nervous system healing, and self-accountability a global movement.
- **Paula Davis** – For teaching sustainable tools for burnout recovery, especially for high-performing women, caregivers, and change-makers.
- **Ben Tannahill (Drunken Buddha)** – For inviting us into emotional honesty, embodiment, and the sacred process of truly feeling our feelings.

These aren't just names on a page.
They are way-makers. Trailblazers. Sacred mirrors.
The ones who dared to ask the questions others were too afraid to ask—
who shattered illusions, cracked open inherited truths,
and gave the rest of us permission to do the same.

Because they spoke, I found the courage to use my voice.
Because they chose truth, I learned to trust mine.
Because they walked first, I recognized the path beneath my feet.

Their impact lives in these pages—
in every sentence I found the strength to write,
and in every reader who now dares to question, feel, and become.

About the Author

Cashea Earls is a rebel of the old systems—
a rule-breaker by necessity,
a truth-seeker by calling,
and a forever student of the body, spirit, and soul.

For decades, she followed the rules.
Played the roles.
Did everything she was taught to do in a world that
rewarded compliance over connection.
But behind the performance was a woman unraveling.

When her body gave out, when her mind fractured, and
when the noise of the world drowned out her truth—
that collapse became her turning point.
And in the silence that followed, God met her there.

What unfolded wasn't a neatly packaged healing journey.
It was a sacred reckoning.
A spiral of remembering, unlearning, surrendering, and
beginning again.
It was falling to her knees in the dark,
only to be lifted by a grace she didn't know she was worthy
of.

Through divine guidance and deep inner work, Cashea came
home to herself—
not as someone who had all the answers,
but as someone finally willing to listen.

Today, she is a Trauma-Informed & Integrative Nutrition
Health Coach, writer, and guide.
Her work blends spirit and science, nervous system healing

and biblical wisdom,
inviting others into a deeper relationship with their bodies,
their truth, and God.

She helps others reclaim their sovereignty, restore trust in
their design,
and build lives rooted in divine purpose—not performance.
Her mission isn't to hand out formulas, but to remind you
that the answers already live within—
placed there by the One who created you.

Cashea believes that true healing is holy work.
That we are not broken, but beloved.
And that transformation begins not when we strive harder,
but when we finally surrender.

When she's not writing or holding sacred space for clients,
you'll find her dancing barefoot in the kitchen,
wandering Texas trails with prayers on her breath,
cooking soul food from scratch,
or resting in the quiet presence of God—
where she is reminded again and again
that she was never alone, never too far gone, and never
without purpose.